To Dexter for his unwavering support and patience.

Icons Used in This Book

Case Study — Examples of this book's advice at work

Quotes — Useful words direct from the experts

Definitions — \di'fin\ *vb* Terminology and jargon explained

Reminder — "Don't-Forget" items to keep in mind

For More Info — Where to turn for more in-depth coverage

See Also — Where in this book to find related information

Hidden Treasures — Family papers and home sources

Sources — Where to go for information, supplies, etc.

Idea Generator — Techniques and prods for further thinking

Step By Step — Walkthroughs of important procedures

Important — Information and tips you can't overlook

Supplies — Advice on day-to-day office tools

Internet Source — Where on the Web to find what you need

Technique — How to conduct research, solve problems, and get answers

Money Saver — Getting the most out of research dollars

Timesaver — Shaving minutes and hours off the clock

Notes — Thoughts, ideas, and related insights

Tip — Ways to make research more efficient

Oral History — Techniques for getting family stories

Warning — Stop before you make a mistake

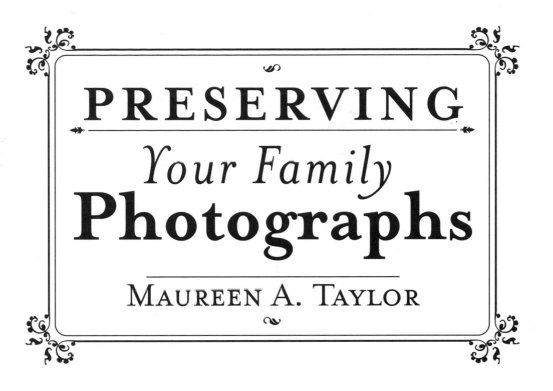

PRESERVING
Your Family
Photographs

MAUREEN A. TAYLOR

How to organize, present, and
restore your precious family images

To Betty —
Maureen Taylor
29 January 2003

BETTERWAY BOOKS
CINCINNATI, OHIO
www.familytreemagazine.com

About the Author

Maureen A. Taylor is the author of several books on genealogy and photo history, including *Uncovering Your Ancestry Through Family Photographs* (Cincinnati: Betterway Books, 2000) and *Through the Eyes of Your Ancestors* (Boston: Houghton Mifflin, 1999). Her columns appear online at FamilyTree Magazine.com, Genealogy.com, and NewEnglandAncestors.org, as well as in *Ancestry*, *Family Tree Magazine*, and *New England Ancestors*. Her national television and radio appearances include *DIY: Scrapbooking*, MSNBC, and *Ancestors* (PBS).

Preserving Your Family Photographs: How to Organize, Present, and Restore Your Precious Family Images. © 2001 by Maureen A. Taylor. Manufactured in the United States of America. All rights reserved. No part of this book may be reproduced in any form or by any electronic or mechanical means including information storage and retrieval systems without permission in writing from the publisher, except by a reviewer, who may quote brief passages in a review. Published by Betterway Books, an imprint of F&W Publications, Inc., 1507 Dana Avenue, Cincinnati, Ohio 45207. (800) 289-0963. First edition.

Other fine Betterway Books are available from your local bookstore or on our Web site at http://www.familytreemagazine.com. To receive Family Tree Magazine Update, a free e-newsletter with news, tips, and resources for genealogists and family historians, subscribe online at http://newsletters.fwpublications.com.

05 04 03 02 01   5 4 3 2 1

Library of Congress Cataloging-in-Publication Data

Taylor, Maureen Alice.
    Preserving your family photographs: how to organize, present, and restore precious family images / Maureen A. Taylor.—1st ed.
        p.   cm.
    Includes bibliographical references and index.
    ISBN 1-55870-579-1 (alk. paper)
    1. Photographs—Conservation and restoration—Handbooks, manuals, etc. 2. Photograph collections—Management—Handbooks, manuals, etc. 3. Photographs in genealogy—Handbooks, manuals, etc. 4. Photography of families—Handbooks, manuals, etc. 5. Digital preservation—Handbooks, manuals, etc. I. Title.

TR465 .T35 2001
771'.46—dc21   2001025369
                                                                                                          CIP

Editor: Sharon DeBartolo Carmack, CG
Production editor: Brad Crawford
Production coordinator: Sara Dumford
Cover designer: Wendy Dunning
Cover photography: Al Parrish
Interior designer: Sandy Conopeotis Kent
Icon designer: Cindy Beckmeyer

Table of Contents
At a Glance

Preface, *ix*

Introduction: Preserving Our Past for the Future, *1*

1   Stories Worth Saving, *5*

2   The Preservation Facts, *18*

3   Cased Images: Daguerreotypes, Ambrotypes, and Tintypes, *41*

4   Photographic Prints and Negatives, *54*

5   Color, *79*

6   The Digital Age: The New Family Album, *92*

7   Professional Help: Conservation and Restoration, *107*

8   Ways of Organizing (Keep It Simple), *133*

9   Safe Scrapbooking, *148*

10   Three Family Collections, *158*

11   Having Fun With Your Family Photographs, *174*

Appendix A: Glossary, *183*

Appendix B: Sources of Family Photographs, *187*

Appendix C: Timeline of Events, *196*

Appendix D: Important Addresses, *199*

Appendix E: Copying and Restoration Services, *209*

Appendix F: Conference Lectures, *211*

Appendix G: Web Sites of Interest, *213*

Appendix H: Professional Study Programs, *215*

Bibliography, *234*

Index, *243*

Table of Contents

Preface, *ix*

Introduction: Preserving Our Past for the Future, *1*

1   Stories Worth Saving, *5*
    • *Retaining the Original Order* • *Photo Identification Techniques* • *Adding to Your Collection* • *A Family Collection Through the Generations* • *Sentimental vs. Market Value* • *Checklist: Getting Ready*

2   The Preservation Facts, *18*
    • *Damage to Photographs* • *Should You Clean Your Pictures?* • *Storage Considerations* • *Take Care of Your New Images* • *Mailing Photographs* • *Choosing a Storage Facility* • *Copying Methods* • *Scanning the Images* • *Printing Digital Images* • *Digital Information Online* • *Know the Law Before You Copy* • *Checklist: The Preservation Facts*

3   Cased Images: Daguerreotypes, Ambrotypes, and Tintypes, *41*
    • *Daguerreotypes* • *Handling Suggestions* • *Ambrotypes* • *Tintypes* • *Telling Them Apart* • *Cases* • *Frequently Asked Question* • *Checklist: Cased Images*

4   Photographic Prints and Negatives, *54*
    • *The Nineteenth Century* • *Identifying the Process* • *Card Photographs* • *Candid Photographic Prints* • *Paper Supports* • *Surface Treatments* • *Resin-Coated (RC) Papers* • *Photographic Albums* • *Negatives* • *Film-Based Negatives* • *Checklist: Photographic Prints and Negatives*

5   Color, *79*
    • *Background* • *Deterioration* • *Instant Color* • *General Suggestions for Color Prints and Negatives* • *Film and Glass Slides* • *Movie Film* • *Hiring a Professional Photographer* • *Frequently Asked Questions* • *Checklist: Color*

6   The Digital Age: The New Family Album, *92*

• *Digital Photography History* • *Computer Files* • *Photo CDs*
• *Online Photo Community* • *Photo Suppliers* • *Preservation Issues*
• *Family Pages and Extended Family Sites* • *Designing a Family
Home Page* • *Privacy Issues in the New Family Album* • *Frequently
Asked Questions* • *Checklist: The Digital Age*

**7   Professional Help: Conservation
and Restoration,** *107*

• *Why You Need a Professional* • *What Can a Conservator
Accomplish?* • *Disaster Preparedness* • *Water Damage* • *What to
Save in Case of Disaster* • *Restoration* • *Airbrush Restoration*
• *Digital Restorations* • *Paper Print* • *Becoming a Professional*
• *Checklist: Professional Help*

8   Ways of Organizing (Keep It Simple), *133*

• *Ways to Organize* • *Finding the Time* • *To-Do List* • *Indexing
Systems* • *Sample Inventory of the Smith Family Collection* • *Photo
Software and Databases* • *Organizing Slides* • *Museum
Registration Methods* • *Chronological Methods* • *Hiring a
Professional Organizer* • *Becoming a Photo Curator* • *Special
Consideration: Organizing Before You Donate* • *Checklist:
Organizing*

9   Safe Scrapbooking, *148*

• *Albums* • *Rubber Stamping* • *Sheet Protectors* • *Stickers* • *Family
Memorabilia* • *Lamination vs. Encapsulation* • *Artifacts* • *Creating
the Scrapbook* • *Digital Scrapbooks* • *Consult the Experts* • *Supplies
for a Safe Scrapbook* • *Rules for Safe Scrapbooking* • *Checklist: Safe
Scrapbooking*

10   Three Family Collections, *158*

• *The Taylor Family Collection* • *The Betlock/Virnig Collection* • *The
Emison Family Collection* • *The Next Step* • *Checklist: Points to
Remember*

11   Having Fun With Your Family Photographs, *174*

• *Using Your Photographs in a Family History* • *Displaying Family
Photographs* • *Family Reunion Activities* • *Creating a Better Family
Photo Collection* • *Checklist: Having Fun With Your Family
Photographs*

APPENDIX A   Glossary, *183*

APPENDIX B   Sources of Family Photographs, *187*

APPENDIX C   Timeline of Events, *196*

APPENDIX D   Important Addresses, *199*
- *Conservators*
- *Magazines*
- *Societies and Organizations*
- *Suppliers*
- *Software*

APPENDIX E   Copying and Restoration Services, *209*
- *Archival Storage Facilities*
- *Cellulose Nitrate Storage*

APPENDIX F   Conference Lectures—Repeat Performance, *211*

APPENDIX G   Web Sites of Interest, *213*

APPENDIX H   Professional Study Programs, *215*
- *Accredited Degree Programs in Library Science*
- *Degree Programs in Archival Training*
- *Digital Photography and Restoration*

Bibliography, *234*

Index, *243*

Preface

I have a confession to make. I have a small photograph collection that is not perfectly organized. Over the years I've tried to work on groups of images but usually lacked the time and money to invest in the collection. The idea for this book grew out of attempts to organize my personal and family photographs. My first photography book, *Uncovering Your Ancestry Through Family Photographs* (Cincinnati: Betterway Books, 2000), explained the process of identifying images. This volume explains the processes of preserving, organizing, and restoring family photographs. Our photographs have a lot to tell us. I hope that if we learn how to identify, care for, and repair them, our descendants will appreciate them.

In the more than twenty years I've worked with photographs as a professional curator and researcher, the number of titles on the history of photography has increased, but there are still topics that need research and publication. One of the underexplored areas in the last 150-plus years of photography is the importance of the medium in family history. I hope that this book helps explain why family historians and genealogists need to be interested in their photographic heritages. I believe that every family collection has a unique story to tell. Each photograph has a fascinating history, including how and why it survived multiple generations. Let's try to take care of these valuable pieces of our history so that others can appreciate them.

This book would not have been possible without the support and encouragement of the many friends and colleagues who responded to a call for their unanswered photography questions. I learned a great deal through them. Parts of this book were a challenge to write because the technology keeps changing. The individuals who shared their expertise and experience to help explain technical terminology and procedures include David Mishkin of Just Black and White; Paul Messier, Boston Art Conservation; Richard S. Wilson, the author of *Publishing Your Family History on the Internet* (La Habra, Calif.: Compuology, 1999); as well as many other patient individuals who felt family photographs important enough to take the time to talk with me.

Lynn Betlock and her husband, Grant Emison, once again opened their photograph collections to me in sharing stories and images. I am extremely grateful that these two people felt comfortable publishing their photographs and family history.

There are people who nudged me during the course of this book. When writing a book, you need friends you can turn to for opinions and suggestions. I am very lucky to know a number of individuals who let me do that including Kathy Hinckley, author of *Locating Lost Family Members &*

Friends (Cincinnati: Betterway Books, 1999); Alison Cywin, director of the Rhode Island Historical Society Library; Helen Bridge; Marcia Melnyk, author of *The Weekend Genealogist* (Cincinnati: Betterway Books, 2000); and D. Brenton Simons, executive director of the Newbury Street Press. Another person lent her support to both projects, encouraged me to pursue them, and offered calming words when necessary. Thank you, Sharon! Finally, thanks to Jane Schwerdtfeger and David Lambert, who share my passion for photo history and love looking at photographs.

Once again I need to thank my husband for his patience and my children, James and Sarah, for their unending curiosity about the world. They ask questions about everything and encourage me to look at life in a new way.

I fell in love with photography and historical images as a young child, and my fascination with the topic has never wavered. It is my hope to pass on this interest to others through the topics covered in this book. Try to find time to enjoy your photographic heritage. It's a great way to relax.

INTRODUCTION

Preserving Our Past for the Future

A woman at one of my lectures stood up and announced that she had a solution for organizing all the photographs she had collected. "Put them on your computer and throw away the originals. That way you don't have the clutter." I spent the next half hour explaining why transferring all your family photographs to a digital format was a temporary solution due to future retrieval problems and the loss of the originals. Her comment made me aware of the amount of misinformation available to the public regarding photo preservation. Others in the class asked questions regarding organization of their photographs. I was supposed to give an introductory lecture on family history but instead spent two hours answering inquiries about family photographs. This group taught me that there is a changing notion of what a photograph is.

In each generation since the daguerreotype appeared in 1839, the definition of a photograph changed as the medium and technique for producing an image evolved. For individuals living at the inception of photography in 1839, a photograph was on metal and appeared black and white and reflective, while for someone living in 1939, the most common images were on paper and may have been a shade of brown, or black and white. Today our family photographs come in a variety of mediums, from a digital image to an instant color photograph to the now more traditional color photograph processed at a lab. The diversity of images in family collections leads to uncertainty over how to organize and care for both the historical images and those we're creating today.

Add to that confusion advertising by companies that sell supplies and materials as acid-free and archival, and it isn't surprising that our family photograph collections are in a state of disrepair. **Acid-free means that the substance is actually free of acid, while archival suggests that it is not harmful.** Since there are no standards to judge an archival process, however, it is best to use specific terms when talking about terminology relating to photographic conservation, preservation, and restoration. The manufacturers end up caught in the mix-up by proclaiming their products are archival when in fact they are not suitable for long-term storage. The history of preservation

\di'fin\ *vb*

Definitions

Figure Intro-1.
The photographs we take today are very different from those of our ancestors.
Collection of the author

methods illustrates that until storage materials are properly tested, consumers should not buy products when they might not fully understand the technical terms and product components.

So what does archival really mean, and why is it important? Don't depend on the staff in most stores to advise you on products to purchase. Even though the label says "archival," it is best to check with the manufacturer to see if the product-conservation professionals have approved the product and that it has passed standards to be used with photographs. To keep your pictures safe, you need to be familiar with preservation methods used in most archives and libraries. Since we all want our photograph collections to outlive us, it can be difficult to know the right approach to caring for our images.

If you were to ask a group of people where they store their family photographs, most would reply that they are in boxes in the closet, the attic, or the basement. They will follow your question with an apology for not knowing what else to do with them.

While genealogists are more aware than ever of the value of their photographs, the next step is understanding how to care for their valuable images. Every picture tells a story of the lives and experiences of our ancestors, so why not pay attention to what we have so that future generations can understand our lives and their ancestors?

There are several reasons our pictures remain in shoeboxes.

1. We produce enormous numbers of images. Every time I take film to be developed, I'm overwhelmed by the choices. Do I want multiple prints? What size? Do I want them on CD-ROM, or would I rather look at them on the Web? So many choices, and yet each one generates a storage or preservation problem.

According to the Photo Marketing Association, Americans take 55 million pictures a day, or more than 20 billion a year. If you were to take 100 rolls of film (36 exposures) in a given year and ask for double prints, you would be generating 7,200 pictures! That doesn't include the negatives and all the pictures you've taken in other years. What are you going to do with them all? You probably send copies to friends and relatives, but what do you do with the rest?

If you select the Web version, you choose the images you want to have printed or print them at home on special paper. Unfortunately, the rest of your images will only remain online for a short period of time unless you pay to have them stored electronically.

By producing a CD, you might think you have solved the space problem. After all, how much space does a single CD occupy? Several years later, however, you discover that you can no longer look at the CD because the technology has changed or suffers from preservation problems.

2. We lack the time to identify the images we produce. If you are like most people, you probably have boxes full of photographs of past generations waiting for identification. Extremely lucky individuals have ancestors who actually placed their pictures in albums and wrote captions on the backs or underneath the pictures. However, the majority of us have produced so many pictures that we are overwhelmed by the time it would take to identify all the images we have taken; never mind the ones we inherited from other family members. You can overcome this by selecting a small group of images to identify and moving on batch by batch.

3. How do we organize them? Whether you decide to organize them first and then identify the images or vice versa, sorting your pictures and refiling them are seen as tremendous hurdles. They don't have to be. There are many different-size prints available, and it seems that each camera produced a different-size print. So how do you create a family photo archive that makes sense and is simple to implement?

Scrapbook hobbyists seem to have an answer. There are new books on scrapbooking published all the time, but if you follow their advice, you could end up with a preservation nightmare. How do you safely arrange your originals so that they will last?

4. How do we know that our solutions won't damage our pictures? Magazines present us with decorating suggestions using our family pictures, from framing arrangements to creating Christmas ornaments. But how do you know if you will be causing more harm? After all, how many of us have those magnetic albums from the 1970s that have caused irreparable damage to our photographs? My mother placed our graduation pictures in frames on a table in the living room. In just a few years, sunlight had caused significant color changes in the images. How do you know what preservation methods are worthwhile?

5. Can any damage be reversed? If you have the time to identify your pictures and organize them, you may still have the problem of damaged photographs. Did a relative place an *X* over the head of your ancestor in a group portrait and then use ink to write the name of the person near the *X* across the face of the neighboring person? Do mold, dirt, or chemicals obscure the face of an ancestor? Has an image faded? Before you attempt to clean any image, remember that the first rule of conservation and preservation is to proceed cautiously so that you don't do more damage. A few basic pieces of equipment such as a scanner, a computer, and special software can help you enhance even the most damaged photographs in your collection. If you require professional conservation or restoration help, do you know how to find the right person?

6. It's too expensive. Purchasing a magnetic album is less expensive than buying one from an archival supplier, but consider the future. I have several albums from the 1970s, and I can vouch for the damage they have caused to my irreplaceable images. Isn't it worth the additional expense to invest in albums from reputable archival suppliers? You don't have to put all your family photographs in a preservation-quality album, but if you don't, are you prepared to lose them? This book outlines some inexpensive solutions for limited budgets.

Given the number of pictures we take, our confusion over definitions, and the ever-changing technology, is it any wonder that many of us put off working with our family photographs? What we need is encouragement and education.

For More Info

This book is the companion volume to my first Betterway book, *Uncovering Your Ancestry Through Family Photographs*, which helped thousands identify their family images. This volume continues the process of working with your photographs by answering the questions listed in this introduction. It also provides a basic understanding of how to care for and organize your family photograph collection. It will outline in easy steps how to add value to your collection by applying the concepts that conservators and photo curators use every day. Most chapters end with a series of commonly asked questions (FAQs) and their answers. This book also

- Provides a set of safe scrapbooking guidelines.
- Furnishes a list of basic conservation supplies.
- Teaches you how to select a conservator.
- Evaluates computer programs that offer organizational solutions.
- Helps you identify the type of damage to the photographs in your collection.
- Talks about the future of photography in terms of electronic archives and home pages.
- Trains you to take better pictures.
- Shows you how to digitally restore your images.
- Explains the legal aspects of family photography.
- Offers suggestions for finding the time to do this.
- Presents some low-cost alternatives.

ONE

Stories Worth Saving

Every family photograph collection has a story to tell and is worth saving. In 1986, the Photo Marketing Association surveyed camera owners to find out why they took pictures. It's not surprising that 95 percent of them responded that they use photography to "preserve memorable scenes."[1] The stories present in our family photographs document important moments. They offer clues about the roles of individuals in the family, as well as provide their own versions of the histories of our families. Look carefully at your photographs.

The information contained in the image and its caption is not necessarily the same data you found in other types of documents used for genealogical research. The photographic narrative needs to be interpreted. What do your images say about your family? For instance, can you tell from looking at a picture of a couple what type of relationship they have? If you are looking at a family group, can you determine the dominant member of the family? This type of background is often lacking from other material.

A group of photographs is the collective story of the family. Think about who is not depicted in your family collection or in individual images. My mother doesn't have any of her baby pictures because her sister who is seventeen years older has the images in her collection. The people included or missing in the photographs add to your understanding of family dynamics.

Reminder

Everything about your family photographs adds to your understanding of their place in the family. Where are they stored? Are they precious enough to be in a location that allows for easy retrieval, or are they buried in the attic? Everyone has at least a few photos that have special significance.

Now consider how you obtained the photographs in your possession. Did a particular relative give them to you, or did you go out and find them?

It is a rare collection of images that stays intact over several generations. Various family members usually ask for a few images to remember deceased individuals or to replace images. One relative recently requested a copy of

Figures 1-1 and 1-2.
These two unidentified photographs depict relationships within a family. What do your photographs say about your family?
Collection of the author

childhood photographs because a fire destroyed his home. You can tell a lot about the history of photographs in your family by discovering the earliest photograph in your collection. This photograph tells a story beyond what and who is depicted. It can enlighten you by tracing its previous owners. If you only own twentieth-century images ask, "Why are there no photographs before that point?"

The answers to these questions inform you of the place of photography in your family. You may not think that answering these inquiries is important to learning how to preserve, organize, and restore individual family pictures. In fact, in each step of the process, you will make determinations about the sentimental value of the images you are going to organize. The answers to these questions will ultimately lead you to additional information and even more images.

Step back from the individual pictures and see your collection as a whole. What types of photographs are there? Who took them and when? What do you really know about the individuals depicted? All of these questions become important when you begin to organize your collection. How do you know which photographs to place in the family album if you can't answer the major question of why they are important?

While there are basic preservation needs for all types of images, some processes require special considerations. Conservation and preservation are ways to prevent future damage. Store images in cases or frames differently than negatives. Each step in the preservation and conservation process asks you to define the parameters of your family. Are you going to purchase supplies for all your images or only those that have special significance? It is advisable to place all of your images in storage, but you may only be able to take extra precautions with a precious few.

You may decide that some of your images require restoration, the process of reconstructing their original appearance. However, professional restoration is a time-consuming and expensive process. By determining the familial importance of certain images, you create a priority list of items to be professionally restored. If you choose to try enhancing your photographs using a software package, you are still determining which photographs are worthy of your time and energy.

The very act of creating an album, scrapbook, or family Web page with images requires that you make additional decisions about your photographs. Why do you include some and not others? You may want to include a statement of your intent as a preface to your final product.

Tip

So how do you reconcile the desire to use all of your pictures with the reality of working with a few at a time? You do this by asking yourself a series of questions about what photographs are most important to you.

- Who are the important people in your life?
- Which images depict events that you want to remember?
- Is there a series of photographs that tells the story of your family?
- Are there photographs of family friends that have special significance?

These are just a few questions. When you look at your collection, whether or not you are aware of it, you are making decisions regarding your photos' future care. You are probably not going to include images of family friends or distant relatives in your albums or pay for expensive conservation of such photos unless those individuals played a significant role in your family life.

To organize your family photographs, there are several steps to follow

Important

WHAT IS THE PAT?

The Photographic Activity Test measures the reactivity of products and their components to photographs. The American National Standards Institute (ANSI) and the International Standards Organization (ISO) issue the standards used in the test. Manufacturers voluntarily submit their products for testing. In the United States, one of the facilities that tests materials is the Image Permanence Institute in Rochester, New York. If you have a question regarding a certain product, you can call the manufacturer or supplier to see if it passed the PAT.

Figure 1-3.
Ask a series of questions about the photographs in your collection before you start to organize them. For instance, what is the relationship between these two individuals?
Collection of the author

so that you create a record useful to future generations. Whether you choose to arrange your photographs in PAT-approved albums or store them in boxes, you still need to caption each image. This can feel overwhelming, especially if you don't know where to start, so in the beginning you may only want to identify small numbers of images.

You need only a few supplies to begin the process. Since these photographs are in part members of your family tree, it is necessary to have your genealogical research available for reference purposes. **When handling the images, it is important to wear clean white cotton gloves.** They are available in most hardware stores or from the suppliers listed in Appendix D. Wearing gloves will prevent further damage from depositing substances from your hands onto the pictures. No matter how clean you think your hands are, you can still transfer oil and fingerprints to the surfaces of the pictures. Years later you may find that you've left a perfect set of fingerprints on the image you touched with bare hands. A good magnifying glass will help you examine each picture for additional details. As you conduct your

Important

genealogical or photo research, be sure to carry duplicates or photocopies of your images on research trips rather than the originals. This will prevent loss or damage. Lastly, use a camera to document the original condition and arrangement of each part of your collection. The proximity and context of other photographs in the collection can help you identify images in your collection.

RETAINING THE ORIGINAL ORDER

Are your photographs in the boxes they were given to you in? If so, then one of the first steps toward organizing your images is to document what they looked like before you disturbed the order. In the Smith family, one member of the family kept separate boxes for papers and photographs relating to different generations of the family. Each box is labeled with the male head of the household's name. This allows the family to use these boxes and their genealogical information to re-create a history of each generation, depending on the materials that still exist. Your first step is to photograph the collection as it is by laying out selections of material. This can become important later when you are unable to recall which box the photographs came from. In addition, label each photograph with the original box number. Place the photograph face down on a clean, dry surface, and write the box number in the upper right corner lightly in pencil. It is preferable to use a soft graphite pencil for this. These can be purchased at art supply stores. **Never use pen on photographs because the ink can run and ruin the image.**

Warning

Figure 1-4.
Try to document the original order of the photographs in order to retain any identifying information.
Lynn Betlock

PHOTO IDENTIFICATION TECHNIQUES

To tell a story, you need to answer the who, what, when, where, and why of the picture. Each image is a photographic mystery waiting to be solved. If you know the identity of the individuals in the picture, caption it. Include the names of the individuals in the picture, when it was taken, the geographic location, and an explanation of why it was taken. Examine the photographs in your possession and see if you can answer all of the above questions. **Most individuals are missing key pieces of information. With a few easy steps, however, you can add to your knowledge about an image.**

Ask other family members if they recognize the photograph. Can they remember why it was taken and when? Do they know the names of the people in the image? Do they know when the image was taken? The clothing clues and photographer's imprint can help you assign an approximate date. Costume encyclopedias can lead you to a time frame. If the photographer's name is present, you can locate a span of dates by researching his business in local city directories. Where are the subjects standing? By examining the

Step By Step

Figure 1-5.
Not all photographs are identified as clearly as this one. You usually have to rely on a series of techniques, including costume dating, to try to associate a name with a photograph.
Collection of the author

THE HAYWARDS.

Photographed by   J. A. FARNHAM.

photograph for artifacts or signage, you can find additional clues that will help you date the image.

In one collection, a pair of wedding portraits was rediscovered. The owners knew who the individuals were, but it wasn't until they determined a date based on clothing and the photographer that it became clear that these were wedding portraits. In this case, the bride was not attired in the traditional wedding dress and veil.

Label each photograph in your collection with a name and date at the minimum so they can be understood in the future. Write this identifying information in pencil on either the album page or the outside of the storage materials. Until you decide how you are going to organize your collection, it is helpful to use a worksheet to track your research and the caption. For additional tips on identifying your pictures, see *Uncovering Your Ancestry Through Family Photographs.*

ADDING TO YOUR COLLECTION

As you lay out your photographs to begin working with them and answering the above questions, it will become apparent that the collection in your possession represents only a small portion of the photographs that were created throughout the history of your family. Each collection of images has been brought together by a seemingly random set of circumstances. Their very survival depended on their value to other members of the family. At each juncture of a family tree, photographs are either lost due to disinterest or damage, or passed on to future generations. Think

Sources

BASIC CAPTION

Person/persons: name(s), life dates, date of the photograph (if known)

Event: family name, occasion, identity of individuals, date of the photograph

Supplies

BASIC KIT

- Genealogical research
- Graphite pencil
- Worksheets
- Photocopies of the photographs
- Magnifying glass
- White cotton gloves
- Camera

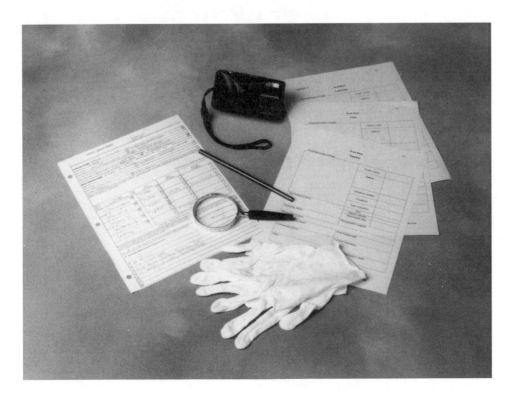

Figure 1-6.
Make a basic identification kit to use when working with your photographs.
Collection of the author

about the images that are currently part of your family photograph archive, and try to imagine what your collection would be like if you had a pictorial representation for each individual. In the Emison family, for instance, there are few images prior to the beginning of the twentieth century. Is this because that is all that survived, or because the family was disinterested in photography until a certain point? The likelihood is that there are other, perhaps earlier, photographs in the collections of distant relatives on the branches of the family tree.

Figure 1-7.
Don't assume that all your photographs are one of a kind. Many individuals ordered multiples to give to family and friends.
Collection of the author

Once you have documented the arrangement of your images and tried to identify some of your photographs, you may want to look for other photographs to enhance what you already have. For instance, the Bessette family collection is divided among several siblings. The photos are primarily images of the siblings as children. There are only a couple of group portraits of their mother and her siblings. Since both sides of the family, the Bessettes and the McDuffs, had large numbers of children, it is reasonable to assume that other family members may have images to fill in the gaps. In fact, one of the cousins has images relating to his father, who was of the same generation as the mother of the Bessette children. If there are photographic gaps in the family record, you might want to try to locate some other family pictures. This might be as simple as contacting all of your known relatives, or it might involve library research. Chapter eleven of *Uncovering Your Ancestry Through Family Photographs* provides examples of how you can build your collection.

As part of an estate, photograph collections are rarely mentioned, and so their dispersal is not part of public record. If you ask various family members, you will find that most have collections of ancestral photographs, ones they were given after the deaths of family members. It is worth the time and effort to track down these missing images and copy them so that they become part of your genealogical documentation.

There are additional sources of photographs that can be added to the family archive. Passports, visas, driver's licenses, and work identification cards can yield additional or new photographs. You might even find an image of a relative in a newspaper or magazine article.

Idea Generator

A FAMILY COLLECTION THROUGH THE GENERATIONS

Once you've surveyed the photographs in your possession, tried to identify them, and attempted to find new ones, you are ready to learn some basic conservation and preservation techniques. **Let's consider what happens to a fictional photograph collection from its beginning to the present.** The Smith family, intrigued by the new invention called the daguerreotype in 1839, sits for individual family portraits. Since these are one-of-a-kind pictures, it is necessary to pose for additional images to have copies for family members. The oldest daughter gives her portrait to her future husband. The father sends his to his elderly mother, whom he hasn't seen in several years. The mother and son hold on to their images. The family becomes fascinated with having portraits taken every few years as the family changes. Soon the collection has expanded to include a variety of mid-nineteenth-century images, such as daguerreotypes, ambrotypes, and small paper photographs called cartes de visite. The son not only sends home a tintype of himself from a Civil War battlefield taken by an itinerant photographer, but he also sends along a few pictures of his friends. The daughter, a young married woman, begins to collect cartes de visite of famous nineteenth-century people. She places them in an album alongside her family photographs.

Case Study

Several years pass. The son and daughter are raising their own families. They take their children to the photo studio for formal portraits, both as a family and individually. Since the siblings no longer live in the same town, they send each other copies of the pictures. Their parents' daguerreotypes are now part of their individual collections. The family photograph archive is now divided between at least two different family groups. Upon their

Definitions

WHAT IS A PHOTOGRAPH COLLECTION?

According to Webster's dictionary, a collection is a "group of objects or works kept together." A photograph collection is therefore the images kept together by a particular family. There is no differentiation between historical images and those currently being created. All are part of your collection.

Definitions

HISTORICAL VS. CONTEMPORARY PHOTOGRAPHS

For the purposes of this book, the word *photographs* refers to both historical photographs and the contemporary ones being taken. Photographic family history is created with each new snapshot. All photographs should be treated with respect and consideration regardless of when they were taken.

deaths, their children divide up the images to create still more photograph collections. This happens for several successive generations until there are boxes of photographs stored in attics, basements, and closets. The original daguerreotype cases are broken or have disappeared to be used for other purposes. The images stored in damp and humid conditions are damaged by mold. Chemical stains from improper washing mar the faces of several by now unidentifiable family members. No one took the time to write identifications on the images. A relative attempts to caption the images based on her own knowledge and places some erroneous names on the backs of the photographs.

It is now the present. You have been helping your parents clean out their attic. You discover several boxes of photographs, some identified and some not. When you ask your parents, they tell you that they know some of the people. The photographs have continued to be damaged by environmental humidity and temperature fluctuations. Your family has moved several times, and some of the mounted and framed photographs are broken or cracked. Another well-meaning relative has taken a pen, placed an X above the one person in the school portrait he knew, and proceeded to write her name in ink on the front of the photograph. Having an interest in family history, you decide to tackle the various issues relating to this collection: identification, restoration, and organization.

This is a fairly typical scenario. The division of the images and the damage they are subjected to happens in most families. What is unique is the composition of individual family photograph collections because photography played a different role in each family.

There are several things that need to be done to stop the collection from disappearing completely. The first is learning how to care for the various types of images in your possession. In the course of caring for them, it is necessary to learn a little photographic history as well.

SENTIMENTAL VS. MARKET VALUE

Every time you look at your images, the sentimental value of the photographs probably comes to mind. They may include the only picture of a great aunt you fondly remember or of your baby's first steps. It is easy to take these photographs for granted because they are part of your family history. But you may not be aware of the market value of some of the images in your collection.

Twenty years ago, you could buy a historical photograph for a few dollars, but today those very same images are being sold for larger sums than you can imagine. Take a look at the photographs being offered for sale in online auction houses and you'll gain a different type of appreciation for your family photographs. In 1998, Swann Galleries sold a family photograph album containing fourteen tintypes of Calamity Jane, her parents, and siblings for $21,850. Rare images are being rediscovered and sold for

W. A. JOHNSON,   THERESA, N. Y.

amazing amounts. Sotheby's sold a previously unknown collection of daguerreotypes by Boston photographers Southworth and Hawes for a record
$3,304,497. The collection was discovered in the basement of a home. Be-
fore you think that preserving your family photographs is an unnecessary
expense, consider the market value of the images.

There are several factors that determine the market value of individual
images and collections, including the condition of the photograph. **When
you look through your photographs, evaluate their sentimental value and historical
worth in terms of the following:**

• **Famous person.** Can you identify the people in your pictures? Does
oral tradition allude to a famous person in your family? Who knows, it
might be true! Once you know a name, consult either online or print versions
of biographical encyclopedias for information. It is possible to discover a

Notes

notable person in your family whose history was lost over the years. Sometimes family stories about an ancestor's exploits are true. Keep in mind that you can find photographs of famous individuals unrelated to your family in albums and collections. It was quite popular in the nineteenth century to collect photographs of famous individuals.

• **Unusual images.** You may own an image that has significant historical value. If you have photographs that are unusual in any way or that depict events, landscapes, or even medical anomalies, they may be valuable. For instance, a photograph of a particular town may be the only known image of a location.

• **Identified photographs.** The monetary value of a photograph increases if the person is identified. There are boxes of unidentified photographs sitting in antique shops, but images with identification attached are less common and therefore worth more.

• **Well-known photographer.** Photographs taken by famous photographers may be mixed in with your family snapshots. For instance, the collection auctioned by Sotheby's sold for such a high sum because the images were in good condition, the poses were unusual, and the work was from one of the first daguerreotype studios in the United States. Researching photographers is explained in *Uncovering Your Ancestry Through Family Photographs*.

• **Unusual photographic process.** Occasionally a photograph is valuable because of the process that created it or its format. Photographic jewelry is uncommon and sells for more than a paper portrait would. Nineteenth-century photographers sometimes used innovative techniques to lure customers into their studios or improved upon existing photographic processes. If you don't recognize the name of a process listed on the back of a photograph, consult the glossary of photographic terminology in Appendix A.

Not every collection of photographs is going to contain images that fall into those categories, but it is worth considering the monetary value of your collection in addition to its significance to your family history. Spending a few extra dollars on a special storage box seems worth the investment for images important both historically and sentimentally. If you think an image should be appraised for its significance, you can contact a professional by looking under auctioneers and appraisers in your local phone book. Museums and historical societies can also provide you with the names of reputable individuals.

By the time you're finished working with your photographs, you will have learned basic photo history, used them to uncover unknown information about members of your family, contacted relatives with other pictures, restored some damaged images to their original lustre, and organized your photos so that generations can appreciate them. It is a long process but not a daunting one. It takes time, patience, and a little capital, but in the end, it is worth it. You'll find that it is also fun. Your photographs are like a puzzle or a good mystery that you need to solve, and you can't wait to discover the ending. The final result of your efforts will be a well-organized story of your family in words and pictures.

CHECKLIST: GETTING READY

Notes

✓ Examine your photographs for their informational content.
✓ Retain the original order of the photographs until you are ready to organize them.
✓ Learn photo identification techniques.
✓ Put together a basic tool kit of supplies beforehand.
✓ Always wear gloves when handling images.

TWO

The Preservation Facts

Warning

T he fictional Smith family photographs incurred damage in the same way that your photographs do. Some of it is the result of a single incident, such as a broken photograph, while some of the damage happens slowly, such as the fading of color images. Most of the injuries our photographs acquire over time are the direct result of three factors: physical, biological, and chemical. Physical damage consists of tears, cracks, warping, and creases. Biological deterioration is a result of insects, animals, and mold. Chemical damage is characterized by fading, yellowing, and staining. **Improper storage materials and environmental conditions such as excess moisture, temperature fluctuations, pests, chemicals, and light influence the rate at which those factors deteriorate the images.**

DAMAGE TO PHOTOGRAPHS
Physical

Every time you shuffle through your images or touch them with bare hands, you cause damage. Moving photographs against each other while looking at them is abrasive and causes small scratches in the surface (see figure 2-1 on page 19). In some pictures, it removes part of the image. Gloves are a necessity when looking at pictures. Handling an image without gloves can leave fingerprints on the surface. While your fingerprints won't be immediately visible, they eventually will be. You probably have the fingerprints of several relatives on your pictures. The oils and dirt on your hands cause deterioration of the image. The best precaution is to handle photographs by the edges while wearing clean cotton gloves. They are available at most hardware stores and through the suppliers listed in Appendix D.

Biological
There are two major types of biological factors that many photographs are exposed to: pests and mold. In both cases, the amount of exposure influences the degree of damage done to the image area. Proper storage

containers and conditions can prevent this type of decay. Mold is discussed in the section on environment.

Pests

Photographs and albums offer animals and insects food and nesting materials. For instance, wood frames can attract insects such as termites. If you want to frame your images, see the list of precautions in chapter eleven. The paper backing on photographs and the adhesive used to mount pictures can encourage silverfish. If you are storing your photographs in an attic or basement, you may not be aware of the mice or other animals that live there. Your pictures provide warmth and supplies for building nests. Finding small animals and insects in your picture collection is an unpleasant surprise. If they decide to nest in the boxes you have in storage, their excrement will stain the images. Proper storage conditions and containers can stop the problem before it starts.

Chemical

Other types of damage are not as apparent. The very containers that we use for storage may seem safe, when in fact they may exude gases that will eventually stain the image. Wood, plastic, cardboard, and other types of materials used to manufacture boxes can produce off-gases. Glue in cardboard boxes can even seep onto your images. For these reasons, you need to take precautions with storage containers. Professional librarians and archivists use boxes produced by the suppliers listed in Appendix D.

One of the common causes of chemical stains is acid from mounting boards and glassine envelopes. Since most paper contains acids from the manufacturing process, it is important to minimize contact with the acids. This is accomplished by placing photographs in storage enclosures that are approved for use with photographs.

Some of the damage incurred by our images is inadvertent. Every time a photo lab processes your film, it is subjected to chemicals. If they are not completely rinsed off during development, they may cause staining. If you have brown stains on your black-and-white images, it is probably due to the chemicals used to develop the pictures. Improper processing marred one couple's wedding photographs. The photographer did not spend enough time washing the prints before drying. The result is an album full of brown-stained photographs.

Environment

Where you store your photographs can determine how long they will last. The amount of exposure to fluctuating humidity, temperature, light, and pollutants has a direct effect on pictures' longevity. Any of these environmental issues can encourage physical, biological, or chemical deterioration. Selecting the right storage area for your photographs is an important decision. Rather than placing your photographs in danger, take some time to consider your storage options.

Humidity

High humidity and dampness allow mold and mildew to grow on images. These can destroy the photograph. Mold and mildew grow on most photographic surfaces, so it is important to maintain a low humidity (see figure 2-2 on page 21). Professional archives maintain their collections between 30 and 50 percent relative humidity. In one library, the rear wall of the brick building was in need of repointing. Unbeknownst to the librarians, the rare books stored in closed glass cabinets on that wall were being subjected to dampness in each rainstorm. Librarians were not periodically checking for damage because the building had a temperature and humidity system. As soon as the staff became aware of the problem, they removed the books to special storage cabinets. Unfortunately, some books sustained substantial mold damage. This is a rather extreme case, but it illustrates the importance of storage conditions. Even if you think

Figure 2-2.
This unidentified photograph was found hiding behind a fireplace during a household remodeling project. It is covered with mold and scratches.
Collection of the author

your photographs are safe from humidity or other damage, it is wise to examine them at least once a year to make sure.

Temperature

High temperature and wide fluctuations harm pictures by accelerating various deterioration factors. Most photographs consist of several layers. The emulsion is the layer that contains the image. Photographs should be stored at a constant temperature no higher than 70°F. The cooler the temperature, the better. The chapter on color discusses the special temperature storage of those types of images. The emulsion of your pictures expands and contracts in the summer and winter, just like the roadway in front of your house does in reaction to temperature changes.

It is fairly inexpensive to monitor the temperature and humidity in the areas where you store your images. Libraries and archives use devices such as hygrothermographs or choose from a wide range of electronic data loggers. They range from expensive, sophisticated models to a low-priced version that can be mounted on a wall or placed on a table. Separate readings for temperature and humidity are provided.

Figure 2-3.
Some damage happens due to substances our images come into contact with. The blotches in the background of this image are stains from the adhesive used to adhere it to an album page.
Collection of the author

Light

Displaying our pictures is such an automatic action that few of us stop to consider what happens to our images when we hang them on walls or place them on mantels. Having photographs of family events in frames for visitors to see is an illustration of our family pride. The bad news is that it exposes the pictures to light and, in some cases, temperature fluctuations. Color is especially susceptible to fading, and color changes due to light, but many nineteenth-century images fade, as well. The lovely blue cyanotypes can fade rapidly when displayed. With some precautions, you can still exhibit those favorite photographs. Some guidelines appear in chapter eleven.

Warning

Librarians and photo curators are now aware that photocopying your pictures should be kept to a minimum. While you will want to bring copies of your photographs with you to visit relatives or on research trips, be sure to limit photocopying. The combination of two types of hazards, heat and light, is inherent in the photocopying process.

Pollution

Don't underestimate the problems caused through exposure to chemical pollutants in our environments. This includes not only the dirt and soot present in air pollution but the materials present in common household cleansers and tobacco. Exposure to these substances can corrode the surface of the images or leave deposits. If you spray air freshener repeatedly near a photograph, you are depositing chemicals on it. You will start to see gradual changes in the picture quality. Just as tobacco leaves nicotine stains on walls and furniture, it will affect the images in your possession. You can prevent damage caused by pollutants by using an air purifier and regularly cleaning the storage area. If you have a substantial family photograph collection, an air purifier can be a worthwhile investment.

Types of Damage	Results
Humidity	Mold, mildew, discoloration, and warping; photographs stick together
Gases from storage containers	Staining, acid migration
Improper photo processing	Staining
Temperature fluctuations	Cracking, warping
Photocopying	Light and heat—keep to a minimum
Handling	Deposits oil, dirt, and fingerprints; leads to staining and marks
Animals/insects	Staining and holes from feeding and excrement
Dust and dirt	Hard to remove from surface without damaging it

SHOULD YOU CLEAN YOUR PICTURES?

As you begin going through your images, you are going to be tempted to clean off the surface dirt and grime that has collected with time. **Stop! There are ways to safely dust off some of the material on the surface of the photographic materials,** but it must be done with care or you will abrade the surface. You can purchase the basic tools at a hardware store or an art supply shop. You can also purchase them from the suppliers listed in Appendix D. Remove surface dust and dirt with a soft bristle brush, gently sweeping it across the image in even strokes. Some of what appears to be grime may actually be mold or staining. If it doesn't come off with gentle brushing, leave it alone. Clean dirt from the card surrounding the image with either a dry cleaning pad for use on documents (available from archival suppliers) or an eraser approved for conservation work. In 1997, an article suggested using Magic Rub and Mars Plastic erasers.[1] They leave little residue on the surface. Do

Warning

Figure 2-4.
Photographs can break during handling. This portrait of a member of the Wilson family has been pieced back together.
Collection of the author

not try to erase the image area, however, because you might end up removing loose pieces of emulsion. Keep in mind that manufacturers constantly change chemical formulations of their products, so before purchasing one, call the manufacturer to verify that the product hasn't been reformulated.

STORAGE CONSIDERATIONS

By now you are probably completely discouraged. Is any place safe for your family photographic heirlooms? The answer is yes! By adhering to a few rules of storage and materials, you can extend the life of your family photographs. If you want to display and frame a few special pictures, go right ahead. Just be sure to follow the guidelines. As you look at your photographs, handle them carefully by the edges and wear special gloves whenever possible.

Each type of photographic process has special storage requirements, depending on the format and the materials. **There are several general tips for all photographs starting with storage environment and types of containers.**

Storage Environment

Of primary importance is where you store the collection. Can you think of any place in your house that meets the criteria of constant temperature, low humidity, darkness, and being out of the way of the hazards mentioned previously? In most homes, the best place to store pictures is on a shelf in a windowless closet. The worst places to store images are basements and attics. Basements can be damp but also periodically flood. One woman lost all of her family photographs when she left them on the basement floor during a move. An unusually strong rainstorm combined with an open window caused the problem. This situation usually requires consultation with professional conservators. They are trained to handle this type of damage. It may be possible to save photographs exposed to water damage. Attics often experience extreme seasonal temperature variations, and roofs can leak. Try to find an appropriate spot in your house.

Avoid these storage areas

1. Basements: There is too much humidity and the possibility of a flood. A woman placed all her boxes of photographs in the basement when she was renovating her house. Unfortunately, when a major rainstorm hit the area, her basement flooded. Instead of calling a conservator for advice, she lost all those pictures.
2. Attics: They experience extreme temperature fluctuations: cold in the winter and hot in the summer.
3. Garages: They expose your photographs to humidity, temperature fluctuations, and toxic fumes.

Containers

There are many suppliers for special boxes, sleeves, and envelopes, but how do you know which ones are best for your images? You will want to select materials that are guaranteed to protect your images. Many suppliers and manufacturers highlight certain items by saying they passed the PAT. This means that manufacturers have tested the reactivity of the components of various types of paper and plastic to photographs. You want to look for this designation whenever purchasing supplies.

Plastics can cause a whole array of problems for photographic materials. When purchasing clear sleeves, make sure to buy polypropylene or polyester ones. Either is fine, but polyester is more expensive. Polyethylene is not approved for long-term storage. Not all suppliers carry polypropylene or polyester sleeves, so verify availability beforehand by calling the supplier directly. Suppliers that are accustomed to working with libraries and museums will readily address your concerns.

Since plastic, wood, and cardboard give off gases that cause a variety of

problems, don't use containers made of these substances. **The best materials are boxes with reinforced corners, which are available from archival suppliers.** Make sure the box tops fit snugly so that dirt and dust do not settle on your prints. Museums and libraries also use baked-enamel metal cabinets for storage.

THE BASICS

All supplies must pass the PAT

Boxes	Reinforced corners or baked-enamel cabinets
Paper	Lignin-free
Plastic	Polypropylene or polyester

Supplies

- Storage containers

- Soft bristle brush

- Gloves

- Hygrothermograph or data loggers

- Graphite pencil

HOW TO SELECT STORAGE MATERIALS

1. Deal with a reputable supplier. See list in Appendix D. 2. Purchase materials that have passed the PAT. 3. If buying plastic sleeves, make sure they are polypropylene or polyester.

What to avoid

1. Unrefined plastic or cardboard boxes: If the storage container gives off an odor, there are gases being emitted that will damage the images over time. Additionally, the glue in the cardboard may seep onto the images and stain them.

2. Acid paper folders or envelopes: This includes brown kraft paper and glassine. There are several dangers. The chemicals used to bleach papers may cause the photographs to fade.[2] If you place photographs in gummed envelopes, the glue can cause stains. The acid papers will over time stain the images, as well.

3. Rubber bands, paper clips, or other objects to keep your images together: Rubber bands deteriorate and adhere to the surface of the photograph, while paper clips rust and cause indentations in the images. Rubber bands can also cause tears in the images.

TAKE CARE OF YOUR NEW IMAGES

These guidelines should be followed for historic family photographs as well as those being created. In addition, there are a number of steps you can take to insure that your new images will be visible a generation from now. The entire chain of buying film, taking pictures, and having them developed has an effect on image durability.

When considering what film to purchase for future photos, use only a high-quality film. Be careful when purchasing film manufactured by an unknown company. It is best to stay with a reputable company. **Magazines such as *Popular Photography* and *American Photographer* regularly publish stories rating the different films.**

Once you have bought the film, try to use it quickly. If you purchased a large quantity on sale, you might consider storing it in your refrigerator. Color is adversely affected by heat. By keeping your unexposed film in a cool place, you are extending its life. Taking a few pictures and then storing your camera for months at a time can hurt the film.

What should you do after shooting the pictures and having them developed? Label them before you place them in storage so that your family won't be wondering who that person in the strange hat is!

What You Can Do to Keep the Pictures You Shoot Now

1. Purchase high-quality film.
2. Choose a reputable lab to process your film.
3. Take care with your film: Don't keep it in the camera for a long time; store unused film in the refrigerator to extend its life (do not place your camera in the refrigerator).
4. Buy storage materials that passed the PAT (see Appendix D for suppliers).
5. Store photos and film at the proper temperature and humidity.
6. Remember to label them.

By following these guidelines for all the pictures in your collection, you are guaranteeing that future family members can enjoy them. The basic requirements of temperature, humidity, and PAT-approved materials are easy to obtain and maintain.

Caring for Your Collection on a Budget

Money is always an issue in caring for a family collection. A few ways to save:

- Compare prices. Ask the suppliers listed in Appendix D to send you their free catalogs, and then comparison shop. Custom-size boxes and folders cost more than those available in standard sizes. Many items are offered in a variety of styles. You can start small and add special items later.
- Buy in bulk and share orders. Find a friend or archive interested in saving money by purchasing in bulk. Most suppliers offer volume discounts on popular items.
- Take advantage of discounts. Companies sometimes offer discounts that are not quantity related. Inquire about them. For instance, Light Impressions has offered me a discount with the last several catalogs. Find out if you qualify by calling suppliers' toll-free numbers.
- Try alternative suppliers. Art supply houses carry a wide variety of materials. In my experience, this is not true for office supply stores.

MAILING PHOTOGRAPHS

Scanners and electronic images make it easier than ever to share images with family members, but if you need to send an original image through the mail, take the necessary precautions.

1. Place each individual image in a protective polypropylene sleeve to protect against abrasion.
2. Sandwich the images in their sleeves between two pieces of stiff cardboard. The photographs should be flat against the surface of the cardboard in their protective sleeves.
3. Select an envelope that will protect the images from bending and from the elements.
4. Write in large letters across the envelope: "Do not bend–Photographs."
5. Mail the package using a method that provides a return receipt and tracking, such as UPS Air, Registered Mail, or FedEx. If the package is lost, there may be a way to locate it. If you send it regular mail and it doesn't arrive at its destination, it may be lost forever.
6. Don't worry about insurance. You can never replace a family photograph, and most insurance will only reimburse for the actual cost of an image.

David Mishkin of Just Black and White, a company that specializes in historic copying and duplication of images, advises his clients to take the following precautions when packing and shipping images.

Quotes

> If you are sending photographs, always include at the very least one piece, or better yet two pieces of corrugated cardboard. Even if the photo is mounted on mount board, this will not provide adequate protection. If you are sending anything with glass, you should wrap it horizontally with bubble packing and then another layer vertically. This should then be placed in a box filled with plastic peanuts. This method will offer maximum protection without adding much to the weight. Once again, the *absolute safest* way to ship your photographs is by FedEx. Don't worry about the extra cost of insurance; they will pay only for the actual cost of the photograph ($10 to $25), not what you claim it is worth to you. Instead, spend your money on the most reliable but more expensive shipping method.[3]

CHOOSING A STORAGE FACILITY

Is your collection too large to store at home, or do you lack the right environment? In this case, you might consider renting storage space at an archival storage facility. Many museums and archives store at least part of their collections off-site. You can find a storage facility in your area by contacting a local library, museum, or conservation lab. Since your collection has sentimental if not monetary value, it is important that you follow a set of criteria to evaluate the facility. These are the same kinds of issues that institutions address before entrusting their collections.

Make an Appointment

In order to properly evaluate storage conditions, it is necessary to visit the facility. It will provide an opportunity to see how other collections are stored. An integral part of a visit is a tour of the storage areas. If your request for a tour is denied, find another facility. In preparation for a visit, estimate how many boxes of material you are planning to keep there and for how long. When you go, bring a checklist of questions. This will help you remember to address the selection criteria.

Cleanliness

Are the storage areas neat and clean? You have the right to ask how often an area is cleaned and by what method. At one facility when I inquired about pest control, the marketing person looked at me oddly and claimed they didn't have any. Since most collections, even those from your home, are exposed to insects and rodents, this was an overstatement on his part. An entire warehouse of collections needs to be regularly inspected for vermin. Ask about the inspection schedule. Be sure to ask about how the company manages pest control. Many storage facilities spray only when necessary, to avoid the toxic and damaging effects of the chemicals. Insect control is a complicated issue. It is important to keep vermin away from photographs, but exposure to insect repellents can damage the pictures. Ask facilities about their policies.

Security

Observe how the facility handles your visit. Do you have to sign a visitor log? You want your collections to be safe from theft, so find out how you gain access to your material. Any warehouse that allows general access without supervision is not a very secure facility. Professional record storage involves procedures for retrieval of items from storage.

Disaster Preparation

What is the plan in case of a natural disaster or fire? You can ask to see a copy of the plan for these events. Well-managed companies update these plans on a regular basis. Does the space have a fire suppression and detection system? Natural disasters usually occur when we least expect them, so it is important to ask questions about the facility's relationship to flood zones. The best storage areas are constructed of inflammable materials and away from locales in danger of floods.

Environmental Controls

Remember that you will be paying to store your collections at this facility, so you want better storage conditions than you are able to supply at home. Of primary concern is the existence and stability of the temperature and humidity system. Air-conditioning and heat are not necessarily adequate for storage unless environmental controls are maintained. It is a good idea to inquire about temperature variation during extreme hot and cold weather. True museum-quality storage areas record temperature and humidity levels.

Retrieval

Accessibility is more than just being able to retrieve items from your collection. Well-organized facilities use systems to keep inventories of material in their care. This enables staff to quickly find items for customers. While you probably won't need to access your material in the middle of the night, you will want to know if there are specific hours for retrieval or if you can stop by anytime. Most facilities ask that clients call in advance of a visit to give them time to locate the material.

Costs

None of these services is inexpensive. When you call to set up a tour, ask the representative how the company charges for space. Depending on the cost, you may want to compromise on certain features such as retrieval to lower your costs. Before you sign the contract, make sure the paperwork doesn't transfer ownership to the facility after a certain amount of time.

As you are about to end your tour, ask for a list of references. You can always benefit from an opinion of a museum or library professional who uses the facility for storage. I've seen all kinds of so-called archival storage facilities. If the staff doesn't understand how to manage a facility with good environmental conditions, pest control, and security, then it probably isn't good for your collection. The worst space was a hundred-year-old warehouse that had wooden floors and walls, had no temperature and humidity control, and was filthy. It was advertised as an archival record management facility. Over the telephone, the place sounded perfect. Then I made an on-site visit.

COPYING METHODS

One of the ways to preserve your photographs is to use copies for display and when you create albums. Just a few years ago, before scanners and digital copiers, there was only one way to make copies of photographs: You had to make a copy negative and then a print. That has all changed. You can now walk into virtually any photo store and make copies yourself using new units such as the Kodak Picture Maker system. You can also copy photographs in your home using a basic scanner.

Photographic Copies

In order to make copies the traditional way, you have to use a piece of equipment called a copy stand and make either negatives or slides of the pictures. This method can be done in a professional photo studio or at home. A copy stand consists of two 500-watt tungsten lightbulbs, spaced

Quotes

LOW-COST STORAGE SOLUTION FROM DAVID MISHKIN OF JUST BLACK AND WHITE

If you can't find appropriate space in your home, consider renting a safe-deposit box. Banks maintain these storage areas at the same environment as their offices, usually at a fairly stable temperature and humidity. Safe-deposit boxes can be rented for a yearly fee, provide dark storage and security.

evenly apart, and a base with an adjustable rod attached that you affix a camera to. The bulbs uniformly light the object being photographed. I prefer this method because you are taking a negative of the print from which additional copies can be made. The print quality is also a little better than the newer direct positive methods.

You can make these stands very simply at home by mimicking the more professional models. On the Internet at <http://www.frontiernet.net/~rja cob/copystnd.htm>, you can even find directions to build your own. If you are going to be making copy prints of photographs in the collections of relatives, you would be wise to invest in one of the portable models. That way you can carry it with you when you visit them. You can also purchase ready-made copy stands from manufacturers and photo stores in a variety of price ranges.

Direct Positive Prints

Another copying method uses a system such as Kodak's Picture Maker to make copy prints while you wait. Kodak's Picture Maker is self-operated. It allows you to crop, enlarge, reduce red eye, and even add creative borders to your pictures. This method is too expensive to use for all of your images but is perfect for a select few. These stand-alone systems make prints, from small wallet-size photographs up to 8″ × 12″. This machine allows you to change the size of the original in seconds. It even works with a variety of photographic formats from prints, photo CDs, and some digital photographic equipment. You can even download the image onto a disk and print it at home. The Kodak Web site, <http://www.kodak.com>, features a search feature so that you can locate a Picture Maker in your area.

Scanning

Now that scanners are more affordable for the home user, they are gaining popularity with genealogists. They generally range in price from less than one hundred dollars to expensive professional models. The inexpensive ones are fine for most family photograph projects and are an excellent way to copy your images. However, **learning the language of scanning is like being tossed into an alphabet soup**; for example, there are several different picture formats: TIFF, PICT, GIF, JPEG. It is a little confusing at first. What does it all mean? In order to understand the basics of scanning, you need to become familiar with a few acronyms for terminology.

- DPI: Dots per inch.
- TIFF: Files viewable on both a PC and a Macintosh.
- PICT: For images to be used on a Macintosh.
- GIF: Usable on a Web site. Images are compressed to save file space and are limited in color. Files are compatible with either computer format.
- JPEG: Usable on a Web site. Images are compressed to save file space. Files are compatible with either computer format.

Sources

BUYING A COPY STAND

Beseler, Bogen, and Testrite manufacture copy stands for the professional and amateur photographer. You can order them through most camera stores. In general, look for one that is compact and portable and fits your budget.

\di'fin\ *vb*

Definitions

For More Info

CONSULT THE EXPERTS

For instructions on making slides and prints, consult the second edition of *Copying and Duplicating: Photographic and Digital Imaging Techniques* by W. Arthur Young, Thomas A. Benson, George T. Eaton, and Joseph Meehan.

For More Info

For an easy to understand explanation of scanning technology, look at Larry Ledden's *Complete Guide to Scanning.*

Factors to consider when choosing a format:

- **Compression:** Does the format compress the image? If so, then choose another format for images you are going to edit, manipulate, or restore later.
- **Image quality:** Some compression methods affect image quality. This can affect editing.
- **Color depth:** Does the format have a full range of color, or is it limited?
- **Special features:** Can you watermark your images or add copyright information?

One expert advises using a simple TIFF format with no compression for saving scans even though it takes up a lot of space. TIFF retains all the qualities of the original image, while JPEG, including the JPEG option under TIFF, drops out some features during compression. Unfortunately, not all photo-editing software will support TIFF. JPEG is a great format for sharing images online because of the compression. It is not true that once you have edited a JPEG image and resaved, it cannot be edited again. GIF is another option, but it is limited in its ability to record color. It is suggested for graphics, not photographs. The best way to see the differences is to try them for yourself.[4]

A scanner uses sensors to measure the amount of light reflected off the image. The size of these sensors determines the resolution or clarity of the picture.[5] The DPI rating of your scanner correlates to the number of sensors per inch of scanning width. A good-quality scanner allows you to adjust the scanning resolution of your picture. The DPI rating of the scanner influences the picture quality of the image. There are other factors that affect the DPI. For instance, you need to know the range of your scanner and the printer when considering DPI. You can scan the image at a higher resolution for printing even if your printer can't duplicate the same DPI. At some point, you will upgrade your printer and not have to rescan the image. In the case of printing an image on the Web, the DPI correlates to the amount of time it takes your computer to download the image. Many Web sites use images scanned at 72 DPI. This results in a readable image and one that can be quickly downloaded.

Some individuals still own handheld scanners, but most of the scanners on the market today are flatbed scanners. That means you can scan images without moving the scanner itself. These work very well for scanning images or flat art. If you have a large number of slides, you might want to purchase a special slide scanner. They are slightly more expensive but worth the investment if the majority of your photographs are transparencies and slides. Before purchasing any piece of equipment, it is advisable to research information regarding the quality of the product. Reviews appear in *Consumer Reports* and computer magazines such as *PC Magazine* and *PC World.* This information is also available online at several Web sites.

In a recent review by *PC Magazine* of seventeen scanners, the reviewer evaluated several features of the scanners, such as color accuracy, the purity of the color white, detail in the highlight areas, clear edges, and that the dark areas had both detail and accurate color.[6] These are the features you want to look for prior to purchasing a particular model.

Color accuracy or color balance in the image is one of the most important considerations. It is the component that captures an image in realistic color. An indication of this is the number of bits a scanner offers. All color is composed of three primary colors: red, green, and blue. A scanner that offers good color quality for home use should have at least 24 bits or 16.8 million colors. A scanner with poor color balance will not show a true white. You don't want to see other colors present in the scanned image of a white dress. You want to scc an accurate copy of the image you are scanning.

A good scanner also provides detail in the image. This is commonly referred to as image resolution. This translates into the DPI rating mentioned above. The higher the DPI, the more detail in the viewable image. This doesn't mean that you have the capability to print an image in the same amount of detail. That depends on the DPI rating of your printer.

Software usually accompanies the scanner, but make sure it is TWAIN compatible. TWAIN stands for "technology without an interesting name." This is a program that will scan the image onto your computer.

The first scanners could produce only black-and-white images, but today most scanners also give you the option of color. This is usually part of the software that comes with your scanner. This software leads you through the step-by-step process of scanning an image. You need to identify what you are copying, such as line art, halftone, a black-and-white photograph, or a color image. Based on your selection, the software will assign certain qualities to that image. However, it is advisable to purchase more sophisticated software if you are going to manipulate the size, color, and features of the image. Two popular programs are Adobe Photoshop and Picture Publisher. They allow enhancement, printing, and processing of the images. Basic features include rotating the image (especially important for large images), cropping, increasing or decreasing the contrast, changing the size of the image, and removing red eye. The best programs will allow you unlimited opportunities to undo any number of changes before closing the program. When you first begin to manipulate your digitized images, you will want to reverse your mistakes. More sophisticated restoration techniques are available in the professional versions of the popular photo software. The applications of these features to your family photographs is covered in chapter seven.

Sources

ONLINE AND PRINT PRODUCT REVIEWS

Consumer Reports <http://www.consumerreports.org; *PC Magazine* <http://www8.zdnet.com/pcmag>; PC World <http://www.PCWorld.com>

SCANNING THE IMAGES

This introduction to scanning covers the three basic considerations in digitizing family photographs: scanning techniques, formats, and storage. First, you must select a scan level. This is the DPI or scan resolution combined with the number of colors or color depth. The suggested format for archiving images is TIFF with no compression, but for sharing, it is JPEG for speed of transmission. The third concern when digitizing your images is selecting

For More Info

CONSULT THE EXPERTS

Web sites devoted to helping consumers learn scanning techniques:
A Few Scanning Tips <http://www.scantips .com>. A great resource. Adobe Technical Guides <http://www.adobe.com/ support/techguides/ printpublishing/scanning/ psscanning.html>. Definitions and tips from the manufacturer of Photoshop, a photo-editing software package. The Scanning FAQ <http://www.infomedia.net/ scan>. Techniques broken down by skill level: novice, intermediate, and advanced.

FEATURES

Flatbed Scanner

A flat surface is essential to scanning photographs safely and accurately. While handheld and sheetfed scanners exist, these will damage the image you are trying to scan and probably won't result in a good image.

TWAIN Interface

Any scanner you purchase should come with a TWAIN driver so that images can be scanned onto your computer.

24 Bits

While scanners come with higher bits, for home use with family images, at least a 24-bit scale is fine.

DPI

The higher the DPI rating, the more detail in your viewable photograph on the computer monitor. Images on the Web work best at 72 DPI. For printing purposes, make sure your printer can support the DPI of the scanner.

Software

If you intend to improve the quality of the scanned images, you need software that will let you crop, rotate, and change the scale of the image, fix the contrast, and remove red eye. It will also allow you to undo errors.

a storage medium that is "archival." You can print your digitized images using certain supplies (explained below) or keep them on CD. Unfortunately, the debate continues on which digital archival storage method will have the best retrieval rate in the future to allow for data migration, which is the transfer to another, newer medium.

PRINTING DIGITAL IMAGES

There are two ways to make prints of your digitized images. You can use one of the photo Web sites mentioned in chapter six, or purchase a good-quality ink-jet printer. In the first instance, you receive prints on regular photo paper, while at home you can use archival paper and inks available from special suppliers.

If you decide to buy a printer, the good news is that most now have the ability to print images. Printing digital images is a technology that is less than a decade old. According to Henry Wilhelm of Wilhelm Imaging Research, Inc., it wasn't until 1994 that the first desktop had the capability.[7] Richard Wilson of *Publishing Your Family History on the Internet* suggests purchasing a printer that has 1,400×760 DPI or higher in order to get a clear picture. He also suggests checking to see if it has a photo print command under setup options when you request a print. It is necessary to select properties to choose the print mode and the type of paper.

While it is relatively easy to produce photographic prints at home on your ink-jet, there are preservation issues that are unique to these prints. The permanence and fading qualities of both the ink and the paper need to be considered separately. The companies that supply inks are not the same manufacturers that produce paper. In the ink-jet print, both ingredients (ink and paper) have different rates of permanence. Archival in terms of printer inks and papers means that the manufacturer intended only for the product to last for a "reasonable" period.[8] These prints using the best-quality inks and papers are still subject to fading, bleeding ink, yellowing, and damage due to high humidity. Wilhelm continues to investigate industry claims and conducts accelerated aging tests to see which products last the longest. His research is available online and is the best source of current data. The choices you make regarding the two components of the home printer influence the stability of your image. These pictures you print yourself can last a long time as long as you purchase products that have been tested. Standard paper and ink will fade in under a year, while special inks and paper can possibly last as long as fifty to one hundred years.[9] In order to increase the longevity of these prints, you need to apply the same basic rules of preservation storage that you use for the rest of your collection.

DIGITAL INFORMATION ONLINE

In the digital realm, it is difficult to keep track of the latest changes. That's why having readily accessible reviews and product information is invaluable. Use the sites below to follow news, obtain feedback from actual users of cameras and scanners, and learn new techniques to make your equipment work for you. According to *Digital Camera Magazine*, there is a lot of digiphoto material available online, but it is user beware. These three sites received top ratings from *Digital Camera*:[10]

- Steve's DigiCams <http://www.steves-digicams.com>
- PC Photo Review <http://www.pcphotoreview.com>
- Digital Eyes <http://www.image-acquire.com>

KNOW THE LAW BEFORE YOU COPY

When I called a photo store to inquire about certain equipment for copying photographs, the salesperson made me promise to tell you about copyright infringement and family photographs. Not that I needed reminding. As a former picture researcher, I dealt with copyright considerations every day in selecting images for print publication. But how does this law affect genealogists? **Copyright is a complicated set of intellectual property laws to protect the interests of the "author."** In general, the author is the person,

Supplies

SUPPLIERS OF ARCHIVAL INKS AND PAPER

Lyson Ltd. <http://www.lyson.com>. MIS Associates, Inc. <http://www.inksupply.com>. For current information on inks and papers, see Wilhelm Imaging Research, Inc. <http://www.wilhelmresearch.com>. This site also contains a list of suppliers for the products he mentions.

Internet Source

Digital Camera Magazine <http://www.photopoint.com/dcm> is also available in print from Digital Camera, Aeon Publishing Group, 88 Sunnyside Blvd., Suite 203, Plainview, NY 11803.

Important

persons, or corporation that creates an original work. The government office that oversees the use and abuse of copyright is the United States Copyright Office (USCO) under Title 17 of federal law. You can find these laws on the Library of Congress Web site <http://lcweb.loc.gov/copyright> or at most large public libraries. USCO also processes and registers copyrights.

Under the law, rules of usage and infringement are the same whether you are creating a family genealogy or a family Web site or copying images to distribute to relatives. Genealogists need to be familiar with the basics of copyright law before attempting to publish any of the images in their collections in a book or on a Web site. An understanding of terminology will help you determine whether or not the photograph you wish to copy or publish is under copyright. For the purposes of this book, a copyright is the legal right of the author, in this case photographer, to resell the images he created. Thus, if you took the picture, you are considered the author. However, if you or a relative went to a professional photographer for a portrait, the photographer owns the copyright. In order to reproduce that image, you have to obtain her permission. It doesn't matter that you paid the photographer for the family photograph; you must still approach the photographer for permission to publish. This also pertains to copies. The photographer will either make the copies at your expense or sign a waiver so you can have copies made elsewhere. Publication of some images will be subject to an additional usage fee known as a royalty. In this case, you have to tell the photographer where the image will be used and why.

There are items that are strictly regulated by law and should never be copied. These include money, Federal Reserve notes, citizenship certificates, passports, postage stamps, revenue stamps, checks, bonds, securities, and government identification documents.

Frequently Asked Questions About Copyright
How does this law concern me?
Let's say that you have a photographic portrait in your collection taken by a photographer who is still in business. According to a ruling made by the U.S. Supreme Court in 1978, the photographer holds the copyright for that image. This means that in order to make copies of the picture or loan it out for display or publication, you must first approach the photographer for the right to do so. You also need to request additional copies from the photographer.

Are there any exceptions?
There is another clause of the law that covers "fair use." There are four criteria for determining whether use of a photograph can be considered fair use. "Work" refers to a photograph.
  1. Is this a commercial or noncommercial usage? (Are you going to make a profit from its use?)

2. What is the nature of the usage? (How will you use it, and where will it appear?)

3. How much of the work are you using?

4. Does this affect the value of the work?

Simply defined it means that you can use the image for personal or educational use without monetary gain. While one of the factors is the percentage of the work being reproduced, this was primarily intended for authors of written works. A good rule of usage is to contact the photographer whenever any portion of an image is going to be published or posted on the Internet. This means that using a copyrighted photograph on your Web site without permission is a copyright infringement.

Does a photographer have the right to use my image without permission?
Professional photographers who sell their work to advertisers and publications usually obtain signed releases from the individuals in those photographs. Reprints of model releases and an explanation of your rights are published in the *ASMP Professional Business Practices in Photography.*

What about alterations?
Any alteration of the image must also be approved by the copyright holder, which means that if you want to use a section of a copyrighted image on your Web site, you need permission to do so. As computer-enhanced images become more common, it is increasingly popular to manipulate an image to add information. This is easily done with digitized images. Photo restorers can show you examples of photographs where the owners asked to have people taken out or added in. Do not

BASIC RULES

Works published pre-1923: In the public domain.

Copyrighted works published 1923–1963: If not renewed, then in the public domain. If renewed, then extended by ninety-five years from date of first publication.

Copyrighted works published 1964–1977: In effect twenty-eight years from date of first publication. Automatic extension of ninety-five years from renewal date (United States Copyright Code 304a and b).

Copyrighted works published after 1 January 1978: In effect for the life of the author plus seventy years (United States Copyright Code 304a). In the case of joint authors, in effect until the death of the last author plus seventy years.

(This is a general overview. Please use the Consult the Experts section for up-to-date information.)

WEB SITE

United States Copyright Office <http://lcweb.loc.gov/copyright/title17>. Find forms and information about Title 17.

A copyright notice should contain the following: The symbol ©, the word *copyright,* or the abbreviation *Copr.;* year of first publication (creation); name of the copyright holder. Example: © 2000 Maureen Taylor. This notice should appear on the item.

view this as a handy way to get rid of the visual evidence of those unsavory relatives or to change history by including a deceased family member in a group portrait. Two famous cases involve alteration of the dust jacket of the book *A Day in the Life of America* and a photograph from the movie *Rain Man.* In the first case, a moon was added to the photograph. In the second, the picture that appeared in *Newsweek* magazine accompanying a story on the movie *Rain Man* and showing Dustin Hoffman and Tom Cruise standing together was a composite of two different images.[11] While you may not consider this a problem, take a moment to consider what would happen to the interpretation of some of your family photographs. Are you changing the history of what is represented in your images by altering them?

If you think that copyright laws don't affect you, see what happens when you take a contemporary family photograph to a photo studio to be copied. In most cases, the studio will request a waiver from the photographer before making reproductions. Professional photographers and photo studios basically agree to uphold the law. Therefore they can refuse to make copies of images covered by the law. Several professional organizations, including the Professional Photographers of America, have agreed to adhere to a set of copyright guidelines outlined by the Photo Marketing Association International. **You can find a complete set of the responsibilities of the consumer and professional photographers on the Kodak Web site <http://www.kodak.com/global/en/ consumer/doingMore/copyright.shtml>.**

When locating images to add to your collection, copyright becomes even more of a concern. Images published in books, in magazines, and on the Web also fall under the parameters of the law. As a genealogist, it is best to be cautious about reprinting images you find elsewhere. For most historical photographs taken prior to 1923, you are safe. They are no longer covered by copyright. An exception is using historical images found in museum collections because they are documents owned by the museum. For the parameters of the law use the Basic Rules chart provided or follow the advice given in Consult the Experts.

If you think you would like to protect some of your images by applying for a copyright, it can be done in three easy steps. Go to the Library of Congress Web site for copyright information <http://lcweb.loc.gov> or write to the U.S. Copyright Office, Library of Congress, 101 Independence Ave., SE, Washington, DC 20559 to obtain the appropriate form. The USCO also has a twenty-four-hour hotline to request forms, at (202) 707-9100. You need to submit two copies of the published image or one copy of an unpublished photograph. The cost of registering is a nominal twenty dollars payable only by check or money order. Holding a copyright entitles you to exclusive rights to make copies, sell and market the picture, display it and allow others to duplicate it as long as you have the proper releases.

Once you publish your images on a Web site, other individuals can copy them. An interesting way to see if anyone is using your pictures without permission is to enter the image file name, including the extension, into AltaVista. It will show you where your image appears on the Web.[12]

Copyright law is a complicated issue, with constant debate. Genealogists need to pay attention to the law when copying or publishing photographs that might be under copyright. Before publishing any photos, make sure you have taken care of any copyright issues.

TERMINOLOGY

Author	Creator of the item being copyrighted
Copyright infringement	Using an item under copyright without permission
Publication	Public distribution of copies
Fair use	Use of a copyrighted work for educational or personal purposes
Public domain	Works no longer covered by copyright

REGISTERING A PHOTOGRAPH

1. Submit Form VA.

2. Include two copies of the work to be registered with a nonreturnable deposit. Unpublished images need one copy, a photocopy, or contact sheets.

3. Enclose the nonrefundable filing fee of twenty dollars (check or money order payable to Register of Copyrights).

4. Send package to Register of Copyrights, Library of Congress, Washington, DC 20559.

Continued on next page

CONSULT THE EXPERTS

When Works Pass Into the Public Domain <http://www.unc.edu/~unclng/public-d.htm>

Copyright Table Compiled by Cottrill and Associates <http://www.progenealogists.com/copyright_table.htm>

"U.S. Copyright and Genealogy" by Mike Goad <http://www.rootsweb.com/~mikegoad/copyright1.htm>

"Who Owns Genealogy?" by Gary B. Hoffman <http://www.genealogy.com/genealogy/14_cpyrt.html>

Stephen Fishman. *The Public Domain: How to Find and Use Copyright-Free Writings, Music, Art and More.* Nolo Press, 2000.

"A Writer's Guide to Using Works in the Public Domain" by Sharon DeBartolo Carmack and Maureen A. Taylor. *Writer's Digest*, September 2001.

CHECKLIST: THE PRESERVATION FACTS

Notes

✓ Find an appropriate storage area.
✓ Use good-quality supplies that are PAT-approved.
✓ Take care of your new images as well as the old.
✓ Be careful of copyright issues when using images.

THREE

Cased Images: Daguerreotypes, Ambrotypes, and Tintypes

A t almost every lecture, someone approaches me with a question about a small box or booklike item he found with the family photographs. Some people arrive with one in hand unsure how to open it. Others know it is a photograph but wonder what kind it is. Paper photographs are familiar, while the images in these small cases are not necessarily part of every family photograph collection. Their images and beauty make them valuable family artifacts. If you have one or two in your collection, treat them with care and respect. They are the earliest types of photographs and provide a glimpse into life in the mid-nineteenth century.

Typically, cases enclosed three types of images: daguerreotypes, ambrotypes, and tintypes. Each has several parts: the case, the image, the cover glass, a mat that creates a frame around the image, and something called the preserver, which is a thin strip of metal with a paper seal that creates an airtight fit of the various pieces. While the glass protects the surface of the image from abrasion, the preserver prevents environmental pollutants from contaminating these images. Unfortunately, this was not always successful. The seal lost its airtight qualities as the tape aged. While you can find a daguerreotype, ambrotype, or tintype in its case, locating one in mint condition is difficult. Cased images are subject to various types of damage, depending on the process.

DAGUERREOTYPES

The first daguerreotypes appeared in America in 1840 in the hands of Francois Gouraud, a contemporary of the inventor Louis Daguerre. Gouraud traveled throughout the United States giving demonstrations on how to create a daguerreotype, the first photographic image.

A daguerreotype is a sheet of polished metal covered in light-sensitive chemicals and exposed to light. The resulting portraits were initially crude and miraculous. Never before had individuals seen such clear and unflattering portraits of themselves. The final product was a realistic portrait of an individual that could be obtained in a short period of time. Unfortunately, the first

\di'fin\ *vb*

Definitions

41

Figure 3-1.
Example of a daguerreotype. *Chris Steele*

For More Info

FURTHER READING

If you want to know more about the fascinating history of the daguerreotype, read Beaumont Newhall's *The Daguerreotype in America.*

cameras had long exposure times. This meant holding a particular pose and expression for a length of time. One move resulted in a blurry image.

These images were one of a kind. The technology did not exist to make multiple copies. Daguerreotypists learned to make duplicates of an image by having an individual sit for additional portraits or by making copies of the original. Mass production of daguerreotypes often became the responsibility of an engraver who made prints based on the images.

Even with this limitation, the daguerreotype became an instant success. Whole industries developed to produce the metal plates, chemicals, and cases necessary for this new process. Anyone with the technical knowledge and the financial resources to purchase equipment and supplies established himself as a daguerrean artist. Enterprising individuals attracted customers to their regular businesses by offering to take their pictures while they were in the store. Itinerant daguerreotypists set up portable studios in more rural areas. America's love of the photograph was insatiable.

Daguerreotypes came in a variety of sizes from a mammoth plate (8½″ in height) to the small ninth plates (2½″ in height). The sizes most popular for portraits were the quarter, sixth, and ninth plates. See page 43 for a chart of daguerreotype sizes.

Individuals not familiar with the different types of cased images often confuse daguerreotypes, ambrotypes, and tintypes. If you have not seen one before, it can be difficult to determine what type of image is in the case. Recently, at a function at a bank, the manager held up a printing plate of

Daguerreotype Sizes	Average Size in Inches
Imperial/mammoth plate	Larger than 6½″ × 8½″
Whole plate	6½″ × 8½″
Half plate	4½″ × 5½″
Quarter plate	3¼″ × 4¼″
Sixth plate	2¾″ × 3¼″
Ninth plate	2″ × 2½″

the founder of the institution and declared it an ambrotype. Since a printing plate has an engraved surface and an ambrotype is glass, it was obvious that the manager had never seen the various types of cased images. Fortunately, daguerreotypes have a distinctive appearance. Their reflective mirrorlike surface makes them easy to identify once you know what to look for. Another clue is that the preservers did not always keep out pollutants and moisture, so the plates are tarnished and in need of conservation. If you have a cased image that is unreadable, you may have a daguerreotype. A professional conservator can chemically reverse this tarnishing.

Notes

How to Identify Daguerreotypes

1. **Shiny, reflective surface.** You will be able to see yourself reflected in the mirrorlike plate.
2. **Must be held at a particular angle to see the image.** You can only see a daguerreotype when it is held at an angle under indirect light. At different angles, the image changes from a negative to a positive.
3. **Usually in a case, although not always.** Daguerreotypists encased the images to protect their surfaces, but you often find daguerreotypes without cases. As the images tarnished, they were removed from the cases and either discarded or mistreated. The later cases with their intricate designs became collector's items.
4. **Sometimes colored or tinted.** Customers wanted the images to look more realistic so daguerreotypists applied tints to the surfaces. You often see pink cheeks and gold jewelry.
5. **Can be confused with cased ambrotypes and tintypes.** Even by using these identification criteria, without taking the image out of the case, you may be unsure whether you have a daguerreotype. Do not attempt this unless you have professional assistance. You can inadvertently damage the image.

HANDLING SUGGESTIONS
Don't clean them yourself!

The dust on the glass of the ambrotype or daguerreotype just seems to be sitting on the surface. It looks easy enough to take one apart and even

Warning

simpler to clean it. Though it is so tempting, don't open one! An individual's attempt to clean a cased image often leads to disastrous results. The person inadvertently causes irreparable damage to the image and loses it forever. What looks like dirt on the glass could be a sign of major deterioration. Contact a professional conservator before attempting any restoration work yourself. The fragile surface of all types of cased images make it difficult to assess how damaged an image really is unless you are a professional.

With these cautions in mind, the best rule to follow is, **leave all restoration to a professional.**

Important

Special Concerns

Conservators can clean a daguerreotype either by cleaning all the parts separately then reassembling them or by chemically restoring the image to its original condition. There are certain conditions that warrant conservation work.

• **Tarnishing.** Metal tarnishes when exposed to air and the chemicals in it. A daguerreotype consists of a silver plate that reacts to sulfur in the air. Therefore, most daguerreotypes have some degree of tarnishing. In the worst cases, it completely obscures the image. Conservators can reverse this tarnish.

• **Weeping.** Another type of damage commonly seen is the glass decomposition or "corrosion." Dust particles trapped on the glass also add to the problem. In these instances, conservators replace the damaged glass or clean dirty glass. When they put the daguerreotypes back together, they replace and secure the paper seal.

• **Abrasion.** The chemicals that create the image rest on the surface of the metal plate. Rubbing, brushing, or exposure to abrasive substances will remove the image and scratch the plate. In fact, photographers could reuse the plates by polishing, thus eroding, the image. Conservators use water-based solutions to clean a daguerreotype. The chemical cleaning of a daguerreotype is considered a major invasive treatment that is not without risk. In most cases, conservators will opt for dusting the surface with a gentle jet of air or rinsing it with deionized water. Most conservators consider chemical cleaning methods only if heavy, disfiguring corrosion is present.

• **Loose preserver.** If you are lucky enough to have a daguerreotype with its original parts, the preserver may be loose. You can gently press the preserver back in place. A better choice is to have a conservator restore your image to its original lustre by cleaning the glass and adjusting the preserver.

• **Halo.** A halo of corrosion on the metal plate forms from exposure to air pollution or high humidity. Depending on the amount of exposure to pollutants and the quality of the airtight seal, the color can range from light yellow to a shade that totally obscures the image.

• **Scratches.** Separate from abrasion are the scratches that occur on the plate through mishandling and neglect. Conservation cannot remove

Figure 3-2.
Here are the elements of an ambrotype. *Chris Steele*

these scratches in the surface of the metal place. Digital restoration can eliminate them.

AMBROTYPES

Another type of cased image is an ambrotype. Popular in the mid-1850s, **they consist of a piece of glass coated with a photo chemical known as collodion, a mixture of gun cotton and ether.** This creates a negative image that when backed with a dark piece of cloth or fabric becomes positive. The rest of the image includes the cover glass, mat, case, and preserver. Just like the daguerreotype, ambrotypes were one-of-a-kind images. They were available in the same sizes as daguerreotypes.

Identification
It is very difficult to tell whether the cased image you are holding is an ambrotype or a tintype. The color of the images is similar. **The best way to identify an ambrotype without taking it apart is to look for missing pieces or holes in the backing material.** These dark areas will appear transparent. The light areas are the collodion.

Special Concerns
A professional conservator should be the only one to clean or tamper with a cased ambrotype. The image only exists as a coating on the surface of the glass, so unless you have extensive experience with ambrotypes, leave it in the hands of a professional conservator. There are several types of damage common to an ambrotype and to other glass negatives.

Definitions

Technique

45

Figure 3-3.
The backing of an ambrotype can flake or lift off the glass. Notice the upper edge of this picture where the backing is missing. *Lynn Betlock*

For More Info

FURTHER READING

For a background history of the ambrotype, consult William Crawford's *The Keepers of Light: A History and Working Guide to Early Photographic Processes.*

• **Missing backing.** When the ambrotype was ready to be encased, the ambrotypist could back the surface with a dark fabric or paper or coat it with a layer of dark varnish. This made the positive image visible to the viewer. As the backing aged, pieces of it separated from the image, causing transparent areas in the image where you can see clear through the glass to the backing. Attempts to replace this backing yourself can pull away any emulsion that has adhered to it.

• **Broken glass.** While the covering glass can break, so can the glass image. If it is in the case and the pieces are together, you should take it to a professional conservator. If it is not in a case, treat it as a glass negative by creating a mat to hold it together. See instructions on page 75.

• **Emulsion lifting from the glass.** Since the collodion emulsion is brushed onto the glass surface to create the image, it can lift off the glass as the surface is exposed to abrasion and fluctuations in temperature and humidity. You can stabilize this damage by sandwiching it between two clean pieces of glass the same size as the image.

TINTYPES

The third type of cased photograph resembles a daguerreotype only because it is an image on metal. Unlike with the daguerreotype and ambrotype, it was possible to make more than one tintype at a sitting. It was inexpensive to produce, and it took less than a minute to walk out of a photographer's studio with one in hand. Some photographers used special multilens cameras to produce additional individual exposures. Tintypes, like daguerreotypes and ambrotypes, were not made using a negative.

History

Tintypes, or ferrotypes, have a fascinating history. It was the first photographic process invented in the United States, and its longevity is only surpassed by the paper print. A chemistry professor in Ohio patented the process in 1856, and it survived until the middle of the twentieth century. While the name suggests the metal was tin, it was actually iron sheets cut into standard sizes. The sizes initially corresponded to those of ambrotypes and daguerreotypes so that in the early period they could be placed in cases. Other sizes were introduced later, such as the "thumbnail" tintype made to fit into a specially created album. These tintypes were literally no larger than a thumbnail, thus their nickname. Tintypes are usually found either in a case, in a paper sleeve with a cutout for the image, or lacking their protective covering.

Tintype Sizes

These are primarily the sizes for cased tintype images. Tintype sizes vary for paper sleeves and mimicked the size and format of card photographs.

Tintype Sizes	Average Size in Inches
Whole plate	6½″ × 8½″
Half plate	4½″ × 5½″
Quarter plate	3½″ × 4½″
Sixth plate	2¾″ × 3¼″
Bon ton with paper sleeve	2⅜″ × 3½″ (could be as large as 4″ × 5″)
Ninth plate	2″ × 2½″
Sixteenth plate	1⅝″ × 2⅛″
Gem or thumbnail	1″ × 1″ (or smaller)

For More Info

FURTHER READING

To find more information on tintypes, read Floyd Rinhart, Marion Rinhart, and Robert W. Wagner's *The American Tintype.*

If you have a Civil War relative, it is likely you have a few tintypes in your collection. Itinerant photographers traveled with the troops and set up to take pictures whenever there was an opportunity. Soldiers often sent these durable images home via the mail without the danger of them breaking like an ambrotype.

Paper prints replaced these images in standard photography studios, but tintypes retained their popularity at tourist resorts until the early part of the twentieth century. Don't assume just because you have a tintype that the image dates from the mid- to late-nineteenth century. Always rely on photographic identification techniques, explained in *Uncovering Your Ancestry Through Family Photographs*.

Identification

Unfortunately, the process of identifying a tintype still in the case uses the process of elimination. If the image is not reflective or missing pieces of backing, then it may be a tintype. However, ambrotypes in pristine condition will have a similar appearance.

TELLING THEM APART

In cases where the primary identifying characteristics are not apparent, the only way to discern the type of cased image is to take it out of the case. In those instances, consult a professional conservator. Be very careful not to damage the case or the image in the process. Removing images from their cases can expose them to deterioration factors in the environment.

MAJOR CHARACTERISTICS		
Daguerreotype	**Ambrotype**	**Tintype**
Mirrorlike surface	Negative on glass; appears as a positive image	Negative on iron; appears as a positive image
Must be held at an angle to be seen	Backed with a dark background	Fixed on a black metal background
Usually cased	Usually cased	Paper mat or case
Image reversed	Image not reversed	Image reversed
1839	1854	1856

Identifying Information in a Cased Image

Occasionally there is a surprise waiting for you when the conservator removes the image from the case—the name of the photographer or other identifying information. Silas Brown, of Providence, included an advertising card as part of the backing in the ambrotypes he created. Other individuals report finding the names of the people represented in the portraits written on the backing. In other instances, the owner of the image inserted a small slip of paper in the case so you could see the name when you opened the case to view the portrait. However, in the vast majority of cased images, the identifying information is lost.

Special Concerns

Tintypes are more durable than ambrotypes and daguerreotypes but are still susceptible to damage. The primary types of damage occur through exposure to moisture, mishandling, and abrasion.

Figure 3-4.
Once the image layer of a tintype is scratched or bent, the iron plate will rust through exposure to humidity in the air.
Collection of the author

• **Rust.** Since the major component of a tintype is iron, it sustains damage due to exposure to moisture. Think about what happens to metal that is left out in the rain. It eventually corrodes due to rust (see figure 3-4 above). The same happens to a tintype if it comes into contact with water or is repeatedly exposed to high humidity. A professional conservator can stabilize rust.

• **Bent plates**. A tintype is created on a thin piece of iron that bends if submitted to pressure and mishandling. Bending can crack the surface of the black coating, exposing the iron plate to corrosive elements.

• **Abrasion**. The image formed by the coating of collodion on the surface of the metal sustains the most damage from abrasion. This can occur when two plates rub against each other and when stored improperly. This friction scratches the image, and in the worst cases, the emulsion flakes off. Digital restoration techniques can repair some of the damage.

• **Cracking of the varnish and emulsion.** Each tintype gets coated with a layer of varnish before the customer receives it. This helps protect the

Figure 3-5.
The surface of a tintype is susceptible to many types of damage and should be handled carefully.
Collection of the author

picture but also leads to another type of damage. The varnish and emulsion crack when mishandled or stored in an area with fluctuating temperatures and humidity. It is important to remember that thin sheets of metal expand and contract in hot and cold conditions. These changes crack the emulsion, and you can lose pieces of the image. In cases where large areas of the picture are missing, photographic restoration on a copy can re-create detail if the majority of the image is still intact.

CASES

There was an amazing variety of case designs in the mid-nineteenth century. Cases refer to any type of unit manufactured to hold ambrotypes, daguerreotypes, and sometimes tintypes. These can range from specially designed photographic jewelry to the cases available in standard sizes. The earliest cases in the 1840s were relatively simple compared to the later, more elaborate "union cases" of the late 1850s and 1860s.

In the 1840s, cases consisted of wooden frames and leather embossed

Figure 3-6.
The surface of a tintype can flake off when exposed to rough handling. *Collection of the author*

with a design. A simple hook and eye acted as a clasp. When opened, the side facing the image was velvet in a rich color, such as red, purple, or green. These cases can still be found in good shape. The leather is worn from use, but it is usually the hinges that fail to hold the case together.

A more fragile case consisted of papier-mâché. Manufacturers tried to make this case waterproof by adding chemicals. They also experimented with making them fireproof. Unfortunately, the chemicals also helped the papier-mâché deteriorate with age. The combination of the acid and lignin content of the paper with the chemical additives created cases that have rarely survived intact into this century.

The most durable case and the one most likely to survive intact was the union case. Patented by Samuel Peck in 1852, it consisted of gum shellac and fiber (wood and other types). At first appearance, these cases appear to be of a type of plastic. They are beautiful. The materials used to manufacture the cases could be molded into any shape. This led to elaborate surface designs. As cased images became less common, the cases themselves became

For More Info

FURTHER READING

The best overview of the development of cases is Floyd and Marion Rinhart's *American Miniature Case Art.*

collectible and usable for other purposes. For this reason, many individuals removed the daguerreotypes, ambrotypes, and tintypes from these cases, thus losing a vital part of the images.

Standard Case Sizes	Average Size in Inches
Whole	7″ × 9″
Half	5″ × 6″
Quarter	4″ × 5″
Sixth	3½″ × 3¾″
Ninth	2½″ × 3″
Sixteenth	2″ × 2″

Broken or Damaged Cases

Since photographers employed cases for protection and presentation of the images they took, the cases sustained most of the damage when viewers dropped or mishandled the images. While you can find examples of cases in perfect condition, the vast majority were damaged. The most repairable cases are the union cases whose hinges need replacing. Papier-mâché usually crumbles and cracks when handled. Unless you consider the case an important family artifact, you probably want to spend time and money on proper storage rather than conservation.

Storage Considerations for Cased Images

Unlike ambrotypes that break and tintypes with an emulsion, daguerreotypes are fairly sturdy images. **The primary concern with all photographic materials is that their storage environment maintain a certain level of temperature and humidity.** There are other precautions for storing these types of material that will lengthen their life spans.

Reminder

After covering photos to protect the materials from abrasion, store cased images in individual boxes with reinforced corners. They can be purchased ready-made from suppliers (see Appendix D) or created from PAT heavyweight paper folded to overlap the case. This fourfold system works well with images in the case or those that lack them. Cased images don't actually need the covering, but since the case is also considered an artifact and identifier, it is preferable to use boxes. An added advantage is having a container on which to write a caption. Having the caption on the outside of the box means you will have to look at the image less, thus reducing wear and tear on the case.

Images that are no longer in cases also need additional protection. After covering the photo with a fourfold paper to protect the materials from abrasion and the ambrotype from breaking, place the object in an acid- and lignin-free envelope. Ambrotypes, not in cases, should be treated like glass negatives. Full instructions appear on page 75.

FREQUENTLY ASKED QUESTION

How can I permanently attach a label to a cased image?

Once you have spent time researching and establishing identifying information on a previously unidentified image, you desperately want to retain it. There are two ways to handle this with a cased image. You can enclose a slip of acid- and lignin-free paper in the case so that it shows when opened, but unless you have a way to slide part of the edge of the slip into the left side housing, this slip will fall out each time the image is opened. Another option is to write the data on the outside of the storage box or sleeve. This has a few benefits. You keep the image in the storage envelope that protects it from damage. It also enables you to see the information without having to handle the image. As long as you don't separate the image from its storage enclosure, the information won't be lost.

CHECKLIST: CASED IMAGES

✓ Learn about the different types of cased images.
✓ Don't clean them yourself.
✓ Use materials that passed the PAT for storage.
✓ Take time to write identification information on the storage materials.

Notes

FOUR

Photographic Prints and Negatives

A ll of us are familiar with paper prints. Every year we produce them by the thousands, documenting our family milestones and vacations. The paper prints of our ancestors and the ones we take today are similar, but the chemicals and processes that create the images are different. Laying out all your prints side by side will create a rainbow of colors, since each photographic process employed different techniques to produce a result. Each of these prints has a couple of things in common. They were all produced with a negative and are susceptible to particular types of damage. By following the basic preservation guidelines presented in chapter two, you can extend the life spans of these images. The negatives used to produce these prints ranged from paper to glass to contemporary film materials. These negatives require protection from damage the same as prints. Understanding the different types of photographic materials in your collection will help you take steps to care for them.

Paper prints fall into several categories. In the mid-nineteenth century, there were basically two types of paper prints: those considered printing-out papers and those called developing-out papers. In the first instance, light-sensitive chemicals applied to paper allow the image to appear during exposure to light. Developing-out papers require chemical processing to bring out the image. There is a revival of nineteenth-century printing-out processes. Some photographers experimenting with these photographic processes are causing a revival of interest in the photographic community. **If you want to try to duplicate the methods that created your ancestral portraits, you can find directions in *Historic Photographic Processes* by Richard Farber.** You can also find historical directions by consulting the bibliographies online at City Gallery <http://www.city-gallery.com>.

For More Info

THE NINETEENTH CENTURY

Capturing images on paper is one of the oldest photographic processes, but it took a couple of decades for it to become popular. At about the same time that Daguerre developed his images on metal in 1839, an inventor in

England, William Fox Talbot, experimented with paper photographs. His very rare prints, called photogenic drawings, used ordinary table salt (sodium chloride). Eventually he discovered a way to make paper negatives called calotypes. This is essentially the same system, negative and paper print, that we use today.

Egg white, another commonly available household substance, played an important role in the development of paper prints. Albumen prints created from paper coated with egg white and light-sensitive silver nitrate became popular from 1850 until almost the turn of the twentieth century. The photographer, immediately prior to use, made this type of paper print on site. Factory-made paper did not become available until the 1870s.

All prints were contact prints, meaning they were the same size as the negatives. When you are looking at an 11″ × 14″ print from the 1870s, that means the negative was also 11″ × 14″. Since artificial light was not available until the late nineteenth century, sunlight was a key ingredient of the photographic process. The right set of environmental circumstances, including adequate sunlight and good weather, became necessary for a good print. Most printing occurred outdoors. Cold temperatures negatively affected the photographic process.

The first twenty years of photography utilized silver compounds to create the image. After this initial period, photographers experimented with the light-sensitive qualities of other chemicals. The platinum print, created with metallic platinum, had the advantage of resisting fading. The lovely blueprint photograph, the cyanotype, consists of iron salts. They fade when exposed to sunlight. Collodion, the same substance used to create ambrotypes, became synonymous with photography. The light sensitivity of the silver halide in the collodion made it useful for prints and for creating glass plate negatives. The composition of photographic papers and techniques employs chemical processes that most of us are unfamiliar with. For that reason, it can be difficult to identify a particular photographic process.

IDENTIFYING THE PROCESS

Conservators and photographic historians invest time in learning to identify the various types of paper prints available in the nineteenth century. For most genealogists, this only becomes important when trying to establish a date for an image; however, as illustrated in examples in *Uncovering Your Ancestry Through Family Photographs*, the other details in the images confirm the date. Correct identification of the photographic method is essential when attempting conservation but is not an integral part of deciding how to store most of these images.

In some cases, identification can be done based on the color of the print. The brilliant blue of a cyanotype is unmistakable. It is not simple to identify prints that changed appearance due to the addition of toning chemicals. Toning can modify the color of the final print by depositing chemicals on the print. Professional conservation workshops teach students to identify

For More Info

FURTHER READING

James M. Reilly's *Care and Identification of Nineteenth Century Photographic Prints* offers a succinct description of the different processes and a color identification chart.

the processes by explaining the composition of the prints. You can purchase a small handheld microscope from the suppliers in Appendix D. It is only with experience looking at a magnified section of a print that an identification is likely. At one of these workshops, a conservator, when asked how he became able to correctly identify photographic processes, replied that it requires time, patience, and experience. For this reason, only a professional with the proper background should do conservation work.

Type of Photograph	Date Introduced	Characteristics
Salted paper print	1840	Yellow-brown, red-brown, fades
Cyanotype	1880	Blue
Platinotype	1880	No fading
Albumen print	1850	Fades; tiny cracks in the image; colors same as salted paper print; paper fibers visible
Carbon print	1860	No fading; large cracks in dark areas
Woodburytype	1866	No fading; some cracking in dark areas
Gelatin printing-out paper or collodion	1885	Purple image; no paper fibers visible
Gelatin developing-out paper	1885	No paper fibers; reflective dark areas a silver color
Matte collodion	1894	No fading; some paper fibers visible

CARD PHOTOGRAPHS

\di'fin\ *vb*

Definitions

Probably the most common type of nineteenth-century photograph in your collection is known as a card photograph. The thin paper of the majority of nineteenth- and early-twentieth-century prints necessitated mounting them to heavy card stock or cardboard to help support the print. These images, regardless of the type of photographic process, came in standard sizes. The cartes de visite are the smallest cards because they resemble in shape and size nineteenth-century visiting cards from which they derive their name. Individuals of a certain economic status would carry small cards engraved with their names to introduce themselves. The duke of Parma decided to use photographic cards and started the trend of the carte de visite. Introduced into the United States in 1860, they became wildly popular, setting off a craze referred to at the time as "cartomania." Our ancestors not only rushed to photographers' studios to have their pictures taken, they began collecting

Figure 4-1.
By the end of the nineteenth century, card photographs came in a variety of shapes and sizes. *Collection of the author*

images of friends, relatives, and notables. Photographers began filling the demand for images by creating sets on various topics. The social ritual of visiting included adding a photograph of yourself to the album on display and spending time looking at the collection.

Photography became more than a way to document family members; it evolved into entertainment. A particular type of card photograph, the stereograph, was part of that transformation. Developed in the 1850s, the term refers to two almost identical images mounted side by side. When viewed through a special lens, the image appeared three-dimensional. Photographers created sets on topics ranging from fictional stories to travel. My mother recalls that during the Depression, her family owned an extensive set of stereographs. She and siblings played with these on a regular basis. Unfortunately they disappeared. The reverse sides of these cards usually contained labels explaining what the images were about. They remained in existence until the early to mid years of the twentieth century.

For More Info

FURTHER READING

William C. Darrah's *Cartes De Visite in Nineteenth Century Photography* presents examples of the various subjects covered by photographers.

SOME TYPES OF CARD PHOTOGRAPHS AND SIZES		
Type	Size in Inches	Introduced
Carte de visite	4¼″ × 2½″	Process introduced in U.S. 1859
Stereograph	3″ × 7″ or 4″ × 7″	Smaller 1859; larger 1870
Cabinet card	4½″ × 6½″	1866
Victoria	3¼″ × 5″	1870
Promenade	4″ × 7″	1875
Boudoir	5¼″ × 8½″	Not known
Imperial (life-size)	6⅞″ × 9⅞″	Not known
Panel	8¼″ × 4″	Not known

CANDID PHOTOGRAPHIC PRINTS

Until the late 1880s, there were two ways to have your portrait taken. You could visit a professional studio or have the amateur photographer in your family take one. These portraits lack spontaneity; it was an involved process. Remember that the size of the print was the size of the glass negative. Show a group of children nineteenth-century images and they will mimic the stiff pose and lack of facial expression. They will want to know why it wasn't fun to have your picture taken.

Kodak changed all that when George Eastman introduced our ancestors to candid photography with ''You press the button, we do the rest'' (see figure 4-2). He eliminated technical knowledge from picture taking.

Figure 4-2.
Kodak cameras allowed our ancestors to photograph their daily lives.
Collection of the author

Each camera came loaded with negatives on a film that you would send back to the factory when you were finished with the roll. Then the pictures appeared in the mail with the camera loaded with a new roll. Our ancestors now had the freedom to depict and play with photography. The box camera that anyone could use without knowledge of photography changed the way our families thought of photography. This changeover is apparent in your family collection. The increased number of pictures and the style of the image reflect that photography became a leisure activity for adults and children. Kodak marketed Brownie cameras directly to children.

Kodak print sizes related to the type and size of the camera used to take them. As long as film remained available, the camera stayed in use. For instance the 101 camera wasn't discontinued until sixty years after its introduction in 1895.

Special Concerns

Different types of nineteenth-century and early-twentieth-century prints develop problems based on the chemical processes used in their creation. Each photograph is a combination of photographic chemicals and paper. Both can affect the longevity of the print as much as storage conditions since their creation.

There are certain types of damage that occur to all paper prints due to improper environment and handling. There are also specific types of damage to which different types of prints are susceptible. Then there is damage that occurs under extraordinary circumstances such as floods.

Most of these prints consist of the image, a paper support, and the adhesive that fixes the print to the support. Each element of this affects the stability and permanence of the image.

• **Improper washing.** My parents' wedding pictures developed horrible brown stains about a decade after they were taken. These stains are the result of the photographer not rinsing the pictures long enough to remove the chemicals. Archival processing includes washing the prints for at least fifteen minutes in clean water to ensure the chemicals won't cause stains. A professional conservator can possibly remove these stains (see figure 4-4 on page 61).

• **High humidity.** Many prints experience various types of damage from exposure to humidity, including curling. In some examples, the highlight areas of the pictures fade and turn yellow. The loss of detail can be significant, and the whole picture will gradually fade from view. Albumen prints are very sensitive to humidity (see figure 4-3 on page 60).

• **Silver mirroring.** Do your pictures have a bluish silver cast to them when held at certain angles? In the worst examples, the entire image disappears beneath this mirroring.

• **Cracked emulsion.** The emulsions of several different types of prints, including those with a gelatin or collodion image, develop cracks in the surface due to fluctuations of temperature and humidity. This can cause

For More Info

FURTHER READING

A complete list of Kodak camera and print sizes appears in Brian Coe's *Kodak Cameras: The First Hundred Years.*

Figure 4-3.
High humidity can cause some photographs to stick together. The lower left corner of this photograph has water damage.
Collection of the author

pieces of the image to flake off. The gelatin prints swell with moisture and become brittle. The image of an albumen print can crack due to environmental conditions. Collodion is also very sensitive to moisture and has a tendency to become brittle and crack.

• **Abrasion.** All photographs experience damage when shuffled against one another or against other types of items. Prints that are already stressed due to humidity and temperature variations are more sensitive to abrasion. Gelatin prints and those with a collodion surface can actually lose pieces of the image area in these conditions. Proper storage with polypropylene sleeves, with acid- and lignin-free paper, and in boxes are all intended to protect images from abrasion.

• **Curling.** Photographs printed on thin paper curl with exposure to humidity or during the drying process. For this reason, most prints were mounted on heavy card stock.

• **Transference.** Examine the backs of the images in your collection. Do

Figure 4-4.
Chemicals used in the developing process that are not completely washed off can eventually stain your photographs.
Collection of the author

you see the ghosts of the images that were resting against them? Platinum prints can transfer their images to others. This happens not just to the reverse of the photo, but when these prints are placed face-to-face, it interferes with the viewability of the image (see figure 4-5 on page 62).

• **Fading.** Light can also contribute to the fading of prints. Cyanotypes are particularly sensitive to light. They should be stored in darkness rather than exhibited.

• **Foxing.** If you have small reddish brown spots on the surface of the print, then you have foxing damage. This is a result of chemical interaction with high humidity, not mold damage. Albumen prints usually show signs of foxing.

• **Mold and mildew.** Leave your prints in a damp environment long enough and they will develop mold and mildew. In order to kill the mold, a professional conservator must treat the picture. You can retard the mold's growth by storing your images at constant temperature and low humidity. Mold and mildew will stain the images.

Figure 4-5.
Turn over a card photograph. You may find a ghostly image of the photograph it was stacked on top of. This is called transference.
Collection of the author

- **Fingerprints on images.** Closely examine your prints and negatives, and you may have fingerprint evidence of the individuals who handled these images (see figure 4-6 on page 63). Handling prints and negatives without gloves allows a thin layer of moisture to build up on the surface. This moisture attracts dust, which adheres to the surface, leaving a lasting impression of friends and relatives. If your contemporary prints are handled without gloves, gently clean off the surface using a lint-free soft cloth.[1]

PAPER SUPPORTS

Around 1865–1870, wood pulp became the predominant ingredient of paper and paperboard available for use with prints to prevent them from curling after processing. The sizes of the images and the mounting boards varied from the small card photographs, such as cartes de visite, to oversize prints suitable for framing.

The primary damage to prints from mounting board and framing mats is exposure to materials containing acid and lignin. Both discolor the image, and the lignin makes the print brittle. Broken photographs are as much a result of the composition of the board as mishandling. When an

Figure 4-6.
Always wear gloves when handling photographs so you don't inadvertently leave a set of fingerprints like this person did.

Collection of the author

acid and lignin mat is used in framing, it leaves a stain the same shape of the mat on the print.

SURFACE TREATMENTS

The third component of the photographic prints is the substances applied to them or the surface treatments done to improve the quality of the print. Photographers added gelatin, waxes, and varnish to the surface of salted paper prints to give them a glossy appearance. Albumen prints naturally have a glossy appearance, but burnishing enhances it. During the processing of albumen prints, they passed through a machine. In order to prevent them from sticking to the rollers, turpentine and castile soap were sometimes applied to the rollers. These chemicals ended up as deposits on the prints.[2]

Hand-Coloring

In the absence of color photography, photographers began to use artistic techniques to add detail and color to their images. The types of coloring evolved with time and experience from simple charcoal outlining to the use of oil and watercolor paints, crayons, and colored powders. Additional substances such

Figure 4-7.
The roses in the hair accessory worn by this unidentified girl are colored red.
Collection of the author

as gum arabic and varnish sealed the color on the prints. These can darken or crack with age. Larger studios employed artists to produce a colorized portrait. Outlining enhanced the image in case of fading. The most common additions are gold jewelry and pink cheeks (see figure 4-7 above). In men's portraits, artists colored collars and shirts white. In some albumen prints, the image has faded, while the color retains its original tones.

Toning

Photographers often toned images on printing-out papers with a solution of gold or platinum to improve the color of the image and increase permanence. For instance, images treated with gold toning changed color from a brick-red to a deeper color such as brown or purple. A combination of gold and platinum toning resulted in a neutral color. The majority of nineteenth-century photographs on printing-out paper were toned.[3]

Adhesives

Photographers had to use something to glue the picture securely to the backing. Their choices included animal glues, gum arabic, gelatin, and starch paste. The best substance on the list is the starch paste. This is still used by conservators today. It causes the least amount of damage to the print. With all adhesives, prints can become rippled from the moisture in the paste, but some of those substances also damaged the appearance of the prints.

BASIC CHARACTERISTICS OF PRINTS	
Type of Photograph	**Problems**
Albumen prints	Brittleness, fading, yellowing, cracking, curling, foxing
Cyanotypes	Light fading, curling
Salted paper prints	Fading
Platinum prints	Transference
Collodion	Especially susceptible to abrasion

RESIN-COATED (RC) PAPERS

Starting in the 1960s, a new type of paper saved processing time and didn't curl when drying. These new resin-coated (RC) papers took around a minute from processing to drying.[4] Kodak was unaware of the deterioration problems of this paper when it was introduced and advertised that it was permanent. Only recently did preservation become an issue for commercial manufacturers of photographic materials. Contemporary RC paper still experiences deterioration, but Kodak has taken steps to find ways to increase the longevity of these papers. Unless you print your own photographs or request (at extra charge) fiber-based paper from a photography studio, your prints will be resin coated. The coating helps protect the surface of the print from abrasion but causes several problems. Fiber-based papers do not have a coating and can be processed for museum-quality storage.

Special Concerns

• **Labeling.** Graphite pencil won't write on RC paper, so you have to use a waterproof pen (**see recommendations on pages 151-152**). Gently write on the back of the image with it facedown on a clean, hard surface. I prefer to use a piece of glass the same size as the print. Make sure the ink is dry before placing against other items because it is permanent.

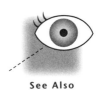

See Also

• **Bronzing.** According to Henry Wilhelm in *The Permanence and Care of Color Photographs*, black-and-white RC prints developed in the 1970s and early 1980s have orange, gold, or yellow discoloration on the prints after only a few years. Sometimes this takes the form of spots on the surface of the print.

• **Cracking.** RC prints can develop stress cracks from handling and environmental conditions. Fluctuations of humidity combined with poor display conditions contribute to this. You can view the cracking by holding the print at an angle or under a magnifying glass.

Framing Concerns

According to Wilhelm, RC prints give off gases that deteriorate the image. When the print is sealed in a frame, it increases the rate of deterioration. RC prints need frames that allow for airflow instead of being sealed on all sides. However, if the print will be exposed to pollutants in the environment, a sealed frame might be best. Most framing establishments should be familiar with the technique. If in doubt about what type of frame to use, consult a conservator.

Storage Considerations for Prints

There are several things you can do inexpensively to protect the paper prints in your possession. While providing a stable environment free from fluctuating temperature and humidity is at the top of conservators' lists of what a collection needs, it is not always possible to provide the perfect setting in the home environment.

Tip

A simple way to protect your prints from breakage is to store same-size prints together either when you organize them or when they are waiting to be filed. This enables the prints to support each other.

Invest in polypropylene sleeves or pages to stop abrasion. The most common form of abrasive damage results from stacking and shuffling through unprotected images. Think about what happens to the surface and edges of ordinary playing cards when they are used repeatedly. The same sort of wear and tear happens to your images.

PHOTOGRAPHIC ALBUMS

It would be almost impossible to find a family photograph collection that doesn't have at least one photograph album. My contemporary photographs are arranged in albums in chronological order. These albums in our collections are intrinsically valuable. The photographs themselves have sentimental value, but don't discount the informational content of these albums. **Examine the ones in your collection in terms of the history of your family and what you can learn from them.**

Notes

1. Who created the album? Check the inside front cover of the album to see if the original owner wrote her name inside. If she didn't, can you determine who created the album based on the captions of the images? Are there any that specifically identify her mother and have a full name? There may be clues to the identity of the owner throughout the album, so keep track of any significant facts.

2. Who is included? When you look at the album, make a list of not only who is included but also who is left out. Omissions can provide clues that add to your understanding of family history. For instance, if one particular family member doesn't appear in any of the photographs, your family research may suggest that the relative wasn't living in the area.

3. What events are depicted? By looking at the album in its entirety, you can develop a feel for what types of events are included. There may be

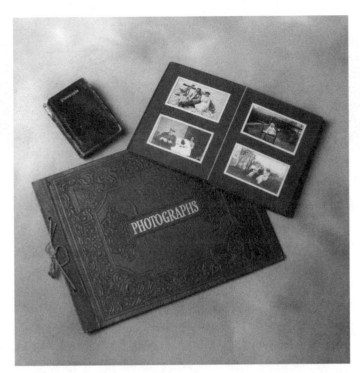

Figure 4-8.
Different-size photographic albums enabled people to organize their photographs. Look carefully at your own albums to see what story they tell about your family.
Collection of the author

wedding photographs of couples followed by their children's photos, or the album may be topical. In one family, a series of albums was created of various relatives holding the same baby. These albums were eventually given to both sets of grandparents and other relatives. This was the only baby in a generation of a family and thus was a very important person.

4. What does your family history tell you about these individuals? What do you know about each individual depicted in the album? It might help you determine the purpose of the album or help you identify when the album was created.

5. Reexamine these images as a total collection. Now step back from the individual images and think about the album. You might discover some surprising facts about the relationships of the various people in the album. Sometimes relatives who fall out of favor are removed from albums. Did you notice any missing images? Captions are helpful when deciphering the content of the album and vice versa. Sometimes the images assist you in completing the caption by providing identification clues.

History

Our ancestors initially used plain-paper albums to arrange their photographs with captions written underneath until commercially manufactured albums became available. These albums figured prominently in the decorating scheme of nineteenth-century parlors, being displayed beside the family Bible for visitors to look at. They usually contain the name of the owner.

These nineteenth-century albums evolved from scrapbook pages to precut albums back to scrapbooks. At first glance, the card photograph albums don't have the same personality as the blank-page albums because the arrangement of the page is dictated by the shape of the album. But at a closer glance, it's evident that the images on those pages were put into a particular order by the owner (see figure 4-9 below). The people important in the owner's circle of family and friends appear in an album as a reflection of the owner's life.

As albums lost their formality and amateur photography became popular, albums became a personal expression. These albums portrayed family unity and were reflective of a personal identity. Albums, with their imaginative arrangements, decorative cutouts, and artifacts, are similar to contemporary scrapbooks.

Throughout the history of photography, there are developments and parallel innovations in the history of presenting images, from the cases for early photographic images to contemporary photographic albums. The introduction of each new type of image enabled booksellers and bookbinders to develop a side industry that eventually burgeoned into mass production of a variety of albums that coincided with the demand for images.

Figure 4-9.
This is an example of an early scrapbook arrangement. The man on the left is probably related to the women on the right.
Collection of the author

Carte de Visite Albums

The first albums designed specifically to hold photographs were imported into the United States in 1860. A year later, an American produced an album that provided a space for a carte de visite and a space for an autograph of the subject of the portrait. Most of the albums manufactured and patented in the decade after 1862 were of a similar design. Each leaf of the album contained windows in which to place the card photographs. These albums typically had leather or cloth covers and brass clasps with decorative tooling. Pages held two photographs back to back in a precut heavy card stock. The bottom of the window was initially sealed, which made it difficult to insert the card. A later improvement included leaving the bottom open so that

ALBUM SIZES[5]	
Size	Number of Images
Octavo	50–100
Quarto	Up to 400 cards; usually held 120–160
Pocket albums	6–12

cards could be slid in. They could be purchased in a variety of sizes depending on the purpose of the album.

According to William Darrah in *Cartes de Visite in Nineteenth Century Photography*, there were four common types of albums. Family albums obviously held portraits of family members, houses, and perhaps even cemetery monuments. Celebrity albums concentrated on a particular type of subject, such as statesmen. The contents of these albums were a reflection of the interest of the creator. There were also travel albums. You could purchase ready-made photographs of popular tourist spots and place them in an album. Shops sold them individually or in sets. The last type of album Darrah identified was the subject album, such as a class book. These were the precursor of the contemporary yearbook and held images of all the members of a particular graduating class. Other subject books focused on wars, art, or whatever topic the creator decided to collect.[6] Matthew Brady, a famous Civil War photographer, sold Brady's Album Gallery, which allowed individuals to purchase prints of his war scenes and arrange them in an album.

CARTE DE VISITE ALBUMS[7]	
Type	Dates Popular
Family albums	1862–1905
Celebrity albums	1862–1880
Travel albums	1862–1885
Subject albums	1862–?

Tintype Albums

The standard sizes of tintypes allowed them to be displayed in carte de visite albums. One exception is the albums created especially for the thumbnail or gem tintypes. They were very popular in the mid-1860s because of the cost. At mid-decade, thumbnails sold for twenty-five cents a dozen and albums for a dollar.[8] This was a fraction of the cost of paper prints and albums. When placed in a paper mount, these "gems" fit into a standard carte de visite album.

Cabinet Card Albums

Cabinet card albums resembled carte de visite albums in the layout and format. They were a larger size to accommodate the different-size prints. These albums resembled in presentation a family Bible. In most homes, the album would be displayed alongside the Bible, a statement of its place in the family.

Scrapbooks

Families who chose to make their own family photograph albums could do so using ready-made journals or by creating their own by stitching together sheets of paper or cloth between two covers. Families either glued or sewed photographs onto the pages. These are the forerunners of the present-day scrapbooks.

Special Concerns

One of the most often asked questions at my presentations on family photographs is what to do with images that are in albums. The first suggestion is to follow the basic rules for extending the longevity of any photographs by placing them in an area that does not experience variable temperature and humidity. You want to be able to maintain the integrity of the album as a total package because of the value of it as a family artifact. According to the International Museum of Photography at George Eastman House, if your albums are older than the 1950s, then most of the deterioration that is going to occur has already happened.[9] Therefore they suggest keeping the album in its original state unless it is extremely damaged. **They advise you to retain the original condition by**

Tip

- Having a professional bookbinder or book conservator repair the damage to the binding or individual pages.
- Consulting a photographic conservator about encapsulating individual pages. See page 154 for an explanation of encapsulation.
- Duplicating the arrangement of the old album in a new one. If the photographs are stuck to the pages, have a photographer make copies of the images for the new album. Transfer the captions by rewriting them.[10]

There are specific types of problems that result from photographs being in an album. Some result from handling, and others from the techniques used to create the album. Then, of course, are the problems resulting from the products used to manufacture the albums.

Abrasion

Every time you look at an album page of photographs that is unprotected by a polypropylene cover, the prints that face each other are subject to abrasion. They rub against each other during viewing or storage of the album.

Acid paper

Unless your photographs are stored in albums constructed of acid- and lignin-free papers, there will be acid migration from the paper to the images. This results in discoloration and staining of the photographs in the album. Other common sources of acid in albums are the ephemeral pieces of our lives that we place beside our images, such as cards, tickets, and documents.

Adhesives

Until the invention of the magnetic album or plastic sleeves, the majority of albums used adhesives to mount the photographs to the pages. The photo collector applied glue to the back of the image itself or to photo corners. When adhesive comes in contact with an image, it causes the image to discolor or buckle from the damp glue. It also makes the photographs difficult to remove from the albums.

Magnetic albums

These dreadful albums are still for sale in photo stores and departments. **They destroy family photographs by exposing them to glue and the gases given off by the plastic sheet protectors.** Your photographs will become stuck to these album pages. They continue to sell because they are inexpensive. A friend's daughter recently purchased some new magnetic albums because of the cost of the PAT-approved ones even though she was warned of the danger to her images.

Warning

Storage Considerations

It is easy to take precautions with the images you have in albums.

1. Try to make sure that all the new albums you purchase are safe for use with photographs. Choose papers that have passed the PAT, and follow the guidelines outlined in the Scrapbooks section to create safe and preservation-quality albums.
2. If you want to save money by not buying albums with their own slip-covers, you can create your own, by wrapping the albums in clean cloths such as sheets. This protects the images from dust and environmental pollutants.
3. Interleave the pages with a thin acid- and lignin-free tissue paper to protect older albums from acid migration and abrasion.

Frequently Asked Questions About Prints and Albums

These are questions that are often asked at lectures and workshops. **The National Archives and Records Administration (NARA) Web site <http://www.nara .gov/arch/faqs/aboutph.html> also features a list of questions commonly asked.**

Internet Source

What can I do about photographs in black paper albums?

According to the National Archives, not all albums should be taken apart. There is a simpler solution. You can interleave the pages with paper or tissue that passes the PAT. The only danger is that you are doubling the size of the album and can break the spine. Tissue available from the suppliers in Appendix D will reduce the bulk.

Can I safely remove photographs from magnetic albums?

At a conservation workshop, the conservator suggested unwaxed dental floss as a way to remove photographs from the pages of a magnetic album. Be very careful not to cut the photographs during this process. You can also try a product such as Un-du, an adhesive remover, to gently dissolve the glue.

I have a large framed image that appears to be a drawing of a photograph.

It is most likely a crayon portrait. These are enlargements that were colored using charcoal pencil, chalk, or pastel. Photographers either hired artists to add detail to the images or did the work themselves. Certain parts of the portraits, especially the eyes, eyelashes, and eyebrows, were enhanced. The hair and background needed even more detail. These portraits were intended for display in the family home and came in a variety of sizes. It was popular from the mid-nineteenth century to the early twentieth.

Most likely the portrait in your possession is on brittle paper backed with a lightweight fabric. It may have pieces of the paper missing and is probably discolored.

In order to stabilize the print, it should be sent to a professional conservator for treatment. If this is cost prohibitive, you can store the picture unframed in acid- and lignin-free materials in a box.

What can I do about rolled photographs?

The only way to permanently unroll these images is through the use of a humidification chamber and then flattening the image. This reintroduction of moisture reverses the curling of lightweight paper. Humidification does not involve immersing the image in water; it merely creates an extremely humid environment that encourages the curling to unroll on its own. This is a conservation treatment and should not be attempted by a nonprofessional.

Generally these images are oversize or panoramic views of groups or landscapes. The rolling occurred because the print is on a lightweight paper that reacts to humidity by curling. It is also possible that someone deliberately rolled the photograph to store it.

These images suffer damage through repeated rolling and unrolling. The emulsion will crack and the image can break. Therefore, do not unroll these images. Let a professional conservator help you flatten them. Exposing such an image to humidity makes the surface tacky and susceptible to damage. Forcing a curled photograph to unroll can result in the image breaking into pieces.[11]

I noticed that magnetic albums now use "Archival Safe" in their advertising. Are they safe to use?

Absolutely not. Unless an album meets the PAT standards, you shouldn't use it for your photographs. More companies are using the word *archival* in their advertising, but the products are not. There is no industry standard for the term archival. Unfortunately, this wording appeals to preservation-conscious consumers who then unknowingly purchase products that do not pass the standards.

NEGATIVES

The history of prints corresponds to the development and history of the negatives used to produce them. After prints, negatives make up a significant part of our family photograph collections. But how many people know about the negatives in their possession? The majority of this material in our homes dates from the era of the Kodak candid pictures to the present. Negatives consist of a base layer and a coating of emulsion. The base layer consists of either glass or a plastic material. It is the emulsion that is the negative of the print in our possession.

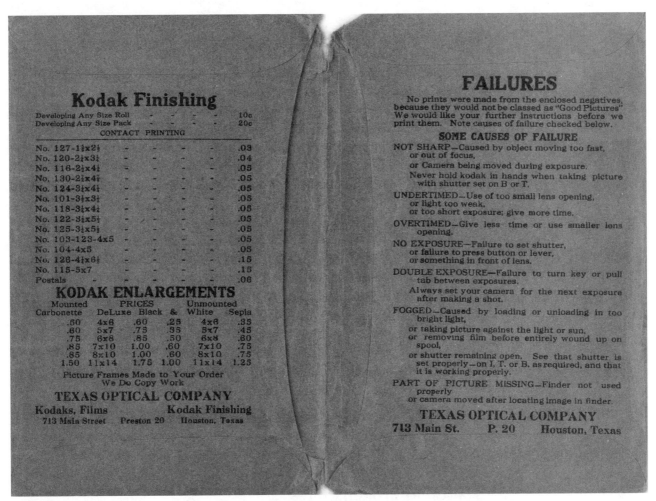

Figure 4-10.
This negative envelope from a Texas company explains the cost of obtaining prints from negatives and some common photo mistakes. *Grant Emison*

REMEMBER WHEN STORING GLASS PLATES

- Store them vertically on the long edge.

- Make sure shelving and storage containers can support the weight.

- Use heavy PAT board to create filler for boxes of negatives.

- Label each box with "Fragile—Heavy Glass Negatives!"

This chart contains the major characteristics of commonly available negatives. All dates are subject to some variation, since photographers generally used up existing supplies before embracing a new technique.

Photographers created their own supply of negatives in the 1850s by coating a piece of glass with a new substance, known as collodion. The light-sensitive silver halides in the collodion captured an image and preserved it during the photographic process. It consists of gun cotton dissolved in ether and alcohol. The combination was used for photography for the first time in 1849. Wet-plate negatives are very heavy to carry around.

GLASS NEGATIVES		
Type	Characteristics	In Use
Collodion, also known as wet plate	Thick glass; edges ground; gray coating; produced by individual photographer	1851–c. 1880
Gelatin dry plate	Thin glass; uniform thickness; edges sharp; black coating; factory produced	c. 1880–c. 1920

Moving Glass Negatives

If you have glass negatives in your collection, they are probably sitting in a box that is too heavy to lift. Photographers used to store these glass plates in wooden storage boxes that had dividers to protect the glass from breakage. Since the boxes contained only a few negatives, they could be easily carried.

Here are a few suggestions for when you have to move or rebox the glass plates.

1. Make sure they have individual envelopes or coverings.
2. Pack them snugly in the box to eliminate accidental breakage.
3. Use small boxes so you can comfortably lift them.

Special Storage for Glass Negatives

There are a few special storage points for glass plate negatives due to their weight and fragility. Store them vertically on a long edge so that their weight doesn't affect the negative on the bottom of the stack. Be sure to check the strength of storage materials, even those with reinforced corners. It is also necessary to make sure that shelving units can safely hold the weight. Since you will only partially fill boxes of glass negatives to insure that the containers will not be overwhelmed by the weight of the glass, you can make filler by using a heavy acid-free card stock. This will prevent breakage when moving the boxes. Negatives larger than 5"×7" need additional reinforcement every five negatives to prevent damage.

Handling Broken Plates

Almost all glass negative collections have broken plates from mishandling. There are things you can do to preserve the images rather than throw them

away. Sarah S. Wagner, senior photograph conservator at the National Archives at College Park, suggests storing them flat in a protective mat cut to the same size as the full negative. These sink mats can then be stacked. An alternative to sandwiching the negatives between glass is to place them between two stiff pieces of cardboard and fold a piece of paper around all four sides. You can also purchase ready-made four-flap paper enclosures from the suppliers in Appendix D.[12]

By re-creating the glass negative by matching the broken pieces, you can have a contact print made of it by a photo lab. Be sure to wear protective gloves to shield yourself from the sharp edges. If the image is in multiple small pieces, your attempts to piece it together may not be worth it. Have a contact print (same-size print) made from the negative and dispose of it.

Home Conservation for Glass Negatives

Technique

If the emulsion of a glass negative is pulling away from the glass, this can be remedied by sandwiching it between two pieces of glass. Be careful trying to piece together broken or cracked glass negatives. There is the risk that the gelatin emulsion will adhere to the glass if it is exposed to high humidity.

1. Buy two pieces of glass custom cut from a glass supplier the same size as the negative.
2. Make sure the glass is clean by washing with a gentle detergent and drying with a lint-free cloth.
3. Gently place the negative between the two pieces of glass. Wear gloves as protection.
4. Seal them together using PAT-approved special tape such as Filmoplast.
5. Take to a photo lab to have a contact print made.
6. Carefully undo the sandwiching before storing in a sink mat.
7. Store in a protective sleeve in a box with reinforced corners. Remember not to overload the box due to the weight of the negatives.

Warning: This process triples the weight of the negative.

FILM (HANDLE WITH CAUTION)		
Type	**Characteristics**	**In Use**
Eastman American film—gelatin	Brittle; edges uneven	1884–c. 1890
Roll film—clear plastic	Nitrocellulose; thin; curls and wrinkles easily	1889–1903
Roll film—clear plastic	Coated on both sides with gelatin to prevent curling	1903–1939
Sheet Film—clear plastic	Machine-cut sheet; rectangular; edges stamped Eastman	1913–1939
Roll film—clear plastic	Cellulose acetate; *safety* marked on the edge	1939–present

Types of Damage

If you haven't looked at your negatives recently, stop right now and pull them out of storage. Just as prints are susceptible to damage, so are negatives. Negatives that are extremely deteriorated may not be printable. It is necessary to take the same preservation precautions with the negatives as with the prints. Negatives are easier to identify than nineteenth-century prints.

Glass negatives are coated with a binder, such as collodion and gelatin, that contain light-sensitive silver halides. Over time and under the wrong circumstances, this emulsion breaks and flakes off the glass. Film negatives are also coated with light-sensitive chemicals that become brittle, and the emulsion and film base can break into pieces. Both types of negatives can develop mirroring, the silver cast to the emulsion when held at an angle.

FILM-BASED NEGATIVES

According to James Reilly in the *IPI Storage Guide for Acetate Film* (Rochester, N.Y.: Image Permanence Institute, 1993), all film-based negative deterioration is dependent on exposure to high humidity and temperature. Once the conditions are right for deterioration, the chemical changes become cumulative and actually rapidly increase. To prevent chemical changes, remove negatives from airtight containers (film cans or sealed plastic bags), which actually exacerbate the chemical breakdown. Conservator Paul Messier recommends a stable temperature and humidity environment with good ventilation.

The characteristics of the deterioration vary depending on the type of negative. Of great concern are nitrate negatives that are not only fragile but also dangerous. It is important to know the type of film negatives in your possession, in case they are nitrate. This type of negative is chemically unstable, and under the right conditions, it spontaneously combusts. **The nitrocellulose negatives, popular between 1889 and 1939, pose a fire hazard.** Most museums and archives copy and store these negatives using special techniques. Special storage warehouses exist to store these potentially dangerous materials. There is no need to panic; the threat to a family collection is not immediate unless there is a large quantity of these negatives in your home stored in an area with temperature fluctuations, such as an attic. Nitrate film can be easily identified by following these steps.

Warning

1. Examine the edges of your negatives to see if the word *safety* appears. If it doesn't, the negative may be nitrate.
2. Using a pair of scissors, snip off a small section of the negative and place it in a nonflammable container, such as an ashtray.
3. Try to ignite the section using a match. If it burns quickly, it is nitrate; if it doesn't, it is unmarked safety film.

If you discover you have nitrate film, have the negatives copied at a reputable photo conservation lab in your area. Federal regulations imposed by

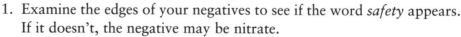

HEALTH RISKS FROM DETERIORATED NEGATIVES

Paul Messier, Conservator of Photographic Materials and Works of Art on Paper

Deteriorated negatives, especially nitrates, can emit a noticeable and noxious odor. Such gasses can cause skin, eye, and respiratory irritations. Allergic sensitivity has also been noted, as has dizziness and lightheadedness. Handle deteriorated negatives in a well-ventilated area. Wear neoprene gloves, remove contact lenses, and limit exposure times. It is also advisable to wear goggles and a respirator with acid/organic vapor filter cartridges.

the U.S. Department of Transportation restrict shipping nitrate because it is considered a fire hazard. Once you have the copies, ask your local fire department how to dispose of the negatives. Most communities mention the disposal of nitrate in their fire codes. How serious is this hazard? Nitrate film can spontaneously combust at 106°F and generates its own oxygen to feed the fire. The gas resulting from this type of fire can be deadly in large enough quantity and is also flammable.

Nitrate deterioration can damage other photographic materials because it produces chemical by-products. There are several phases to nitrate deterioration.

1. Amber discoloration appears on the film base. Image has faded.
2. Film base is brittle and sticky.
3. Bubbles are apparent in the film base. Negative emits an acrid smell.
4. Film disintegrates into a brown acrid powder.[13]

Safety Film

Cellulose acetate film shares some of the signs of deterioration of nitrate films, such as brittle films, bubbles, chemical by-products, and an odor. In safety films, this is known as the "vinegar syndrome" due to the vinegar smell. The film base can also shrink, producing waves, or "channels," in the emulsion. Unlike nitrate, safety film is not a fire hazard.

Storage of Film Negative Materials

There are several considerations when storing negatives. First is the environment. Negative deterioration is slowed when the material is stored at a constant temperature and humidity. The life span of negatives stored at 70°F and 40 percent humidity is about fifty years.[14] Lower temperature and humidity increases longevity but is not usually practical in a home setting. Cold storage conditions that can be created using a frost-free commercial freezer further extend the life span of these materials. Follow the storage recommendations for color prints and negatives on pages 84-85 for proper storage in cold environments.

The second consideration is that negatives range in size from panoramic

Tip

sheets of several feet in length to 35mm negatives. Each size needs to be stored separately so that the weight is evenly distributed.

As with all photographic material, wear lint-free cotton gloves when handling the negatives. This protects you from cuts from the glass negatives and from depositing oils and dirt on the negatives. Gentle brushing with a soft bristle brush can remove surface dirt prior to placing them in sleeves. Never brush negatives that are deteriorating due to chemical changes or glass negatives that are losing their emulsion. Use handling recommendations for chemical decomposition under Health Risks From Deteriorated Negatives on the previous page.

Here's a summary of the guidelines for storing negatives.

1. Use buffered envelopes.
2. Lightly brush the negatives with a soft brush to remove surface dirt. Use lint-free cotton gloves for handling good-quality negatives. See Health Risks From Deteriorated Negatives.
3. Place negative in the envelope with emulsion side away from the seam.
4. Store negatives upright in boxes. Do not mix sizes.
5. Do not pack them tightly.
6. Use boxes with reinforced corners.
7. When storing glass negatives, make sure the box can hold the weight.
8. Cut rolled negatives into lengths, and store them in polypropylene sleeves.

Frequently Asked Question About Negatives
Can I store them in the jackets from the lab?

If you are concerned about losing the information from the jackets, such as the dates, you can transfer the negatives and information to either polypropylene pages or to the special negative holders from the suppliers in Appendix D. This protects your negatives from the acid and plastic in the folders from the lab.

CHECKLIST: PHOTOGRAPHIC PRINTS AND NEGATIVES

Notes

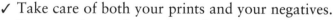

✓ Take care of both your prints and your negatives.
✓ Pay attention to the context of the photographs in your family albums.
✓ Learn to recognize the different types of damage that destroy photograph collections.
✓ Handle all prints and negatives by their edges only.

FIVE

Color

Walk into any home and you'll see color photographs on display either standing in frames or hanging on walls. They are pictures of graduations, family vacations, and other events significant to the owner. What might not be immediately noticeable, depending on how long the photographs have been exposed to light, is that they are all in various stages of fading. It happens so gradually that most people don't notice the change in color quality until they compare the print to a newer color image. If you were to place two identical photographs side by side with the difference that one was displayed in a sunny room and the other stored in darkness, the change in color would be immediately apparent. However, once we place our images on display, we overlook the color changes until we compare the displayed photo to a new print or the change is dramatic.

Damage to our color photographs is not limited to those we place out for public view. Images in storage can also show signs of aging. For instance, slides and instant color images such as Polaroids deteriorate differently than standard color prints.

Unfortunately, some of our color photographs will incur damage even if we use proper materials and keep the prints in temperature- and humidity-controlled environments. This can all be very confusing and disturbing to the family photographer. After all, you have spent time and money investing in documenting family milestones. You probably hoped that generations of your family would appreciate your efforts. However, the instability of these prints and slides is inherent in the qualities of the color photograph. Color images consist of three basic colors—cyan (blue), magenta (red), yellow—and sometimes black. Each of these colors fades at a different rate in dark storage.

These color shifts occur due to one or both of a couple of reasons: chemical instability of the color process and exposure to light. Different types of color images deteriorate at varying rates, depending on the type of processing and materials. If you are of the generation whose childhood was captured on film using color processes, then you have probably discovered that those images are now totally destroyed due to their instability. Manufacturers such as Kodak, Fuji, and Polaroid issued new products to consumers without informing them that these color images had limited life spans. Professional photographers and family photographers bought and used some of the same materials with the identical result: Pictures faded or discolored as they sat in the family album or on display. The good news is that film companies are responding to their customers' concerns about their color photographs.

BACKGROUND

Early photographers tried to invent a color photographic process but were unsuccessful. It wasn't until 1862 that the basic theory was developed that red, yellow, and blue are the basis for all other color combinations. Louis Ducos du Hauron, a Frenchman, designed a camera that could produce negatives in the three separate colors. While photographers were not able to use his invention to produce color photographs, printers used the process in lithography. Chromolithographs, or color prints, appeared in advertising and in magazines.[1]

More than forty years later, Auguste and Louis Lumiere introduced the first color photographic process, the autochrome, in 1904. Many people have never seen autochromes. Professional photographers utilized them in their work, but these first color slides are rarely seen in family collections. These one-of-a-kind positive glass images appear primarily in museum collections. They were typically used for landscape photographs and occasionally to photograph individuals. A special viewer, a diascope, was necessary to look at the images.[2]

Family photographers had to wait until 1936 for the first Kodak Kodachrome slides, although 16mm motion picture film appeared a year earlier.[3] Negative film became available from Kodak in 1941 and was the first color still film sold directly to the consumer market. According to Douglas Collins in *The Story of Kodak*, in the 1950s Kodak experienced its greatest period of economic growth.[4] Annual net earnings doubled in the four years from 1953 to 1957 to $100 million dollars. Kodak accomplished this by investing in research and development that resulted in new consumer products.

Taking photographs in color required new skills. In order to take a good-quality photograph, clothing choices became important. The family shutterbug had be concerned with color balance as well as background. In order to help its customers adjust and to teach them to appreciate photography, Kodak printed instructional manuals for family photographers that included easy-to-use charts to ensure photo quality.[5]

DETERIORATION

Color pictures are composed of two elements: the negative and the image. The negative is the film, while the image is printed on different types of paper. Today most photographs are printed on resin-coated (RC) papers. This means that the image is printed on a paper coated with a substance that protects the surface of the print from abrasion. Over time, these RC papers develop cracking.

Henry Wilhelm and Carol Brower, in the voluminous and technical publication *The Permanence and Care of Color Photographs: Traditional and Digital Color Prints, Color Negatives, Slides, and Motion Pictures*, present evidence on the deterioration of color family photographs. Their groundbreaking exposé is a story of lost pictures, family photographic memories destroyed by the very elements that consumers purchased to preserve them.

For More Info

- Kodacolor film used between 1942 and 1953 has one of the worst preservation records. Today those negatives are irreparably damaged and unprintable. The prints made from those negatives are now almost illegible due to yellow staining.
- Ektachrome slides used from 1959 to 1976 have by now experienced fading and color shifting.
- Agfacolor Color Type 4 paper produced and used between 1974 and 1982 by discount photo processors and commercial studio photographers has also dramatically faded.

These are only three of the color photographic processes used by family photographers.[6] But as disturbing as these three examples are, it is the instant picture that deteriorates the fastest.

INSTANT COLOR

Until 1947, amateur photographers either sent their rolls of film to labs for developing or did it themselves in home darkrooms. Edwin Land's patent for "instant" black-and-white pictures that developed in a minute changed that. Photographers could shoot a picture, watch it develop, and decide whether to take a new one. In the 1970s, Polaroid patented a color film that did essentially the same thing. Consumers shot approximately a billion Polaroids in 1974. Close to 65 percent of that number were color images.[7] In order to continue to meet the needs of its market, Polaroid offered new cameras and films every couple of years.

The problem with these new instant color pictures would not surface for several years. Unfortunately, the life expectancy of a color Polaroid can be limited to only five to ten years if storage conditions include environmental fluctuations. The deterioration of these pictures occurs whether or not the images are stored in the dark. Their very composition causes the problem. The chemicals that form the image are stored between two pieces of plastic. When the picture passes through the rollers of the camera, the chemical reaction starts to produce the image. Unfortunately, what happens in a relatively short period of time is that the process breaks down and the images begin to deteriorate. While all Polaroid prints deteriorate over a short time, the SX-70, Spectra HD (1991), and 600 photos experience the most problems.

A friend bought an SX-70 camera as soon as it was introduced and began taking snapshots of his family and friends. He completely abandoned traditional color prints in favor of the convenience of Polaroid's new cameras and films. For twenty-five years, the only camera he used to document the important events in his family was a Polaroid. This constitutes a substantial investment of equipment and supplies. Since Polaroid pictures do not fit in precut photo albums, he also purchased the albums specially made by the company for his images. Most of his collection is now in various stages of deterioration, including cracked images and staining. Since a Polaroid is a one-of-a-kind image, there is no negative from which to make another print. Many of his originals are in no condition to be copied and so are lost.

Polaroid films are also susceptible to temperature and humidity prior to exposure. There is some hope, however. There are a few precautions consumers can take to lengthen the life spans of their Polaroid prints and film. Written on the film's packages is a set of instructions for handling the film. See chapter two for guidelines on storing other types of color film prior to using them.

PROPER HANDLING OF POLAROID LAND FILMS

1. Store unopened film in a cool, dry place, for example, a refrigerator. Never freeze the film.
2. Allow film to warm to room temperature prior to use.
3. Use film before the expiration date on the package.
4. Never cut or bend the images. This may release the caustic chemicals contained in the image. This can result in alkali burns.
5. Follow package directions for use.

Notes

Special Concerns of Color Photographs

• **Fading.** Color photographs and slides are extremely susceptible to fading. Some of the Kodak paper available in the 1950s through 1970s fades regardless of where it is stored. However, to reduce fading of color prints, store them in the dark at cool temperatures and low humidity.

• **Discoloration.** In addition to fading, color prints and slides experience discoloration. The color of the shift in tone varies depending on the type of print. Some look more red and others more yellow. This can be an allover color change or just an intensification of certain shades in the print. This can be reversed using digital restoration.

• **Cracking.** Color prints on RC paper can crack under the same conditions as black-and-white RC prints. Polaroids can develop cracks in the emulsion between the plastic layers, which can destroy the image (see figure 5-1).

• **Moisture and temperature.** Color prints on coated paper are susceptible to heat and humidity. High heat and humidity cause the prints to stick together. It is best to interleave the prints with acid-free tissue or place them

Figure 5-1.
In just a few decades, Polaroid prints can crack through exposure to fluctuations in temperature and humidity.
Lucien Montaro

in a recommended album. To avoid the problem entirely, store the prints in a proper environment and in individual sleeves.

• **Fingerprints.** Make sure your hands are dry before touching a color print. Damp hands cause you to stick to the print and may also cause an area of discoloration, leaving a lasting reminder that you looked at the image. Fingerprints on color prints can occur due to sweat, oils, and salts from your hands. While most color prints are coated, this does not mean that fingerprints won't stay on the images. Polaroids often contain fingerprints from individuals who fail to handle the images by their edges during development.

• **Poor-quality plastic.** Color prints, negatives, or slides stored in plastic sleeves that are not polypropylene suffer damage from the plastic breaking down and depositing droplets of plasticizer on the images themselves. When buying plastic pages, stay away from any that exudes an odor. The gases given off by these pages will damage the images. Protect them by buying materials from the suppliers in Appendix D.

• **Surface treatments.** Some color prints are lacquered after processing to prevent them from sticking in framing and to prevent surface damage from handling. This treatment also added texture to the surface of the picture. Unfortunately, the lacquer also causes discoloration of the image.

GENERAL SUGGESTIONS FOR COLOR PRINTS AND NEGATIVES

Color film is inherently unstable, which means that unless steps are taken to safeguard your prints and films, they will fade. **By following a few basic**

Tip

principles of caring for them and avoiding special types of damage, you can extend the life of the materials, including Polaroid instant prints, in your family collection. The basic rule of color deterioration is that the amount of light, temperature, and humidity affects the rate of deterioration. Therefore, use these guidelines from libraries and archives.

1. **Do not expose images to sunlight.** Any exposure to sunlight fades the images and changes the appearance of the prints. If you want to display a photograph, have a copy made from the original negative or photograph and use that. Sunlight accelerates the deterioration process by attacking the dyes in the color film. Fluorescent light can emit high proportions of ultraviolet rays that can affect the color quality of color photographs. In order to reduce the amount of ultraviolet rays, do not use fluorescent light, but if it is unavoidable, purchase special sleeves to mask the bulbs. Most libraries and museums use these sleeves for their collections. You can purchase the sleeves from the suppliers listed in Appendix D.

2. **Store images in a dark place with a stable environment.** The standard preservation advice for color prints is to store them in a cold place at a stable temperature in the range of 30°F. Low temperature and humidity slows the deterioration of the image. Finding a perfect environment in your house can be difficult, so try to find an area without fluctuating temperature and humidity.

3. **Retain the negatives.** Negatives provide insurance. Since prints discolor over time, it is important to retain the negatives so that you can make new prints. Color negatives have special storage needs, as well. The best storage materials consist of individual acid- and lignin-free paper sleeves designed for that purpose sold by archival product companies. Negative pages are not recommended since the negatives can adhere to the sleeves over time due to changes in temperature and humidity. If you decide to use pages, stick with those manufactured with polypropylene.

Cold Storage

Cold storage of color materials has been around for a few decades. The leading authorities on cold storage of color photographic materials are Henry Wilhelm and Carol Brower. They found that cold storage discourages the fading and deterioration of color photographs. Many large museums with extensive color collections, such as the John F. Kennedy Library in Boston, have extensive cold storage facilities. You may think that cold storage is impractical for family collections; however, under the auspices of a grant from the Smithsonian, Wilhelm Research is testing storing photographs and motion picture film in commercially available non-humidity-controlled (frost-free) freezer units. These are essentially the same type of unit we use in our homes to store food. If you have a large number of color pictures, slides, and motion picture films, you may want to invest in a small freezer to literally freeze your images to prevent further damage. Set temperature at 0°F and keep the door closed. Each opening of the door causes temperature fluctuations that can damage the pictures.

COLD STORAGE AT HOME

For cold storage in your home, you need a freezer, some zip-locking storage bags of polypropylene, cotton gloves for handling the images, and metal storage boxes. All of these materials, with the exception of the freezer, are readily available from the suppliers in Appendix D.

Supplies

- Freezer (frost free)

- Zip-locking airtight storage bags of polyethylene or polypropylene

- Cotton gloves

- Metal storage boxes

Instructions

1. Purchase a frost-free freezer that can maintain a stable temperature of 0°F.

2. Double-wrap the photographs in PAT materials to protect them from temperature and humidity fluctuations. Then place them in freezer bags that zip close.

3. These precautions will dramatically change the rate at which color materials deteriorate. When removing materials from cold storage, follow the recommendations from the National Archives.

The National Archives follows these rules for removing materials from cold storage.[8]

- Remove the items from the freezer to an interim space away from direct heat to allow the materials to gradually warm up.

- Do not remove the photographs from storage bags until they feel room temperature.

- Wipe bags clean of any excess moisture before opening.

Don't want to do this at home? You can rent storage space from a commercial cold storage facility called Hollywood Vaults. See Web site <http://www.hollywoodvaults.com>, or call (800) 569-5336. In 1984, the owner of this company responded to a need in the movie industry for a cold storage warehouse. This is not the same cold storage that warehouses food but a state-of-the-art facility for preservation storage. The company maintains its vaults at 45°F and 25 percent humidity. In addition an air-filtration system cleans the air so that the materials are not exposed to pollutants. Movie studios, professional still photographers, and museums store materials here.

Basic Display Guidelines

According to conservator Paul Messier, color photographs, negatives, and slides are susceptible to physical, chemical, and biological deterioration the same as black-and-white materials. However, the chief damage is fading through deterioration of the dyes. For this reason, protect your original images by not displaying them and by following guidelines to extend the visibility of your copies.

1. Display out of direct sunlight and preferably in rooms that don't receive excessive amounts of sunlight.
2. If you have fluorescent lights in your home, consider covering them with ultraviolet (UV) filters. See list of suppliers in Appendix D.
3. Use proper framing techniques as outlined in chapter eleven, including a UV-filtering glass.
4. Display only copy prints or duplicates.

FILM AND GLASS SLIDES

There are basically two types of slides, those on glass and the film ones we have today. Both are one-of-a-kind original images that need to be protected from various types of damage. While you can make copies of both types of slides, the image quality will not be the same as in the original. If you need to send a slide to anyone, have a duplicate made. You wouldn't want the original slide lost.

Glass slides are a standard size of $3\frac{1}{4}'' \times 4''$. They are often confused with glass negatives, but there are two important differences. These glass slides, called lantern slides, are a positive image and a standard size. Glass negatives come in a variety of sizes and are negatives. Each lantern slide consists of a positive image sandwiched between two pieces of glass with a paper mount and sealed by tape around the edges.

The first photographic lantern slides, introduced in 1849, allowed for the projection of photographic images. Earlier versions of glass slides were scenes painted on the surface of the glass and predate photography by centuries. William and Frederick Langenheim patented the glass slide in 1850, calling it a Hyalotype. Their slide shows became entertainment, and the public paid to see these shows. Lantern slides were usually produced on a particular subject and in addition to providing entertainment were used for

Type of Process	Introduced
Lantern Slides	1849
Autochrome	1904
Kodachrome (slides)	1936
Kodak color negatives	1941
Polaroid SX-70	1974

educational purposes. Individuals could see a show on ancient antiquities or even scientific pursuits. Early movie theatres projected coming attractions using slides.

Black-and-white or hand-colored slides can be found in libraries and archives on a variety of topics. Early color processes such as the autochrome became available in slides around 1907. You may even find them in your home. Amateurs could produce their own slides or purchase sets and projectors. My public library recently stumbled on a set of lantern slides created of views of the town around 1900. They were sitting in a storage area in wooden boxes and envelopes. They were part of an illustrated lecture of the history of the town.

The National Museum of Photography, Film and Television in England suggests that owners of lantern slides examine the condition of their slides. The key things to look for are ripped or missing tape, broken glass, and uncleanliness. If in good condition, the materials are relatively stable, but if the cover glass is cracked or broken and the tape loose, then moisture, dirt, and other pollutants can cause damage.[9]

You can repair some of the problems yourself. You can replace broken glass as long as you can find glass of similar thickness and reseal the image using PAT tape. Do not under any circumstances attempt to clean the image itself. It is coated only on the surface of the glass. Photographers used a variety of methods to create the transparencies, and it is important to use a professional conservator for repairs to the actual image. Clean the cover glass with a lens tissue or small pieces of cotton. Store the slides in their original wooden boxes to protect them from breakage. If the boxes no longer exist, store the slides vertically with a support between every few slides.

Lantern slides remained popular from 1850 to approximately 1950 and are still used today in many academic disciplines. Inexpensive film slides introduced in the 1950s replaced lantern slides. But it wasn't until color photofinishing was available that color slides became inexpensive to produce and develop.

Contemporary slides consist of the image and a mount. In 1936, Kodak introduced Kodachrome slide film. Lacking a way to mount the slides during processing, Kodak sent slides back to consumers to be glass mounted by hand. It was another three years before cardboard mounts were available. There are three types of mounts currently available. You can glass mount slides yourself by transferring your images from cardboard ones to glass. This protects the surface from abrasion. Most slide film processed by commercial photofinishers is packaged in cardboard. This acidic paper mount can be replaced by a plastic mount but will be expensive and time-consuming. If you take your film to a commercial photo lab frequented by professional photographers, your slides will probably be mounted in plastic. While the quality of the mount will eventually affect the image, the majority of damage to slides occurs through handling and improper environment.

Technique

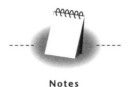

Notes

Guidelines for Handling Slides

1. **Handle by the edges only.** This prevents scratches and fingerprints.
2. **Store film slides in the dark.** Glass slides are more stable. Both types need proper temperature and humidity to last.
3. **Limit the projection time.** As recommended by Kodak's *Conservation of Photographs* (Rochester, N.Y.: Eastman Kodak Co., 1995), do not project slides or use them on a light table for more than a minute. A light table is a piece of equipment that sits on a tabletop and backlights the slides so that projection isn't necessary. The combination of heat and light will fade the images. Use copies for projection. Just leaving slides exposed to sunlight will fade the images. Projection times accumulate and cause fading.
4. **Never send originals.** Since these are unique images, once they are lost they are irreplaceable. Have copies made when you need to send images to someone.

Notes

Basic Guidelines for Slide Storage

1. **Use polypropylene pages for storing slides.** Using pages helps protect the slides during handling. Stiff pages or flexible ones made from polypropylene are best for slides. Other types of plastic deteriorate with time and deposit chemicals on the surface of the slide. In addition, adequate ventilation between the slides and the storage materials reduces the slides' contact with the sleeves and prevents condensation.
2. **Find a proper environment.** Temperature, humidity, and light cause a significant amount of damage to color materials, including slides.
3. **Purchase films with a proven storage record.** Protect your slides before you take them, by purchasing film that lasts. Kodak Kodachrome slide film is suggested. You can also use the film longevity charts in Henry Wilhelm and Carol Brower's *The Permanence and Care of Color Photographs*.

MOVIE FILM

While, technically, home movies are not photographs, they are often part of a family photograph collection. In fact, it would be difficult to find a family without at least one reel of 16mm or 8mm color movie film. Caring for this film is as important as preserving the still images in your collection. The basic rules of preservation apply to home movies. They need an environment with stable temperature and humidity. Since your still images need the same sort of storage area, it makes sense to keep everything together.

Movie film first became available in 35mm formats that the early commercial films were made on. If you own any 35mm motion picture film, please contact the National Center for Film and Video Preservation at the American Film Institute, 2021 N. Western Ave., Los Angeles, CA 90027,

(323) 856-7600 <http://www.afionline.org>. Since nitrate film was produced from 1889 to 1939, most of the early movie film is unstable and needs to be transferred to safety film.

Another reason to contact a film archive about any nonstandard film is that you could be holding a copy of a missing film. The National Center for Film and Video Preservation estimates that less than 10 percent of the movies made in the 1910s exist. Each new cache of commercial film that is discovered in someone's attic or basement may be valuable to historians studying the history of motion pictures.

Important

Since all color film fades, whether it is still film or motion picture film, it is necessary for you to follow a set of guidelines to slow the deterioration of your home movies. Films for the commercial market, such as Ektachrome, Agfa, and Ansco, fade in less than ten years. The good news is that Kodachrome movie film sold to consumers since 1940 does not fade as quickly.

1. **Identify your film.** Is the film in your collection black and white, or color? Is it marked as safety film? Do you have it stored in the original packaging that identifies the brand?

2. **Examine the film.** Does it show any signs of damage? The film base will shrink over time, buckle, or become brittle. Projecting the film may have caused scratches and broken sprocket holes. Someone knowledgeable about film conservation methods can repair tears and perforations in the film. Conservators can also copy film onto a new base. Before you are tempted to use videotape as a long-term storage medium, read pages 105–106.

3. **Rewind the film emulsion side out.** Be careful not to wind the film too tightly; if it is brittle, it will break.

4. **Use metal storage cans for long-term storage.** They can be stored flat in a stack no more than a foot high. These cans are available from library suppliers.

5. **Label the outside of the cans with a permanent marker** so that the identification information remains with the film. Transfer any information from the original storage box, such as who is in the film and where and when it was taken.

The number of color images and the variety of formats in our home collections are dependent on when the family became interested in documenting events and individuals. In some families, there has always been an interest in photography, so their collections will be varied and probably contain both still and motion pictures. Economic status is also a factor. In order to take photographs or home movies, you had to purchase equipment, buy film, and spend money on expensive processing.

HIRING A PROFESSIONAL PHOTOGRAPHER

There are times in your life when you hire professional photographers to document important events, such as weddings, or to take formal family portraits. But how can you tell if these professionals are following procedures to ensure the longevity of your images? You can start by asking them a few simple questions. When considering hiring photographers to take pictures of special events and family members, interview them about their procedures and final products (see page 91). As the customer, you can request information. Just be aware that special treatment of your prints may create additional costs.

Frequently Asked Questions

How can I copy my Polaroid pictures?
Since a Polaroid print is a one-of-a-kind image, you need to make duplicate prints or use a scanner. Most photo labs now have the ability to make direct positive prints. You can also do this on a Kodak Picture Maker system. Locate a system near you on Kodak's Web site <http://www.kodak.com> or calling its customer service department (800) 939-1302.

How can I stop my color prints from fading?
Some color prints fade even when stored in the proper environment, but the best thing you can do is keep color materials in a cool, dark place. See storage guidelines on pages 84–85.

Can I have film developed that has been sitting undeveloped for years?
You can have the film developed, but the quality of the prints may not be what you are hoping for. The length of time the film sat undeveloped and the environment it was stored in affect the quality of the color and the degree of fading.

Can I store my slides in slide carousels or trays?
The preferable way to store slides is in polypropylene pages. Carousel trays give off gases from the plastics they're manufactured from but also give slides an opportunity to breathe. Storing slides in trays in boxes, to protect from dirt, is better than using poor-quality slide pages that deteriorate with time.

How can I make prints from my slides?
Before the days of digital imagery, the only way to make a print from a slide was to first make a negative (called an inter-negative) and then a print. Today, thanks to computers, you can make a good-quality print from your slide without making an inter-negative. This results in a better print. Each time you make a copy from an original, it is called a generation. For instance, the process of making a negative of a slide and then a print is considered two generations. If you were to make another negative from the print, it would be an unnecessary third generation. Each generation results in a loss of detail. Now the whole process can be done in one step either by a photo lab or at home with a scanner and a slide adapter.

QUESTIONS FOR A PROFESSIONAL PHOTOGRAPHER

What type of photo paper do you use, and how long does it last?

Photographic papers fade at different rates, and some are better than others. Once you know what type of materials the photographer uses, go to a professional photo store and find out if it has information on the best types of paper. Photographs of extra importance should be printed using the processes recommended by Henry Wilhelm and Carol Brower in *The Permanence and Care of Color Photographs*, such as UltraStable permanent color prints, Polaroid permanent color prints, or EverColor pigment prints. For the most up-to-date information on color permanence, consult Wilhelm Imaging Research online <http://www.wilhelm-research.com/>.

Do you water-process or chemically process your prints?

Water processing is the better choice because it cleans chemical residue from developing from the surface of the prints and negatives.

How long do you store negatives?

This is important information if you ever need reprints. Under current copyright law, you must go to the photographer who took the photograph to have reprints made. Photo labs will not infringe on this copyright by making duplicate prints from your positive prints. See an explanation of the copyright matter on pages 35–40.

Do you use lacquer to coat the photograph or to create texture?

You may be able to ask that your prints not be coated.

Is the photo studio going to frame the prints?

You may be able to make this optional and take the print to a professional framer to ensure that your print is framed according to methods used in museums.

Are the images going to be presented in an album supplied by the photographer?

You may decide to purchase and supply your own album from one of the suppliers in Appendix D. Ask the photographer where he purchases albums to see if they pass preservation standards.

CHECKLIST: COLOR

✓ Follow the recommended storage guidelines for color images.
✓ Make copies of valuable photos.
✓ Don't display original color photographs.
✓ Be aware of the different ways that color photographs deteriorate.

Notes

SIX

The Digital Age: The New Family Album

A growing number of individuals feel like the woman in my lecture who insisted that placing her family photographs on compact disc and throwing away the originals is a viable solution to the preservation and space dilemmas posed by our collections. Yet, as convenient as this may seem to some, it raises a lot of issues about our family images, not just those taken with a digital camera but those that bypass the traditional print and are maintained by a photographic Web-based company. There are preservation problems, retrieval issues, and the sheer lack of aesthetics of looking at a digital image. Yes, it is easier to share pictures, e-mail copies to relatives, and set up family Web sites, but what is really happening is a changing notion of the nature of a family photographic album.

The popularity of the new family album is gaining converts as digital technology becomes accessible and less expensive. According to a recent Maritz research poll, thirty-five million people use the Internet for family research, about half of the total number of individuals who use the Internet. There are no concrete figures for the number of users of photo-sharing sites, but if you consider that ownership of digital cameras is on the increase, then there may be millions. If you don't already own a digital camera, it is probable that you will in the near future. Some models now sell for less than one hundred dollars.

DIGITAL PHOTOGRAPHY HISTORY

Here's a snapshot of where digital photography was ten years ago. In 1991, only a select few professional photographers had access to electronic cameras. The reason: They cost twenty thousand dollars and came with a shoulder pack that weighed eleven pounds due to the hard drive. They had black-and-white screens. Today, professional cameras sell for less than a thousand dollars and have an internal hard drive and a color screen. Sales of digital cameras increased from 245,000 in 1996 to two million in 1997.[1]

COMPUTER FILES

As fascinating as digital photography is as a new photographic medium, the whole process creates preservation problems. There is no doubt that storing photographs on computers is a space saver. It eliminates the problem of piles of photographs around the house. However, **the major concerns are retrieval and preservation.** Storing digital images takes an incredible amount of hard disk space. Does anyone remember 8-track tapes and 5¼" computer disks? If you do, then you know there is very little equipment left that can play the tapes or retrieve the information on the disks. The same might be true for digital photography. How long before your computer is obsolete and you have to move all that information, including your digital images, to a new one? Sure, you can transfer the information from one computer to another, but if the software to read the images changes, you may have an incompatibility problem. You have to be sure that the newer system can read the format in which your images are stored. And what happens if you want to donate your family photo archive? Will the facility be able to read the computer data, or would it prefer having hard copies of your images? I bet it would prefer actual photographs over computer data. One archive has collected television newsfilm for the past fifty years. Its collection consists of film in a variety of formats and videotape. It's a wonderful visual history of the last half century; it is, if the archive had the equipment to read the videotape and some of the film formats. This is a different type of material than a still photograph, but if you transfer all your images to a digital format, will anyone be able to read them in fifty years?

Warning

PHOTO CDs

Then there is the problem of photo CDs. Initial testing of the first CDs gave them a life expectancy of only five to ten years. Today, manufacturers are creating CDs that according to their estimates will last thirty to one hundred years. Companies used accelerated aging tests to predict the stability of their products under certain conditions. What they found is that longevity depends almost entirely on proper storage conditions, careful handling, and limited exposure to light. **You increase the life span of this material by storing your CDs in the same environment as your photographs.** A temperature of no more than 77°F and at 40 percent relative humidity is suggested. CDs are quite susceptible to scratching and should be handled by the edges only. Just as light damages the layers in a photograph, it deteriorates one of the components of the CD. The larger issue with CD-ROM technology is the retrieval of the material written on one. Again, the question is whether the equipment will be around to allow you to look at it in five, ten, or twenty years. Even if the material lasts to the outside date of three hundred years, will anyone really be able to look at your photo CDs?[2]

Important

If you think this is alarmist, just stop and consider the history of technology in your lifetime. Whether you are young, old, or middle-aged, there are pieces of equipment that have become quickly obsolete in a relatively short period of time, such as 45 and 33 rpm records. The public is not fully aware of the ramifications of switching completely to digital formats. In a recent conversation, a friend laughed when I raised these issues. He said he would just copy all of his data each time the technology changed. However, the costs of this conversion far exceed the inconvenience of having boxes of photographs around the house.

ONLINE PHOTO COMMUNITY

What is the future of our family photograph collections? At this particular moment, as consumers, we have a wide variety of choices. Walk into any camera store and try to make a decision about your future picture-taking habits. You can choose to be a traditionalist and stay with a camera that uses film, select a video camera, or buy a digital camera that offers still or moving images. A few months ago, I spoke with a marketing person at a then brand-new company who told me the future of family photographs is digital video cameras. He assumed that Web sites would incorporate this new technology and feature not only still images but movies and video e-mail. I agree that technology looks promising, but will that company, let alone that technology, still be current a year from the date of publication of this book, or will the market have changed due to the invention of a new medium?

As a family photographer, it is difficult to figure out this exploding market. Each day there are new digital photography related sites. At the moment, the digital photographic community online consists of community sites where individuals share images, photofinisher sites that produce images from digital formats as well as film, and sites that do both. These are the sites that are trying to quickly incorporate as much new technology as possible. It is quite likely that the final format of these photo Web sites will combine photofinishing services and live video and that the sites will become online communities that allow you to selectively share with other family members. This seems to be the trend.

PHOTO SUPPLIERS

Most of the major photo companies have jumped into the digital photography market by offering services via their Web sites. Kodak, adapting to the digital marketplace, now offers customers a choice of services either from home or through a Kodak photo-processing retailer. For instance, if you use film, you can take it to be developed at a retailer and select your usual prints and negatives or select two online options. Kodak PhotoNet online <http://www.photonet.com> will place your images on the Kodak Web site

Tip

PLANNING FOR OBSOLESCENCE

1. Upgrade your equipment every few years. 2. Transfer your photographs from one media to another when the technology becomes available. 3. Acknowledge the limits of the technology. 4. Make additional copies on different media, such as photo prints, disks, and recordable CDs.

Sources

Figure 6-1.
Online photo companies offer many services and options for consumers. *Photopoint.com*

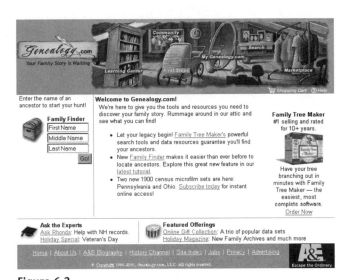

Figure 6-2.
Genealogy.com is just one site where you can create and post a free family Web page. *Genealogy.com*

and allow you to share photographs with others. You can also take advantage of AOL's "You've Got Pictures" by supplying your AOL screen name then viewing your developed pictures on AOL's site. As is true with many photo suppliers or processing sites, you can order personalized gifts or re-prints without using a negative. There is also a feature for uploading digital photographs to the Kodak site using the Print@Kodak link <http://www.kodak.com>. While Kodak currently offers more options than competing retailers, others will follow. Agfa <http://www.agfanet.com> and Fuji <http://www.fujifilm.net> also provide services for consumers through their Web sites. Agfa allows you to upload digital pictures to its site and buy prints. In order to access your pictures online at the Fuji site, you must take your film to a Fuji film-processing retailer and use your roll number and password to access the online film.

There are a lot of options and it's a personal choice. However, it is advisable to evaluate these sites prior to use. Since so many new sites are being posted each month, there is tremendous competition for customers. Newer companies offer customers all types of incentives to use their services, such as free film processing, scanning your images to place them online, free downloads, and storage space. It is difficult to estimate which of these photo-processing sites will be long-term survivors. Whether you use traditional film or digital formats, there are a few questions to help you evaluate what the companies offer.

1. How do they process your film and make images accessible online?
2. Can you upload digital images?
3. Can you download images from their sites?
4. How long do they store the images?

Company Web Site	Film Processing	Uploading	Sharing	Comments
http://www.agfanet.com	Yes	Yes	Yes	
http://www.fujifilm.net	Yes; traditional prints and negatives; also scans prints	Yes	Yes	
http://www.kodak.com	Yes; traditional prints and negatives; also scans prints	Yes	Yes	Related Web sites: AOL's "You've Got Pictures" and Kodak PhotoNet
http://www.ofoto.com	Yes; traditional prints	Yes	Yes	
http://www.photoworks.com	Yes; traditional prints and negatives; also scans prints	Yes	Yes	Formerly Seattle Filmworks

Community Sites

Sharing your family photographs online is another facet of the rapidly expanding digital photography industry. More established companies are entering the field as well as small entrepreneurs who recognize the potential of this market. According to a recent online article comparing many of the sites, these companies are able to supply free services by generating revenue through advertising, selling you print and other photographic products, renting you space for additional photos, and selling your user profiles.[3] As the competition between these companies increases, the number of features these sites are able to offer expands. Some of the best sites offer you the ability to edit your images, organize them into albums, add captions, send copies via e-mail, print them, and even password protect your site. **Before deciding to use a community site for all of your family images, you should evaluate the site and the company.**

Notes

• **How long has the company been in business?** Since this is a fairly new medium for family images, most of the businesses are fairly new, but their financial backers might be older, more established companies. While this does not guarantee longevity and economic stability, it is an indication that the company was worth the investment. You can also ask about the company's business model. Find out how it supports its product. If it is completely supported through advertising, you might want to look elsewhere. In the new reality of the online community, very little revenue is actually raised through advertising.

• **What happens to your electronic files if the company ceases to exist?** This is not a topic that is currently being dealt with when a site is reviewed but one that will have growing importance. There will be winners and losers in this e-commerce venture, so before posting valuable family images on a site, why not ask if it can transfer your images to another site of your choosing? Of course, you probably can download your images to a disk or CD yourself. If you have used an online company for the photo processing, you may not have negatives to make prints from in the future. Fujifilm.net offers long-term storage of digital images for one year.

• **Are photo-editing tools offered?** Some Web sites offer a variety of editing options, from creating your own scrapbook pages and family Web sites to simple features such as cropping and rotating images. Make a list of the features you want to use, and see if the site offers them. Be sure to check back regularly because the number of options generally increases the longer the company is in business.

• **How easy is it to look at your images?** If you don't have fast Internet access, you may have trouble using your files. If a picture is a large file, you have to think about how long it will take to download it. Try a few of these companies prior to signing up for a service. Most have demos online for potential customers. If you don't see demos, contact customer service departments for access.

• **Are you limited on the number of files?** This becomes important if you are going to upload a large number of images. You'll want to know if the company has a limit to the number and size of the images that you can post. Ask companies to elaborate on the "free" offers; they may have finite definitions.

• **Is there a maximum size at which you can display or print?** According to the reviewer at Dygraphics.com, this is a factor if your images are going to be reprinted on objects such as T-shirts and mugs.[4] If the site compresses your digital images, it can affect the final product when you reprint.

• **Are your albums completely private or open to the public?** Some people don't mind if everyone sees their family photographs and has access to them. For most of us, images are private, to be shared only with individuals who are relatives and friends. Before you decide to make your genealogical information and photographs public property, consider the privacy issues presented in this chapter.

• **How long does the site maintain your images?** The business model for these sites allows most of them to provide basic services for free for the moment. This is apt to change as more people make use of these sites and additional services are added. The Kodak site is the only one to currently charge for space on a regular basis.

• **Does the company resize your images?** If you shoot all your images with a digital camera, do you want the site to resize and compress your images? This may not affect your ability to view them on the Web but will change their appearance when you request copies. A couple of sites compress images for storage purposes. This policy may not be specifically mentioned on the site.

• **How are vertical images handled?** Unless you are an unusual photographer, at least some of your images will be vertical rather than horizontal.

For More Info

CONSULT THE EXPERTS

See how some of the sites compare to each other by reading reviews regularly conducted by magazines such as *Digital Photographer*.

How to display these vertical images becomes an issue whether you are using a standard photo album or an online one. Some sites offer you the option of rotating your images and some don't. If you take verticals shots, you don't want to have to tilt your head to see the pictures; you want to be able to view them comfortably.

Of course, the best way to determine if a site suits your needs is to try it out. You can experiment with online demo versions on most Web sites. Some companies even offer to send you starter kits to introduce you to their services.

OVERVIEW OF PHOTO-SHARING SITES

Adobe ActiveShare <http://www.adobeactiveshare.com>

Club Photo <http://www.clubphoto.com>

Ecircles.com <http://www.ecircles.com>

Ememories.com <http://www.ememories.com>

GatherRound.com <http://www.gatherround.com>

Homestead.com <http://www.homestead.com>

PhotoLoft <http://www.photoloft.com>

PhotoPoint.com <http://www.photopoint.com>

PhotoWorks.com <http://www.photoworks.com>

Shutterfly <http://www.shutterfly.com>

Snapfish <http://www.snapfish.com>

Zing <http://www.zing.com>

PRESERVATION ISSUES

Unavailability of equipment to retrieve images and incompatible software to read the medium are only two problems for the digital medium. Of growing concern are the Web sites that offer to host your images, acting as family photo archives online. While it is possible to place your images on one of these Web sites, there are a couple of things to consider. First, while these sites are initially free to new users, there is eventually a cost to store images or make prints. Another, more serious issue is trying to determine, in the rapidly expanding e-commerce world, which of these companies will survive. **In the worst case, you would store your images online, the company would fold, and you would lose all of those images.** A professional who works in the

Warning

industry claims that many of these new small start-ups will be absorbed to form larger companies and the digital archives transferred. If this expert is wrong, you won't have the actual photographs to look at with or without technology. Simply stated: Most photographs are more permanent than digital storage mediums.

FAMILY PAGES AND EXTENDED FAMILY SITES

A natural extension of the photo-sharing Web site is a family Web site that shares both images and genealogical and general information. So you are anxious to join the vast numbers of people creating family Web sites, but what do you need to know before you begin and how do you get started? Sure there are sites that offer you space for free, but before signing up, you need to evaluate the sites and determine what type of site you are going to create.

Professional Web designers refer to a site's information architecture, the how and why a site is constructed. With any site, you need to outline your goals and parameters.

DESIGNING A FAMILY HOME PAGE

Notes

1. Why are you creating the site? You can develop a site that has just genealogical information and images, or one that acts as a great family meeting place online. Take a look at other sites to see how other families use their home pages. Having a Web site is a great way to communicate your family research and photographs. If you want to hear from others about their research, list an e-mail address on your site.

2. What type of equipment do you have? Some of your decisions will be based on the type of equipment you have. If your computer is not current and lacks a fast modem, you are probably going to need to upgrade. All you really need is a computer (with a modem); access to the Internet via phone line, cable, or DSL (Digital Subscriber Line); and a good-quality printer. The faster the modem, the quicker you can download pages. To add photographs to your site, you will need a scanner or a digital camera or you will need to post your pictures on one of the photo-sharing sites (see earlier section) and upload them to your site. Most computers come loaded with software for viewing the Web and receiving e-mail. Even with this software, you will need to sign up for Internet service with an ISP (Internet Service Provider). You can find one in your local area by using your phone book or by searching online. Ask friends how satisfied they are with their services before committing to one.

3. Are you designing your site yourself? One of the primary issues is the design of the site. Before you start working with Web design, look at pages already on the Internet to get ideas for your own. This is simple to do. Using a standard search engine, type "family Web site" into the search field. You will uncover all types and styles of family Web pages along with articles on how to create them. Keep in mind that Web pages are subject to copyright laws, so you can't copy the pages exactly, but looking at them will help you decide how to organize your information and photographs. Some Web-hosting services offer hints on creating a site and provide tools to help you with the process. Commercially available Web-design software, such as Microsoft's Front Page, is a good choice. You can also enlist family members in the process. Teenagers are, in most cases, quite familiar with the Internet and would welcome an opportunity to design a Web page.

4. How will your site be maintained? Once you have posted your information on the site, it is time to start thinking about the next phase of the project. In order to keep your site up-to-date, you will want to make regular changes. Will that be your responsibility, or are there other family members who can help with the task? The best sites are those that are updated regularly. This takes time, but if you want to have a well-respected site, it is worth the effort. A good way to see how often other Web sites are changed is to search for them using AltaVista. That search engine supplies you with the date of the last upgrade.

Once you have decided on the purpose of your site and have a general idea of what you want it to look like, you will need to find a host for it. There are many options, from extended family sites that offer free hosting to paying a monthly fee through your ISP.

Evaluating a Site for a Family Web Page

1. Is it free, or is there a fee? When you first see an advertisement for a free Web service, make sure there really is no cost. One of the advantages

FAMILY WEB SITES

Ancestry.com <http://www.ancestry.com>

Angelfire <http://www.angelfire.com/register.shtml>

eFamily.com <http://www.efamily.com>

FamilyPoint <http://www.familypoint.com>

Genealogy.com <http://www.genealogy.com>

GeoCities <http://www.geocities.com/join.html>

MyFamily.com <http://www.myfamily.com>

RootsWeb.com <http://www.rootsweb.com>

SuperFamily.com <http://www.superfamily.com>

SuperGroups <http://www.supergroups.com>

Tripod <http://www.tripod.lycos.com>

to paying for space through your ISP is that it allows you to name your own site and have a unique URL (Uniform Resource Location) with an e-mail account.

2. Are there space limitations? Some free services limit you to 10MB of space and then assess fees for additional space. For the average person, this is probably enough space, but once you start adding images, you may need more storage.

3. Can you design your own page? Does the site provide you with a template you must use, or are you able to use your own design?

4. Does the site provide design software, or can you use your own? Some sites provide you with Web design software to use on their sites, while others let you use your own program.

5. What are the privacy conditions? Privacy is an important concern. See Privacy Issues in the New Family Album below and on pages 103 and 104. You want to make sure that you can password protect your family information so it isn't available to everyone. If you don't see a privacy statement, e-mail the service for a copy before you sign up.

Creating the Site

Whenever you create a Web site, remember to include certain basic components, such as a title, a background, text, an e-mail address, and, for visual interest, graphics. Consider your page an online publication and treat it as such. It should be user-friendly and attractive. When adding pictures to your site, use a low DPI (72) so images load quickly. It is also important to name each image so that if your users can't view the image they have a sense of what is supposed to be there. Graphics provide an opportunity to be creative with the material on your site. Just remember to follow the copyright guidelines presented in chapter two so you don't inadvertently use someone else's image.

Try not to overwhelm users with too many images that aren't relevant to their searches. According to Matthew Helm in *Genealogy Online for Dummies*, put each photograph on its own page and link to it from your main page. Include thumbnailed images with the links on the main page. This saves people from looking at images they are not interested in. Helm also suggests using a twenty-five-year rule. This means not posting any photograph less than twenty-five years old. It is important to respect individual privacy, credit the photographs, and not use images without permission.

PRIVACY ISSUES IN THE NEW FAMILY ALBUM

As you begin to create your family Web site, there are certain steps you should consider to protect your privacy on the Internet. As genealogists, we are excited about the possibility of sharing information with individuals looking for similar data. After all, isn't part of the fun of genealogy meeting all the long-lost cousins on the family tree? However, in recent years, there has been increased attention by the media to identify theft and the Internet.

Reminder

Reminder

BASIC COMPONENTS OF FAMILY WEB PAGE

Title, background, text, e-mail address, graphics

GUIDELINES FOR PUBLISHING WEB PAGES ON THE INTERNET

Recommended by the National Genealogical Society, May 2000

Appreciating that publishing information through Internet Web Sites and Web pages shares many similarities with print publishing, considerate family historians

- apply a single title to an entire Web site, as they would to a book, placing it both in the <TITLE> HTML tag that appears at the top of the Web browser window for each Web page to be viewed, and also in the body of the Web document, on the opening home, title or index page

- explain the purposes and objectives of their Web sites, placing the explanation near the top of the title page or including a link from that page to a special page about the reason for the site

- display a footer at the bottom of each Web page that contains the Web site title, page title, author's name, author's contact information, date of last revision and a copyright statement

- provide complete contact information, including at a minimum a name and e-mail address, and preferably some means for long-term contact, like a postal address

- assist visitors by providing on each page navigational links that lead visitors to other important pages on the Web site, or return them to the home page

- adhere to the NGS "Standards for Sharing Information with Others" regarding copyright, attribution, privacy, and the sharing of sensitive information

- include unambiguous source citations for the research data provided on the site, and if not complete descriptions, offering full citations upon request

Tip

- **label photographic and scanned images within the graphic itself, with fuller explanation if required in text adjacent to the graphic**

- identify transcribed, extracted or abstracted data as such, and provide appropriate source citations

- include identifying dates and locations when providing information about specific surnames or individuals

- respect the rights of others who do not wish information about themselves to be published, referenced, or linked on a Web site

- provide Web site access to all potential visitors by avoiding enhanced technical capabilities that may not be available to all users, remembering that not all computers are created equal

Continued

Continued from page 102

- avoid using features that distract from the productive use of the Web site, like ones that reduce legibility, strain the eyes, dazzle the vision, or otherwise detract from the visitor's ability to easily read, study, comprehend, or print the online publication

- maintain their online publications at frequent intervals, changing the content to keep the information current, the links valid, and the Web site in good working order

- preserve and archive for future researchers their online publications and communications that have lasting value, using both electronic and paper duplication

The majority of these cases involve unscrupulous individuals obtaining Social Security numbers and credit card offers. Although there have not been any reported incidents using genealogical information, **it is advisable to take a few steps to safeguard all your living relatives.** Creating a Web site of family information and photographs is a big responsibility and one that needs to be taken seriously.

Important

First, think about what you put on the site. The Texas GenWeb Project suggests not including information on living persons. Its slogan, "Protect Your Living Relatives—Don't Mess With The Living," is straightforward and full of common sense. Let's apply that guideline to cover responsible use of family images on your Web site.

1. When using family photographs on a Web site, be sure to ask for written permission from both the owner and the subject of the photograph beforehand. Professional photographers obtain signed releases in order to use images. If you need sample forms, consult *ASMP Professional Business Practices in Photography*, issued by the American Society of Media Photographers.

2. Select photographs carefully. You wouldn't want to cause anyone discomfort or embarrassment with your choice of images. Let photographic jokes remain private.

3. Use photo-editing tools to erase excess identifying information from the images. While it is acceptable to state someone's occupation as schoolteacher, is it within reason to exclude the name of the school in a photograph?

4. When writing a caption for an image, be careful not to include too much identifying information on living persons.

5. Educate others about proper use of photographs on the Internet. Once you post them, others have access to them.

If you doubt the importance of this issue, ask yourself the following questions:

- How would you feel if someone used your photograph without your permission?
- How would you feel if it were copied by an unknown person and posted on a non-family-related site?
- How would you feel if pictures and information on your children were posted elsewhere?

These can happen.

Before you post any genealogical information to accompany family images, remove data on living persons from your GEDCOM file. There are several filtering programs that can do this for you. GEDClean32, GEDLiving, GEDprivy, and Res Privata all clean your files of genealogical information on living persons.

FILTERING PROGRAMS

GEDClean32 <http://www.raynorshyn.com/gedclean>

GEDLiving <http://www.rootsweb.com/~gumby/ged.html>

GEDPrivy <http://hometown.aol.com/gedprivy/index.html>

Res Privata <http://www.ozemail.com.au/~naibor/rpriv.html>

Tip

Internet Source

CONSULT THE EXPERTS

Myra Vanderpool Gormley, CG, "Adventures in Cyberspace" <http://www.ancestry.com/columns/myra/Shaking_Family_Tree07-09-98.htm>.

A good general rule to follow is to exclude information on individuals less than one hundred years old. For instance, WorldConnect at RootsWeb eliminates data outside that cut off unless you ask to override it.

Before sharing information and photographs of living persons with "relatives," be a little skeptical. Don't provide this data in e-mails and GEDCOM files without first establishing the recipients' right to know. After all, if they are researching family history, do they really need to know all about your immediate family? Even if you trust these individuals, how do you know they won't pass this material on to another researcher without consulting you or submit it for inclusion on a CD or Web site? Using one of the more powerful search engines, such as Google.com, search for your name. Find any hits? Do the same with the large commercial genealogy sites. You might be surprised to see your private family information listed in a public place.

The digital family album offers possibilities that our ancestors couldn't even imagine. We share photographs, communicate with several family members simultaneously on extended family sites, and reach out to forgotten relatives. Use the technology wisely with regard to historic family photographs, and do not throw the originals away. Think of digital albums as another way of using your family images, not a replacement for the traditional family image.

Special Concerns

City Gallery is a Web site that features information of great value to genealogists interested in photography. One of its new columns, "Digital Album," publishes articles on the preservation of digital images. In one particularly thought-provoking item, the author discusses the meaning of archival in terms of digital media. The article also offered guidelines on choosing a format.[5]

- Durability: How long will the format you select last? Have you researched the preservation aspects of your choice? No digital storage media currently available will outlive a nineteenth-century print on a stable medium.
- Reliability: Prints that you can hold are reliable. Can you say the same for your computer?
- Erasability: How many times have you accidentally written over a computer disk full of information? Make sure whatever medium you select can be write protected to prevent that from happening.

There are plenty of positive aspects to the digital album: You can share images, make copies, store large quantities of images compactly, display them without handling originals, and restore them. Just don't expect your digital albums to be viewable by your great-grandchildren unless you take the steps to make that happen.

What Is the Future of Family Photography?

How do you as a consumer figure it all out? My advice is to have fun with your family photographs and not worry about the technological future. **If you treat your images well, they should last at least one lifetime regardless of the format.** As you experiment with all this new technology, remember to document your family's important moments using a technology with some longevity so that future generations can enjoy your family's moments. Our descendants may have more photographs of family members in 1890 than they will of us living in 1990 because the photographs were relatively stable. In the meantime, I'm going to try to invest wisely in photographic technology and keep reading the current consumer journals to follow the trends.

FREQUENTLY ASKED QUESTIONS

Can I have traditional photographic prints made from digitized images?

Yes. Most photo labs and online vendors can produce prints on regular photographic paper of your digital images.

What about the videotapes I have in my collection?

Videotape is a type of magnetic tape that consists of metal oxides on a clear polyester tape. The images are recorded on the magnetic metal oxide and the VCR plays it back. This is a fragile medium. The surface area is subject

Quotes

A few words from the Texas GenWeb Project <http://home.sprynet.com/~harrisfarm/warning.htm>: "It is the policy of The TXGen-Web Project to protect the rights and privacy of our living relatives. We strongly encourage all involved to do their best not to place information on the Internet about anyone who is still living, unless you have their express permission to do so."

Reminder

Warning

to abrasion, and repeated playing wears away at the metal oxides and degrades the images. Dirt that builds up on the VCR also scratches the tape. Videotape is susceptible to several other types of damage, too, such as blocking (where the tape sticks together), dropout (when pieces of magnetic material are missing), and deterioration of the base for the magnetic material. **This is a temporary storage medium; all tapes are unplayable in under a decade.** The cheaper the tape, the less likely it is to last that long. The only way to preserve the image is to copy the tape before damage becomes noticeable. In general, conservationists recommend not storing the tapes near any magnetic source that will erase the material on the tape. Videotape is not suggested as a preservation storage medium.

The Clarke Library <http://www.lib.cmich.edu/clarke/pres.htm> at the University of Michigan has published some helpful information online for consumers. The library suggests buying brand-name tape, checking it once a year for damage, making a preservation copy, and cleaning your VCR regularly. In addition, you should rewind and check the preservation copy yearly to anticipate when you will have to copy it. If you haven't followed this advice, you need to look at all your important family videotapes and copy them before it is too late.

Notes

CHECKLIST: THE DIGITAL AGE

✓ Plan for built-in obsolescence.
✓ Make regular photographic prints of valuable images.
✓ Research online services before using them.
✓ Use common sense when including images on family Web sites.

SEVEN

Professional Help: Conservation and Restoration

U nless you are extremely fortunate to have a collection in mint condition, at least a few of your family photographs will need to be professionally restored or conserved. There is a lot of confusion about these two processes. Companies that claim to conserve your images may be misrepresenting their services. Digital restoration is not conservation. The two terms are not interchangeable. Restoring an image is the process of re-creating the appearance of the object. Conservation has several steps that include examining the object, scientific analysis, research, and evaluation of the condition. All conservation work involves treatment to prevent future deterioration. Both conservation and restoration are time-consuming processes. Unless you are a trained chemist with a background in photographic conservation or a specialist in photographic restoration, you will want to hire someone else. **It is important that someone trained as a photographic conservator handle conservation work.** Attempting to remove damage from the surface of your images can destroy them.

Photographic conservators are specially trained individuals. Their backgrounds include working with all the mediums that appear in the history of photography, such as glass, metal, wood, paper prints, albums, and plastics.

Important

WHY YOU NEED A PROFESSIONAL

There may be daguerreotypes in your collections that are covered with tarnish or prints covered with stains. Stains due to acid storage materials or mold can gradually affect your pictures. A conservator can reverse some of the damage in these cases.

In other situations where photographs have been exposed to catastrophic events such as floods or fires, a conservator can assist in the recovery of your valuable photographs. Waterlogged images and those exposed to smoke will require special help.

It is necessary to find a properly trained photographic conservator to work with your images. Since there are no laws that regulate this profession, it is helpful to find someone affiliated with a professional organization.

One such group is the American Institute for Conservation of Historic and Artistic Works (AIC). Members of this organization must adhere to the AIC's Code of Ethics and Standards of Practice. The AIC requires its members to perform their jobs at a high level of professionalism. One of the AIC's sub-groups is the Photographic Materials Group (PMG). The AIC operates a Conservation Services Referral System, which will send you a list of members in your area. Since they represent conservators from a variety of backgrounds, be sure to ask specifically for photographic conservators. There is no charge for this service.

Within the AIC, there are various levels of membership (fellow, professional associate, or associate). Fellows and professional associates have agreed to follow the ethics outlined by the organization and have passed a peer review.

Many museums have small conservation labs to work with their in-house collections. **They may be willing to refer you to a conservator.** However, it is important to follow certain guidelines for choosing a conservator.

Tip

Choosing a Conservator

According to the AIC, there are specific questions you should ask conservators before hiring one. As a potential client, you have the right to ask questions and expect answers. After all, this is an important decision. You will be turning over irreplaceable family photographs to someone else's care. This is not the time to be shy about the interview process. You need to find out about training, experience, professional activities, and availability. **Ask for references and be sure to contact them to see if they are satisfied with the work.**

Tip

Evaluating Conservators

1. What is their training for photographic conservation? You want to learn more about their professional backgrounds. Did they study in formal programs or learn through participating in apprenticeships? Are they specifically trained in photographic conservation? Do they regularly attend conferences to keep up-to-date with new developments?

2. Ask for lists of references and call them. Conservators who actively accept clients will have lists of individuals they have recently done work for. Following up by calling those references is a necessary part of the hiring process. It can save you time and money later.

3. How long have they been involved in photographic conservation? Conservators who have many years of conservation experience will be able to use that to anticipate treatment problems. They have also developed networks of other professionals they can call on if necessary.

4. Is conservation their primary business? You need to find out if conservation is their business or just a hobby. This can make the difference between a well-conserved item and a project gone awry.

5. Do they have experience working with the type of image you have? Ask for examples. There is a wide variety of photographic materials in

family collections. You want to make sure that the person you hire is familiar with the item you are trying to have conserved.

6. What is their availability? Good conservators usually have a backlog of clients. The project you want to undertake may not be a complicated one, but because there are other clients, it can take a while until work begins.

WHAT YOU SHOULD EXPECT

1. The conservators will examine the item before advising a treatment.

2. They will supply you with a written preliminary report that contains a description of the treatment, results, and estimated cost.

3. Some conservators charge separately for examinations. Clarify whether the examination costs are deductible or separate from the future contract.

4. They should be able to explain risks, insurance, payment schedule, and shipping.

5. If the work is more involved that originally projected, you will be notified.

6. When the work is completed, some conservators provide a treatment report, while others require the client to request a copy. It contains a list of treatments and materials, as well as both written and photographic documentation.

WHAT CAN A CONSERVATOR ACCOMPLISH?

These two examples illustrate the different approaches involved in conserving different types of material. In both cases, the hard work and expertise recovered these "lost images." Before you throw out the damaged materials in your own collection, consider obtaining the advice of a professional conservator.

Case Study

Damaged Daguerreotype Recovered

The First Baptist Church in La Grange, Georgia, discovered a daguerreotype in a time capsule in the 1856 cornerstone during demolition of the building. When found the image was completely tarnished. Not a single one of the four sitters was visible.

The Church Archives Committee, with the guidance of the Troup County Archives, decided to send the daguerreotype to the Northeast Document Conservation Center for treatment. For well over a century, it had been exposed to high humidity, fluctuating temperatures, and probably water. All parts of the daguerreotype package had deteriorated. The brass mat and preserver were corroded brown with a few green spots. The glass cover was intact, but was very dirty and had mold

Figures 7-1 and 7-2.
Here are before and after conservation photographs of a daguerreotype found in a time capsule in a church cornerstone in La Grange, Georgia. Cleaning the image allowed for identification of the men in the image. *Courtesy of the Troup County Archives and NEDCC*

growth on it. The plate, itself, had mold deterioration (greenish spots), water lines across the image, and some uneven brown and blue tarnish. The paper on the reverse of the plate was completely disintegrated.

The Northeast Document Conservation Center was given the daguerreotype to treat. A senior paper conservator reduced the surface soil using dry cleaning techniques and cleaned the plate electrolytically in a strong ammonium hydroxide solution. The image of four men became clearly visible.

The brass mat and preserver were cleaned in ammonium hydroxide, and then washed and varnished in shellac. The daguerreotype package was resealed using a new cover glass and Filmoplast P90 tape.

Since NEDCC's treatment of the daguerreotype, staff of the Troup County Archives identified the man on the left as Phillip Hunter Green, a noted local builder, and the man in the center, Reverend Elder B. Teague, minister of the church. The other two men are still unidentified.

Church leaders had anticipated a capsule in the 1922 cornerstone, placed when the church was renovated, but were unaware of the one in the 1856 cornerstone, placed when the church was built. In the earlier stone in an opening chiseled out of the granite a cardboard shoe box was found. Gary Sheets, building superintendent, said, "I was nervous as a long-tailed cat in a room full of rocking chairs when we were taking out the box." Unlike the contents of the 1922 stone, the articles found in the older stone were in poor condition. They included the daguerreotype treated at NEDCC, a small bible, a small wooden box which may have originally housed the daguerreotype, some remnants of a tapestry-like fabric, and some unidentifiable deteriorated "crumbs."

When the new First Baptist Church is built it will include another time capsule in its cornerstone. Inside that time capsule will be a photographic copy of the daguerreotype.

Reprinted with permission from NEDCC, 100 Brickstone Square, Andover, MA 01810 <http://nedcc.org>, *NEDCC News* 7, no. 1 (Winter 1997). (See figures 7-1 and 7-2.)

Negative Deterioration

The method employed by the Chicago Albumen Works to salvage these deteriorating negatives involves three steps. First, the emulsion is chemically removed from the di-acetate base. The pellicle (the removed emulsion) is then set in a carefully controlled solution which allows its folds and furrows to relax. Finally, the flattened pellicle is duplicated with our standard duplication procedures, producing an archival film interpositive and an accurate duplicate negative. The pellicle itself can also be returned to the collection.

Reprinted with permission of the Chicago Albumen Works, Front St., Housatonic, MA 01236, (413) 274-6901 <http://www.albumenworks.com>. The Chicago Albumen Works offers negative conservation for individuals and institutions. (See figures 7-3 and 7-4.)

Figures 7-3 and 7-4.
The Chicago Albumen Works specializes in salvaging damaged negatives. Shown here are before and after views of a negative of Clark Gable and Margaret Mitchell at the premiere of *Gone With the Wind*. The image is shown as a positive to illustrate damage.
Atlanta History Center

DISASTER PREPAREDNESS
What to Do When the Unexpected Happens

For many of us, living in certain areas of the country means exposure to many types of natural disasters, such as hurricanes, tornadoes, and earthquakes. There is a predictability to the fluctuations of the weather. Then there are the unexpected events that change our lives, such as fires and floods. These disasters usually affect our belongings, including our photograph collections. Several individuals I know experienced damage to their photograph collections during heavy rainstorms while their house was being renovated.

So what can be done to prepare your collections for damage? **In the words of a salvage expert, there are four parts to a disaster planning process: prevention, preparedness, response, and recovery.**[1] Most museums, libraries, and archives have disaster plans just in case the unexpected occurs. Many others are

Notes

INTERVIEW WITH PAUL MESSIER, A CONSERVATOR WITH BOSTON ART CONSERVATION

What is the basic component of any conservation work?

A conservator stabilizes a photograph so that no further deterioration can take place.

When should a photograph be considered for conservation work?

Like any other artistic or cultural object, photographs require conservation treatment to address active deterioration. Active deterioration typically falls under three broad categories: chemical, physical, and biological. Some examples: Chemical deterioration can relate to the presence of acidic enclosure or adhesives. Such materials can cause progressive staining and/or fading of photographic images. Perhaps the most significant cause of chemical deterioration is long-term exposure to elevated relative humidity, which can cause deterioration to photographic binders (the image such as gelatin), the paper base, and the silver-based imaging materials. Physical deterioration usually takes the form of tears, creases, and overall embrittlement, making handling and displaying the piece risky. Biological deterioration typically takes the form of mold and insect activity that can cause staining. These are all manifestations of active deterioration that require conservation treatment in order to stabilize the condition of the piece.

How long does the process take?

Usually a conservation treatment will have two major phases. The first phase typically deals with addressing the various forms of active deterioration in order to stabilize the object. Once the piece is stabilized, then treatment might shift to compensating for areas of loss or doing other restoration work. The first phase can often be achieved after one to five hours. Depending on the amount of restoration needed, the second phase can take minutes to any number of hours.

What can a conservator accomplish?

It varies depending on the type of photograph and the type and amount of damage.

Tintypes

For instance, there is not much a conservator can do to repair abrasive damage to a tintype. If the tintype is rusting, conservation treatments can stabilize the chemical deterioration of the image. It can be consolidated to help prevent lifting off of the image.

Continued

Continued from page 113

Ambrotypes

When the backing of an ambrotype is flaking away, consolidation treatments can re-adhere it into place.

Paper Prints

A conservator can repair physical deterioration by mending tears with Japanese paper and wheat paste. When the damage is severe, the entire print can be removed from its original mount, lined, and remounted on Japanese paper or a sturdier mounting board. This protects the photograph from further tears.

When the damage is the result of chemical deterioration, such as staining or silver mirroring, a variety of treatments can help. Silver mirroring gives the print a silver or iridescent appearance when held at a particular angle. The silver mirroring may be removed from the surface or coated by saturation of the mirroring. In both cases, the mirroring can be significantly reduced.

Stains due to biological damage can be reduced by washing in deionized water or bleached using light. This is a challenge for certain types of prints, depending on their sensitivity to water.

Missing pieces of emulsion due to abrasion, cracks, tears, or insect damage can be compensated for with a technique called inpainting. First, the area of image loss is consolidated using a substance, then the inpainting medium, such as watercolor, pastel, or colored pencils, is applied. The goal is to make the area of image loss as minimally distracting as possible. In all cases, the inpainting should be reversible.

If you could give one piece of advice about caring for photographs in a home, what would it be?

I think long-term exposure to elevated relative humidity and poor-quality housing materials are the most significant factors that cause deterioration of most collections. Avoiding these conditions is critical for the preservation of photographs, whether in a public institution or in the home.

How expensive is conservation work?

If someone has a photograph of sentimental value in their collection, they should not be discouraged from approaching a conservator. Stabilization can be done in a few hours of treatment. Often it is the cosmetic work, such as inpainting, that becomes expensive. If need be, a person can have a conservator stabilize the print from future damage and have the cosmetic work done at a later time.

Paul Messier is a professional associate of the American Institute for Conservation. His Web site address is <http://www.paulmessier.com>.

creating them. You can, too. When the next natural disaster strikes, you will know how to save your valuable collection from destruction and whom to call for assistance.

Follow the example of the professionals who think the best way to prepare for disaster is to take steps to prevent it. This simply means storing your collection in an area of your home or in a facility that will limit certain types of damage. In other words, in addition to looking for an area with stable temperature and humidity, store your photographs in an area away from water pipes, chemicals, and electrical wires. Accidents have a tendency to happen when we least expect them, and that water pipe may end up causing damage to your collection.

Preparation is the next step in disaster planning. First, do you know whom to call if your photograph collection is damaged due to flood or fire? Obviously there will be other things that need taking care of before you get to your photographs, but eventually you may need to contact a professional experienced in dealing with damaged materials. You can obtain a list of conservators in your area by contacting the American Institute for Conservation of Historic and Artistic Works, 1717 K St., NW, Suite 301, Washington, DC 20006, (202) 452-9545. This is a free service of the organization. Conservators will charge for their services. Before assuming that one of these individuals will be able to assist you, call them and ask if they work with home collections. If they don't, ask them for a reference.

Prepare a simple checklist of items to do when faced with a disaster. Include such items as knowing where the main water shutoff to your residence is located, the number of the fire department, and of course the number of a local conservator.

Knowing how to respond to an unexpected disaster will minimize the damage to your photographic materials. Each type of damage requires certain responses and an assessment of the problem.

Tip

WATER DAMAGE

You can minimize the loss of images if you know how to respond to water damage beforehand. I know several people who decided that their photographs were not salvageable because they were immersed in water. This is not always the case. It depends on the length of time the materials were submerged, the condition of the water, and the type of material. Remember that most photographic developing involves water, so you may still be able to save your collection. You will need three things to save parts of your collection: time, space for drying, and a few supplies.

1. Clean up water. To assess the damage, you will have to clean up the water. Make sure that the electrical supply to your residence is shut off before attempting to stand in the water, just in case there are any electrical wires. Use whatever method you can to empty the area of excess water, such as pumps and special wet vacuums.

Technique

CONSERVATION OF A PAPER PRINT

These before and after photographs of a damaged portrait in figures 7-5 and 7-6 illustrate what a conservator can accomplish. The sample report provides you with an example of what a client can expect.

SAMPLE CONDITION AND TREATMENT REPORT

Condition Report and Treatment Proposal

File #: 99033
Type: Crayon enlargement
Title/description: Portrait of a Man
Artist/origin/date: Unknown American, ca. 1915
Dimensions: approximately 19″ × 16″ oval
Owner: Jean M. Washington
Examined by: Paul Messier
Report date: 8/7/00

Condition: The photograph is in poor condition. It is split into four major pieces, and several smaller fragments. The pieces are adhered to a paperboard mount. There are losses, punctures, tears, and staining. There are several losses to the photograph, all located along the outer edges. The largest losses are as follows: 4½ × 4½ × 2½ inches, triangular, located to the left of the sitter's head; 2½ × 2½ × 1 inches, triangular, located near the sitter's left shoulder; 1½ × 3 × 3 inches, triangular, located above the sitter's right shoulder; 1 × 1½ × 2 inches, triangular, located at the upper edge. There are three punctures in the photograph. They each measure approximately one inch and are located above the sitter's left eye, at the lower left edge, and 2½ inches from the lower right edge.

Continued

Figures 7-5 and 7-6.
These photographs of a damaged portrait illustrate the conservation process.
Reports courtesy of Paul Messier, photograph courtesy of Keith Washington

Continued from page 116

There are several tears throughout the photograph. The largest of these are as follows: 3 inches vertical, located at the right shoulder; 2½ inches vertical, located at the lower edge; 4 inches, diagonal, located to the left of the ear.

The photograph appears to have suffered some minor water damage. There are dark brown stains at the lower edge. There is minor media loss near the mouth.

Treatment Report

File #: 99033
Type: Crayon enlargement
Title/description: Portrait of a Man
Artist/origin/date: Unknown American, ca. 1915
Dimensions: approximately 19″ × 16″ oval
Owner: Jean M. Washington
Treated by: Paul Messier
Report date: 8/7/00

Treatment: The photograph was split from its acidic mount using a metal spatula. Remaining paper was removed from the reverse of the photograph with poultices of methylcellulose. Losses were filled with paper toned with acrylic paints. The fragments were assembled together and adhered on the reverse with Japanese paper and wheat starch paste. The photograph was lined overall to a sheet of Japanese paper with wheat starch paste. Following lining, it was placed between blotters and under weights to dry and flatten. Once dry, the photograph was mounted to a 2-ply board using heat set tissue.

Types of Material	Drying Method[2]
Cased images	Dry face up if water and debris inside. Contact a conservator for disassembly. Do not blot dry.
Glass negatives	Dry emulsion side up if cracked or emulsion is peeling; dry vertically if in good condition.
Acetate negatives	Dry emulsion side up.
Prints	Dry face up on blotters.
Slides	Remove from mount. Dry emulsion side up.
Sheet film and negatives	Gently hang to dry.

2. Assess the damage. At this point, you need to answer a few questions.
- What type of water damage (broken pipe or dirty flood water)?
- Are the materials partially dry, damp, or wet?

Supplies

EMERGENCY SUPPLIES KIT

- Blotter paper or un-printed newsprint
- Disposable plastic gloves
- Distilled water
- Fans
- Dehumidifier
- Clothesline
- Plastic clips
- Plastic bags
- Sponges

For More Info

CONSULT THE EXPERTS

See the Disaster Plan for the British Columbia Information Management Services. Betty Walsh, "Salvage Operations for Water Damaged Archival Collections: A Second Glance," *WAAC Newsletter* 19, no. 2 (May 1997) <http://palimpsest .stanford.edu/waac/wn/ wn19/wn19-2/wn19-206.html>.

- Was the water dirty or contaminated with chemicals? If so, what were the contaminants?
- Has mold started to grow on the materials?
- Were they wet more than forty-eight hours before you salvaged them?

The answers to these questions guide your next steps. If the material was contaminated by more than just water, you need to call a conservator for advice. Photographs wet in humid, warm conditions can grow mold in just a few days. It is important to prevent mold by controlling the environment.

3. Control the environment. As quickly as possible, you need to reduce the humidity and temperature in the area that sustained water damage. Failure to do so will result in mold and mildew. You can do this by lowering the heat (in winter) and by using dehumidifiers to reduce the amount of moisture in the air. A few strategically placed fans to circulate the air will speed up the process.

4. Contact the experts. Before you attempt to salvage any photographic material, you should know which materials benefit from air-drying and those that require cold storage until professionally conserved. Some materials will need to be frozen until conservation can take place. This should not be done without the advice of a professional. All packing of this material should be done under the assistance of a conservation expert. This is when you call the local conservator on your checklist or contact one of the labs listed in Appendix D.

In general, the following photographic materials should be air-dried immediately: ambrotypes, daguerreotypes, tintypes, and prints. You can safely rinse off dirt in clean distilled water. Some negative materials and color items have components that dissolve in water, so consult a professional. Whenever in doubt, consult a conservator.

Find a large, clean, dry work area to begin your salvage operation. Air-drying is accomplished by placing the images face up on blotting paper or unprinted newsprint to absorb the moisture. Negatives need to be emulsion side up. Glass negatives should dry vertically. Cased images that have water inside the cases should be gently taken apart. Be careful not to lose the identifying information. Prints that start to curl when drying can have small weights placed on the corners of the prints.

It is recommended that materials be salvaged in a particular order to increase recovery rate. The materials affected most by water should be dried first, such as daguerreotypes, ambrotypes, tintypes, and collodion negatives. Dry the rest of the materials as follows: color prints, black-and-white prints, negatives, and transparencies. Wear disposable plastic gloves when working with the images. Handle the images and negatives by their edges. The emulsion is soft and susceptible to damage from improper handling.

Materials that have already dried and stuck together should be reimmersed in water before you try to take them apart. Trying to pull them apart when dry will damage the emulsion.

PREPARATION FOR DRYING

1. Set up a clean work area.

2. Gently rinse dirt and debris off the items using clean distilled water.

3. Wear disposable plastic gloves for handling materials.

4. Handle images by the outside edges only. Never touch the emulsion.

5. Lay out images in a single layer. They will stick together if dried as a clump.

Important

FAMILY PHOTOGRAPH DISASTER PLAN

- Make a list of emergency numbers: fire, police, conservation lab, names of friends who can help.

- Know how to shut off the main switches for water, gas, and electricity.

- Prepare an emergency supplies kit.

- Have a disaster plan.

WHAT TO SAVE IN CASE OF DISASTER

The hardest part of a disaster plan is deciding what to save if you only have a few moments. I know that I'd grab my negatives and the small box of historical photographs. I can make prints from the negatives, and the historical images are irreplaceable. In order to be able to grab them and run, I need to put them in an easily accessible spot. But how do you make that decision if you have a large group of material?

There are digital solutions. Some individuals advocate digitizing your photograph collection as a type of insurance. Since digital media stores large numbers of images in a compact format, you can easily grab the CD and reprint the images later. A part of the disaster plan for every computer department is storing backup tapes and disks off-site. Why not double your insurance by making a copy of the CD and placing it in a safe-deposit box or leaving it with a good friend? This way, if you have to leave without your images, there is a chance you will still have them.

Another solution is to publish your family history and illustrate it with pictures from your collection. You can do this by including copies in a typescript and donating it to a local historical society, by formally publishing the material in book form, or by creating a family Web site with extensive graphics. There is a solution for every budget.

Idea Generator

RESTORATION

Like with conservation, there is a professional organization that monitors photographic restoration experts. The Professional Photographers of America (PPA), established in 1880, offers certification for individuals who join as Art Tech members. Art Tech is a subdivision of the main organization that covers retouching and restoration both digital and photographic.

Flip through any genealogical magazine and you will find companies that advertise restoration services. Unbeknownst to most consumers is that there is a wide variety of services that fall under restoration, from airbrushing to digital manipulation. You want to be sure that your expectations match the restorer's expertise. After all, you are entrusting this company or individual with a photograph that has sentimental if not monetary value. Evaluate the company before you engage it. Ask questions about training and equipment. You want to be an informed consumer. Find out the full range of services. If the company defines photographic restoration as digital manipulation but your image needs to be re-created by creating a duplicate and airbrushing, then this is not a good match. Don't be afraid to ask for references and to see samples of the type of work done for other clients.

Notes

Evaluating Restoration Experts

1. What is their training for photographic restoration? Do they have backgrounds in photography or computer science? Have they taken classes to enhance their skills? Restoration is too expensive to hire an inexperienced person. The PPA maintains a free referral service on its Web site <http://www.ppa.com/PPA_F.htm> to help you find a certified Art Tech professional in your area. Go to the Find a Photographer option, select "General Art Tech" from the Retouch menu, and supply your Zip code in order to obtain a list. Ask if the person you are considering hiring is a member. The PPA offers members an opportunity to attend events and sponsors continuing educational opportunities.

2. Ask for lists of references and call them. All professional companies maintain lists of clients. Ask the restorers whether they have individuals you can talk with about their services. Then call them. In addition to speaking with their references, ask to see before and after examples of their work.

3. How long have they been involved in photographic restoration? Photographic restoration is not a new business, it is just that digital techniques have made it more accessible to the public. If a particular company does only digital restoration, you probably want to look elsewhere. Simple digital restoration can be done at home with a scanner, a computer, and a software package. If you have a large number of pictures, it is worth the investment of time and money to learn to do it yourself. A professional restoration expert has experience manipulating prints digitally and enhancing them with photographic techniques and airbrushing.

4. Is restoration their primary business? Ask about their other services. In order to get the best-quality restoration, it is advisable to hire a person whose primary business, rather than sideline, is restoration.

5. Do they have experience working with the type of image you have? If they show you examples of restoration work on nineteenth-century prints but you have a daguerreotype, you want to be sure they have experience working with your type of image. Restoration is only part of the process. They need to know the proper way to handle your original when it is in their possession.

6. What is their availability? Reputable, experienced restorers may have a waiting list of clients. If you need something in a hurry, it is best to ask up front about the wait.

What you should expect:

1. The restorers will examine the object prior to suggesting a restoration method.
2. You will receive a written estimate prior to the start of work.
3. They should be able to explain risks, insurance, payment, and shipping.
4. They will handle your photograph with extreme care.
5. You will be notified if the job exceeds the original estimate.

What Can a Restoration Expert Accomplish?

The strategy used to restore an image depends on the amount of damage apparent in the image. Each photograph survives a different set of environmental hazards and amount of handling; therefore, the condition of each one is unique. A typical restoration has several phases. The first documents the original condition of the print by making a copy negative or a scan. Second, a new print is made so that airbrushing and other embellishments can take place. In the end, the new print will be restored using a variety of methods. The original photograph is never directly worked on. Upon completion of the work, the original is returned to the owner. You should also be given a copy negative of the restored print and the print itself. You can make additional prints from the negative without having to touch the original.

AIRBRUSH RESTORATION
Daguerreotype

This daguerreotype of a woman from 1845 to 1850 (see figures 7-7 and 7-8 below) is showing some damage on the surface glass due to decomposition of the glass. The costume details date this image. The woman is wearing her hair looped over the ears in the style introduced in 1845. Her cape collar is called pelerine. She would change the white collar and cuffs daily. The

Figures 7-7 and 7-8.
This is an airbrush restoration of a daguerreotype showing decomposition of the cover glass.
David Mishkin, Just Black and White

**COMMON TERMINOLOGY DEFINED BY
DAVID MISHKIN OF JUST BLACK AND WHITE**

Restoration

There are two types of restoration—digital and airbrushing.

Digital Restoration

This uses a computer as the tool to fix or repair a damaged photograph by scanning an image and re-creating detail through use of photo-editing software. The process produces computer files that can be printed on different types of mediums, such as paper, photographic films, or digital files.

Airbrush Restoration

In a restoration done with an airbrush, a pressurized (usually from an air compressor) paintbrush is the tool. The restorer fills the airbrush with pigment and sprays it onto a copy print in a fine or coarse spray to cover the defects you are trying to eliminate. The final product is a work print that can be used as is or copied.

Photographic Enhancement

The contrast in a faded print can be improved using special film, filters, and chemistry. A very faded image can be brought back to original clarity using this technique.

addition of costly neck ribbon finishes the costume and establishes that she is not lacking financial resources.

Airbrushing removed the distracting marks from the image. There were several steps to the process. First, a photographic copy print was made of the daguerreotype in its original mat. Then an artist using airbrushing applied paint to the surface of the copy print. The final result has a new background and is free from lint. Great care was taken not to disturb the informational content of the image so that the costume details remain intact. The client then received a new copy negative of the restored daguerreotype, a photograph, and the original daguerreotype. No work is done to an original print or object using airbrushing. Copy prints are always made first to protect the condition of the original.

DIGITAL RESTORATIONS
Tintype

The examples on pages 125 and 126 are tintypes with different types of damage. In both cases, a professional artist using digital photo-enhancing software eliminated all traces of age and decay.

INTERVIEW WITH DAVID MISHKIN OF
JUST BLACK AND WHITE IN PORTLAND, MAINE

When should a photograph be considered for restoration work?

It is purely subjective. Because of the expense, you need to determine the sentimental value or strong historical value of an image prior to the financial commitment.

How long does the process take?

It usually takes three to four weeks depending on several factors, such as the amount of restoration work and my workload.

Are there different types of restoration work?

You can have a photographic enhancement (which is not considered a restoration), digitally restore an image, or use airbrushing.

Why is a restoration so expensive?

To produce a restoration that looks real and professional looking requires the skill of an artist. Whether it is done by airbrush or done digitally, the person doing the work must be highly skilled in either medium. Individuals with those skills charge rates based on their training and expertise, sometimes in excess of fifty dollars per hour.

When is a photographic enhancement appropriate?

When an image is extremely faded, manipulation of filters, film, and chemicals can bring back some of the original detail.

Are there any faded photographs that can't be enhanced?

Most faded photographs are pre-1900 and are usually salt or albumen prints. Insufficient washing at the time they were made can cause the image to fade. There are also photos that appear faded but were either printed too light or were taken with a camera that had light leaks. If an image is faded (generally pre-1900 pictures), it might benefit from photographic enhancement. This is where we take a faded photograph and enhance it using photographic methods. There are instances where an image is too faded to be enhanced, such as underexposed prints or those that experienced light leaks.

Is there any type of damage that doesn't benefit from restoration?

If you can't see the face, you can't do a restoration. In a digital restoration, we are re-creating detail from what is already present in the image. For one client, the eyes and nose of the tintype were too scratched to be able to re-create. In these cases, it is an artist's guess what the original features were.

Continued

Continued from page 123

What about airbrushing?

Airbrushing is when we create a duplicate print of a damaged image and using artists' techniques apply paint to the surface of the duplicate in an attempt to re-create detail or eliminate damage. Airbrushing is good for filling in cracks and missing pieces, making new backgrounds, and eliminating things. This is the most expensive form of restoration and usually costs a few hundred dollars.

If you could give one piece of advice about caring for photographs in a home, what would it be?

The best thing you can do is to have a copy negative and an archivally processed print made of valuable photographs.

What else should a person do?

After a high-quality copy negative is made, store the original in a place like a safe-deposit box because it has all the elements of proper environment. Most safe-deposit vaults maintain a stable temperature of 68°F and 50 percent relative humidity. In addition, the box allows you to store the collection in a dark and secure place. Safe-deposit boxes are also an economical storage solution.

What about digital prints rather than photographic copies?

The quality is there in a digital reprint, but it requires expensive computers and materials. I think it will be at least ten years before digital methods match the copy negative. Many companies provide their customers with either a digital reprint or the print plus the file. The caution with digital mediums is that technological changes may make those files unreadable.

What do you consider the most important ways to keep a photograph safe for future generations?

We already mentioned two: (1) Have a copy negative made of significant photographs. Make sure the negative is archivally processed. (2) Store photographs in a safe-deposit box for environment, safety, and economy. (3) Place the images in protective sleeves made of acid- and lignin-free paper, polypropylene, or polyester. This will protect them from handling and abrasion.

In your experience, what is the most common form of damage that you restore?

Scratches and folds. People keep photographs in wallets. They get lots of cracks and scratches.

Continued from page 124

What about oversize pictures?

If someone gives us a panoramic picture, we digitize it, make a copy negative and then an enlargement print. Since it is another generation, it loses some of its focus. In this case, it is best to provide the client a large digital output (at least 36 inches) instead of a photograph and a copy negative. We give them the image as a digital file (Zip file). Another option is a traditional one, to skip the digital process and create a copy negative. We use airbrushing for the restoration and then make a new print of the airbrushed result.

Do you have anything else you'd like to add?

The most important thing we do is give someone an archivally processed negative of an image so that they can have copies made.

In the first set of tintypes of the elderly man, the costume detail is clear. He is wearing a striped shirt without a collar and a type of jacket known as a sack coat. It appears to have braided trim. This dates the image to the mid-1860s. The placement of his hands is interesting. He may be hiding one due to an injury.

His tintype has a few notable features. The clipped corners and halo image suggests that this tintype was originally in a case. Over the years, pieces of the emulsion came off the iron plate and those areas rusted. There is also some scratching of the image due to abrasion. The most puzzling piece of the damage is the hole in the upper right of the image.

Idea Generator

WHAT CAN BE ACCOMPLISHED DIGITALLY?

- Damage disappears or is diminished.

- Color balance can be restored.

- Negatives can be scanned and printed as positive images free from damage.

Figures 7-9 and 7-10. Digital restoration can dramatically enhance a damaged tintype.
David Mishkin, Just Black and White

In the tintype of the younger man, the plate is so damaged that the costume is almost completely illegible. It is difficult to date an image in this condition. He is wearing a small pointed collar with his shirt and no tie. The lapels of his jacket are not visible, although he is wearing either a loose jacket buttoned at the top or with a vest. More detail must be visible to make a definite identification. The surface of this tintype is pitted due to contact with an unknown substance.

In the elderly man's portrait the artist re-created all the detail, such as the missing pieces of shirt. The restorer emphasized the halo effect to give the photograph the appearance of a painted portrait. The problems with the background, such as the hole and the abrasion, are gone. The artist had to re-create or enhance all the detail in the image to restore the tintype.

The tintype of the younger man required the artist to re-create the entire look of the photograph based on the little remaining undamaged detail. The restored version is a digital portrait with the appearance of a painting.

Figures 7-11 and 7-12.
In this tintype, the image is barely visible. Look at the effect after digital restoration.
David Mishkin, Just Black and White

PAPER PRINT
Photographic Enhancements of Faded Prints

In each of the examples, the original photographs exhibit varying amounts of fading. If you were to take a faded print to have copies made, the prints would look like the first view of the faded examples presented here. By selecting a photo lab with experience with photographic enhancement, you can make clear, new prints of the faded originals. Photographic enhancement uses a combination of filters, film, and chemicals based on the condition of the originals to re-create the images. The techniques vary based on the type of print and amount of fading.

The two prints of the railroad men are late-nineteenth-century prints (see figures 7-15 and 7-16 on page 128). The photographic method used to create them is not known. Fading happened due to exposure to light, environmental fluctuations of temperature and humidity, or instability in the photographic process. Whatever the reason, the enhancements were successful. Each client received a new print that made the scene visible. Once again, the right combination of skill and photographic techniques accomplished the end result—a beautiful print!

A Complex Problem

Sometimes it takes a combination of photographic enhancement and digital restoration to re-create a photograph. This image of Lucille McDonald (see figure 7-13 below) was folded up and stored in a wallet for many years. It is the only picture her daughter has of her mother, so it has great sentimental value to the family. Since the print was faded due to wear and tear, the first step was to photographically enhance the image to strengthen the quality of the picture. Digital restoration filled in the cracks, reconstructed the missing corners, and removed scratches and stains. The final product was a photographic print. Additional prints can be made from the digital file if necessary.

Figures 7-13 and 7-14.
After years of being stored in a wallet, this image of Lucille McDonald required both digital restoration and air-brushing to make a print that looked brand new.
Victor Lewis

Digital Restoration at Home

Not all digital restoration work needs to be done by a professional. The whole process can be cost prohibitive, **so there are a few things you can do at home with a minimal financial investment.** It might be worth the investment of time and money for equipment if you have a file of images that are damaged. However, the results might not be as dramatic as in the examples presented here.

Everyone has photographs that need restoration or improvement. The

Money Saver

Figures 7-15 and 7-16.
The contrast in faded photographic prints can sometimes be improved using special filters, film, and chemistry.
David Mishkin, Just Black and White

photo-editing programs available for amateur use have improved so that you are only limited by your imagination.

Digital image manipulation helps you turn a poorly composed photograph into a keeper for the family album. Be patient with yourself; it will take some time to learn how to restore images. A certain amount of time is necessary to learn all new techniques. In this case, you will be exposed to terminology and techniques with which you will be unfamiliar. The good news is that you can find tutorials online or find a book on the topic to guide you through the initial steps.

It is possible to enhance and repair historical images in your family collection with a few basic maneuvers. You can change the exposure of a photograph by adding or deleting highlights and shadows. Do you wish that you could drop out that distracting background in the image of your aunt? Most programs allow you to change the focus of different elements of the picture or even delete whole sections. I find the most valuable tool in photo-editing software is the ability to repair damaged images. With digital restoration, you can remove cracks, fill in missing persons, enhance faded images, and even change history by removing people from pictures. You can also take out the X over someone's head and replace missing parts of emulsion. These programs are powerful enough to allow you to change the visual history of your family by adding or subtracting people from your images. I don't advise it, but if you must, then label each image appropriately.

Most software packages allow you to do all that and more. More types of programs are incorporating photo-editing tools with other materials, such as greeting card software. Generations, a popular genealogical software package, now comes with a photo editor. These built-in editors usually feature some basic options so that you don't need to purchase a more sophisticated and expensive program. For simple at-home digital restoration, use the software that comes with your scanner. Professional-quality restoration packages are expensive but offer more options. In general, the more expensive the program, the more features and control you will have over complex changes. Here are some general guidelines regarding photo-editing software.

1. Save each picture as a new file so you don't change the original scan.
2. Use a photo editor that allows for unlimited undos.
3. Choose a package that has the option of looking at two views of the same image at once.
4. Get software that allows you to blow up a specific detail to work on it.

Tools and How to Use Them

Airbrush: Models an actual airbrush.

Auto repair: Will enhance the contrast, brightness, and color (if color photo) of a faded original.

Blur: Allows you to soften harsh images (e.g., remove crosshatch pattern from scanned newspapers).

Clone: Allows you to copy texture/colors from other areas.

\di'fin\ *vb*

Definitions

129

Color mapping: Contrast and brightness.
Copy: Replicating area within a specified area or mask.
Eyedropper: Picks up color from the image to fill in another area.
Lasso: Identifying an area, then enhancing it, or copying it and moving it to another place.
Lighten/darken: Enhancing small areas.
Painting: Using artistic tools to digitally paint in areas.
Sharpening: Making edges more distinct.
Smear: Smoothing or blurring edges with painting tool.

When to Stop

While photo restoration can do many things, it can't bring the picture back to its original unblemished condition. There is only so much manipulation that can be done digitally. This is a reality that all restorers using digital manipulation have to accept before they begin to work on images. The limits are set by the condition of the images prior to scanning. You will be able to improve or eliminate certain problems, but at some point, you will realize that you've reached a conclusion.

BECOMING A PROFESSIONAL

If you decide you want to train to be a professional conservator or restorer, there are programs and organizations that can help you pursue that dream. Both professions are technical in nature and require that individuals enroll in formal programs to learn the profession. After obtaining your degree, it is necessary to take classes, attend workshops, and maintain membership in a number of organizations to stay current with changes in your chosen field.

Becoming a conservator is a time-consuming and challenging choice. The American Institute for Conservation has a couple of brochures for potential students. One outlines undergraduate prerequisites for admission to a training program, and the other lists all the conservation programs in the United States with financial aid information and a bibliography.

Since conservators conduct scientific and technical work when restoring an image, it is important to have a background in science. Typically undergraduate coursework in both general and organic chemistry is necessary. Some programs also require studies in other sciences, physics, and mathematics. Most programs also expect degree candidates to have a background in the humanities and art and be able to read at least one foreign language. Applicants should have exposure to the profession by working in a conservation lab as an intern, volunteer, or paid employee.

Still interested? Conservators are highly trained professionals who work with irreplaceable materials, so the graduate degree programs are demanding. According to the AIC, programs require four to six semesters, summer work projects, and a year-long full-time internship outside the classroom. Students specialize in a particular type of conservation. This internship enables them to work with professionals in their specialties.

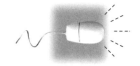

Internet Source

CONSULT THE EXPERTS

A Photoshop tutorial by Carla Rose is available on the Adobe Web site <http://www.adobe.com/web/tips/psmagazine/main.html>.

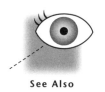

See Also

See Appendix H: Professional Study Programs

SCANNING IMAGES AT HOME

What You Need to Do This at Home

- flatbed scanner

- computer

- ink-jet printer

- photo-editing software

Steps Involved

1. Select the image.

2. Scan the image at a high resolution (1,000 DPI) to pick up the details.

3. Save it as two separate files—one you work on while the other is an archive copy.

4. Resave the image.

Digital Manipulation You Can Do Yourself

- improve contrast

- correct color imbalance

- fill in small areas

- rotate

- eliminate distracting background spots

The requirements for degrees in retouching and restoration are not as difficult to meet. Undergraduate and graduate programs in photography usually offer the option of learning some of the techniques employed in photographic restoration. However, the PPA sets standards for anyone who wants to apply for its certification process. Applicants must pass a written test as well as demonstrate general knowledge of photography and retouching. They must also provide both personal and business references. A panel of the association's members will examine a sample of an applicant's work to see if it meets professional standards. If so, then the panel awards certification for five years. In order to maintain that certification, you must meet continuing education requirements by attending educational programs offered or approved by PPA. This includes class work and hours of hands-on instruction. You can take classes from a PPA affiliate school that offers special classes one to two weeks a year and earn continuing education points. For a complete list of conferences and educational opportunities, consult the Education pages on the PPA Web site <http://www.ppa.com/PPA_school.htm>.

The organization has a disciplinary procedure for any member found to violate its code of ethics. If you have a complaint about one of the members, put it in writing. A committee meets to decide on a course of action from censuring to a loss of membership.

CHECKLIST: PROFESSIONAL HELP

Notes

✓ Understand the differences between conservation and restoration.
✓ Ask questions before hiring a professional.
✓ Try basic digital restoration techniques at home.
✓ Have a copy negative and photographic print made of images before and after conservation and restoration.

EIGHT

Ways of Organizing (Keep It Simple)

O ften the hardest part of organizing your family photograph collection is finding the time to do it. However, by breaking the entire process down into a series of steps, it can be easily accomplished. Dedicating a half hour here and there adds up until you are finished. A way to save time is to employ a basic rule of organization: Keep your system simple and flexible. Everyone who needs to use it should be able to comprehend the organizational system. Not just you should understand how it works. That's why it is important to streamline the process so that you avoid overwhelming users of the collection and yourself with complicated arrangements. Flexibility is a key element so that you can add new materials without having to reorganize.

Part of the planning process is evaluating your collection. Take into consideration the sizes, shapes, and number of images you are organizing. Before starting any new project, I try to look for potential pitfalls by asking myself a series of questions that helps me assess the collection. First, think about how you use the images. Do they sit in a closet untouched for months at a time, or do you regularly go through them reminiscing about people and activities? If you are like most people, you use some of the collection all of the time and only look at the older photographs occasionally. Each question helps identify storage needs and suggests ways to organize your photographs. Don't become discouraged. **This part of the process only takes a little while and will actually save you time later on.**

• **How many group portraits are there?** If your entire photograph collection comprises group portraits, then some organizational plans won't work. You may have to create an index of people and number each picture. Since group photographs are usually oversize, knowing the number will help you gauge the sizes and quantity of the boxes.

• **What types of photographs are in the collection (e.g., daguerreotypes)?** One family collection had one hundred daguerreotypes! That is more than exists in many small museum collections. The owner had very few contemporary photographs in his possession since he was not actively photographing his family. In this case, special storage boxes were recommended for all his cased photographs.

Timesaver

- **How many different sizes of pictures are there?** Since photographs come in a variety of shapes and sizes, it is necessary to gauge the contents of the collection. There are so many storage options for photographs that you want to be frugal in your purchase of boxes and albums. Counting the number of similarly shaped images enables you to plan what you need. Storage needs are related to how you organize the photographs.

- **Are there documents related to the images?** Every photograph collection is different. Some individuals inherit or collect the documents that relate to the events and people depicted in photographs. So when you think about organizing your memorabilia including pictures, are you going to separate the photographs from the related items or include them? Many archives create integrated storage plans for large family collections. You may want to visit an archive or museum and ask to see how it organizes its photographs.

- **Are several different families represented?** Some family collections contain a wide variety of images relating to maternal and paternal sides of the family for several generations, while others focus on an immediate family group. The more families that are included, the more precise filing and labeling will need to be.

- **Are the photographs of individuals or events?** What is your family photographic style? You may not think that you have one, but some individuals photograph specific people while others prefer to focus on events and places. This personal style and the contents of your historical photographs will influence how the images are organized. Depending on the types of images in your collection, you may decide to arrange them chronologically, by surname, or possibly even by event.

WAYS TO ORGANIZE

There are many different ways to organize a photograph collection, and the variety of methods and techniques changes as new technology becomes available. At the moment, you can arrange photos alphabetically by name, use your genealogical numbering system, store them by medium and create an index, use a genealogical software package or the Internet. **Bear in mind that there is no perfect solution. Each organizational method has problems that need to be overcome.** If you have a large and complex collection, you may end up using more than one system, depending on the types of materials in your possession.

Reminder

Family

Probably the most common way people organize their photographs is by family in albums according to events. My albums are a chronological history of vacations and school events and follow my children from babyhood to the present. Short descriptions provide names and dates and little else. This is fairly typical. The majority of my images are just of our nuclear family group. This system works well for us at this point but does not incorporate all the photographs we receive from other people and our historic family pictures. However, as soon as we inherit pictures from family members, I will need to add to this simple arrangement.

As a former photographic curator, I have seen all kinds of organizational attempts. One of the simplest and most logical ways to organize your pictures is used in museums and libraries for large groups of unrelated images. Arranging your photographs by surname and alphabetically by first name is a great system for family photographs. A strictly alphabetical system makes it easy to locate people by name as long as there are limited numbers of them. In cases where there are large numbers of images of a single person, you need to incorporate chronological or topical information into this system so you can find series of photographs from specific events. This will prevent you from wading through hundreds of photographs looking for the right one. This can be accomplished in just a few steps.

Let's see how that works with the fictional Smith family presented in an earlier chapter. John and Betsy Smith and their children, James and Eliza, appear in all types of family photographs from individual portraits to weddings and holidays. They also took pictures of their family pets. Each Christmas they received images from a variety of Smith relatives and from Betsy's family, the Joneses.

Case Study

A theoretical way to organize their images is to start with the alphabetical arrangement by surname and within that by first name. That way John, Betsy, James, and Eliza would all have separate files. Similarly, any other surnames would also be filed in the same way. The integration of the pictures occurs only on the family tree information. If you primarily take photographs of individuals rather than events, you can use the alphabetical system subdivided by year or topic. If there were large numbers of pictures taken in various years, then the first names would be subdivided chronologically. This system is both simple and flexible. New family members and photographs can easily be incorporated, even cousins and friends, because the photos are organized by surname.

However, you may also have images of events, in which case you will need a separate file arranged by topic, event, and/or year. Either arrangement can be stored in albums or special boxes as long as you include labels or index tabs of acid- and lignin-free paper. Each tab should include the full name of the person, including a maiden name (in parentheses), and life dates for easy identification of family members with the same first name.

This system works well with contemporary images of relatively the same size and medium, but what happens if your photograph collection contains large oversize wedding pictures and cased images such as daguerreotypes? By now, you've probably decided this is too much work and the project should be abandoned. But wait—there is a way to handle all the different types of photographs that are in your collection. After all, museums and archives are faced with this task daily. It doesn't take a professional to manage a picture collection, just time, patience, and organization.

Medium

The key ingredient to any arrangement is flexibility. You are using the same principles that professional archivists and librarians implement with collections in their facilities. Instead of assigning record group numbers, you are using surnames.

Step By Step

The initial step is to create a list of the types of images in your collection and count how many of each you have. Instead of specifically identifying the photographic method, you are concerned with size and shape. For instance, you may have five daguerreotypes, six tintypes, a dozen oversize prints from 12″ × 18″ to 20″ × 24″, and a large number of color photographs taken in the last twenty years. Museums seek to retain the original order of the materials, and you should, as well. Since daguerreotypes, tintypes, and contemporary color prints are about the same size, you can arrange them in similar-size storage boxes. The daguerreotypes and tintypes require special storage material, such as individual boxes. The oversize prints can be stored together in a container that is the same size as the largest prints. Placed in individual folders, it doesn't matter that their dimensions vary. Just make sure the largest prints are on the bottom with the smallest ones on the top to prevent creating stress on the images. It is necessary to limit the number of photographs in each box so that there isn't a lot of weight on the images on the bottom. Arranging materials by medium within the family system still enables you to find images quickly and easily. In this way, you are using size to determine your storage while retaining the primary filing strategy. It just means that you have several boxes of images that may all contain images of the same people. You're probably wondering how you are going to sort them out. The answer is very simple.

FINDING THE TIME

Keeping your organizational scheme simple and flexible requires a little preplanning. Reorganizing images once you've already started wastes hours of good work time. **A little additional effort in the beginning to outline your plan results in extra time.**

Step By Step

Planning

Now that you have an idea how to organize your images, lay out your plan on paper. A little preplanning will prevent you from making costly mistakes of time and money. Look at your organizational scheme as if you knew nothing about the individuals in the images. Can you still find people and specific events? If you have trouble separating yourself from the information, ask a friend to look over your plan. See if he can understand how the pictures relate to each other. If you are a hands-on person, try to organize a small part of your collection and see if it works. Start by making a list of all of the people, places, and events in the pictures. This will help you group individuals in alphabetical order. You will also develop a sense of the size of the project you are undertaking.

Creating a Work Space

Whenever you are working with your family material, it is important to find a spot in the house where you can spread out. Remember that it needs to be clean and provide space for boxes and your other supplies. You can save time by having this separate area ready to use whenever you have a few moments. If you have to set up the area each work session, you will have wasted precious minutes to make progress. If space is at a premium, a card table in a corner of a room can be helpful. You can cover it with a clean cloth in between sessions. Efficiency experts suggest having everything you need within reach to eliminate a major time waster—looking for missing items.

Supplies

Looking through your photographs helps you estimate your storage needs. Follow the guidelines for each type of photographic material outlined in the appropriate chapters. You can order materials from the suppliers listed in Appendix D. It is advisable to buy in bulk whenever possible since most suppliers offer discounts for quantity buying. Try asking a friend or a local historical society to share an order so that both of you save. Not sure how many boxes you need? Call the suppliers or look at the descriptions listed in their catalogs. Most will provide information on how many items fit comfortably in a box or album. All of the suppliers listed in the appendix provide catalogs free of charge.

Supplies

The Sort

Now that you have an idea of the system you want to use and have tried it out with a few photos, you are ready to start implementing your plan. First, depending on how you decided to organize your images, you will begin sorting them by medium, by size, or alphabetically by surname and first name. Since you are probably going to use a combination of size and surname, you should start placing images of the same dimensions and names in boxes. Since you created a list of who is included in your system, you know how many separate boxes you need for this part of the process. I suggest using PAT boxes with reinforced corners so that you can stop whenever you need to and stack the boxes on top of each other in order to leave a clean work space.

Idea Generator

Labeling and Boxing

Another time-saver efficiency experts recommended at a class I attended is to move a single piece of paper only once. It is difficult to do with photographs, but if you apply their advice to labeling, you'll be surprised how much progress you can make. Using your paper system, label each card divider before you start so that you are ready to start filing your images. Remember to include the full name of the person and life dates, such as Eliza (Smith) Will 1855–1910. Maiden names are listed in parentheses.

If you are using albums, include additional information as well near the

**SAMPLE LABELS
FOR DIVIDERS**

Person: full name (life dates)
Scene: full place-name (town, state, or other descriptor)
Event: subject and date of the event

images. Just in case you can't find the images after you have filed them, a good backup system is to create an index to the materials in your possession. Be sure to label each photograph prior to filing using the techniques recommended on pages 151–152.

Create a File of Unidentified Images

As you begin to label and file, you will uncover photographs that you are unable to identify. Hopefully this is only a small number of images. Place these pictures in a box labeled "to be identified." Using the techniques outlined in *Uncovering Your Ancestry Through Family Photographs*, you can work on them one image at a time.

Create a File of Pictures in Need of Conservation or Restoration

No collection is in perfect shape, so you will find images that need professional evaluation. Rather than put them to one side, photocopy the images and create a separate file. Images that are identified should be filed in their appropriate locations, while those that are unidentified can go into your "to be identified" box. Familiarize yourself with the points raised in chapter seven before deciding which photographs get extra attention. You can then set up a triage list of these images selecting certain ones for conservation and others for restoration.

TO-DO LIST

Part of starting an organizational project is making a to-do list. This is another tip I learned from professional organizers. I never start a project without one. It helps me stay focused and not get distracted by other project needs. For instance, a sample list for the Smith family is as follows:

1. Look through all the images, and make a list of people, places, and events.
2. Decide on an organizational plan, and try it with a small group of images.
3. Estimate the supplies you need (most supply catalogs list the storage capacity of boxes and sleeves).
4. Purchase them in bulk (save time and money).
5. Set up a work space.
6. Begin sorting.
7. Create a file of images in need of identification.
8. Create a file of photocopies of pictures requiring conservation or restoration.
9. Start labeling and boxing.
10. Create an index (if necessary).

INDEXING SYSTEMS

There are several different types of indexes, from card files to inventories and database systems. Each system has strengths and weaknesses, but all have the same purpose. They help you find the photographs you need when you want them. While creating indexing systems takes time, you will save minutes if not hours when you begin looking for an image.

Card Files

A card file is a simple system that uses index or other cards with information. It resembles a library card catalog in telling you what can be found where. Each card has a single name, life dates, as well as where certain images can be found. For instance, pictures of Eliza (Smith) Will (1855–1905) are found in boxes 2, 8, 11. This goes across the top of the card. In the body of the card, you can get more specific, such as Wedding photos Box 8. This can immediately direct you to the appropriate box rather than you having to look through three boxes. You can even color code the family cards if you want. Just to avoid any confusion, Eliza (Smith) Will would have a card in both the Ws and the Ss.

The weakness with any card file system is that the cards tend to get misfiled and can become jumbled if they are dropped. You can remedy these problems by using a large ring or an old card catalog drawer that has a rod running down the center of the drawer to hold the cards in place.

Inventories

You could create an inventory of the collection and use your genealogical research as a guide. Ideally your index/inventory will help future generations locate items in your collection. An inventory is merely a guide to all the different types of material in your collection. If you have twelve different boxes and all of them contain pictures of family members, how are you going to locate what you need and quickly? An inventory enables you to do that.

Idea Generator

There are several key parts to an inventory, such as organizational scheme, provenance, and index. Provenance refers to the history of ownership of the photograph. An inventory system is used in many museums and archives. You are applying their time-tested techniques to your home collection.

The first part of the inventory explains your system so that others understand it. Suppose a family member can only find eight of the twelve boxes. Your explanation tells them that they are missing four more. If you have managed to keep it simple, it will be easy to explain. The provenance of a collection describes how the materials came to be in your collection. One of the most fascinating parts of a photograph collection is how it is passed on within a family. There appear to be no rules of inheritance when it comes to images, so it is important for others to understand how all the pieces fit together. This data can help you identify the subjects of some photographs. You need to explain how different pieces of the collection came together.

The final part is the index. In this you mention the name of each person and in which box, folder, or album his images are located.

Case Study

SAMPLE INVENTORY OF THE SMITH FAMILY COLLECTION

Organization

The twelve boxes of the Smith Family Collection are arranged by size or type of photograph and organized by surname. Subdivisions are first names, year, or event. Each division is labeled with the full name of the person, including maiden name and life dates.

Provenance

These images are in the possession of Alexander Smith. Other family members owned various parts of the collections until Mr. Smith inherited the material.

Contents

While the collection contains images of the Smith and Jones families, there are also photographs of individuals unrelated to these families. The collection spans the years 1844 to the present, with the majority of the material from 1950 to the present. There are daguerreotypes, tintypes, and black-and-white and color prints in the collection.

Index

Name	Box
Betsy (Jones) Smith	1, 2, 8, 12
Eliza Jane (Smith) Will (1855–1905)	2, 8, 11
James William Smith	2, 8, 9
John Henry Smith (1825–1870)	1, 5, 8
Unrelated miscellaneous individuals	12

PHOTO SOFTWARE AND DATABASES

There are many different types of software on the market that can help you organize your contemporary or historical photographs.

Databases

If you already own software that allows you to create relational databases of information and individual images, such as Microsoft Access, you can use it to index your photographs. It can be accomplished by selecting and renaming specific fields. You can then scan your images into the database and merge the photographs with the data for worksheets. These programs allow you to re-sort information and print reports. These programs can be used to search for specific images.

Scrapbooking Software

The program you use to organize your photographs depends on how you want to use it. If one of your future projects includes creating a series of scrapbooks that you can share electronically, you may want to invest in software for that purpose. The scrapbook resources listed in Appendix D can help you locate various packages.

Genealogical Software Packages

By using a genealogical software package, you are connecting your images, documents, and information within a single program. The technical photo-indexing systems are helpful, but it is important to make sure you are using a flexible system. There are special considerations to bear in mind when purchasing or using various packages or Web-based products.

The key features most genealogists should look for in a program, according to Rick Crume, a software reviewer, are price, computer requirements, ease of use, source documentation, file management, reports, and research help.[1] If you are using the program to help manage your photo files, you should purchase a program that also has the multimedia features you need.

Evaluating Software

In order to evaluate software in terms of photography, you want to look for a program that allows you to link images to information, has a photo editor, and is easy to use. Most of the programs on the market come with these features, but beyond the basics, there are differences. Ask yourself yet another question: Are you going to use the multimedia feature of the program? Are you going to upload images to a family Web page or create your own site? How many photographs are you going to include in the program?

Features to look for

- **How many photographs can it handle?** You want to purchase a program with the most capabilities at the price and ease of operation that you need. If you have a collection of images tracing a family member from birth to death that you want to link to the genealogical data, purchase a program that allows you unlimited images per individual. The majority of genealogy software allows you to place your images and captions in scrapbook pages linked to the family group sheet.

- **Can you link photographs to events?** Rather than just link images to specific individuals without regard to events, wouldn't it be wonderful to link a baby picture to the birth information and a wedding photograph to the marriage data? Unfortunately, no genealogical program on the market today allows that degree of flexibility.

- **Does the program allow you to caption each image?** Just as you document each piece of data, it is necessary to create a caption for the images you are scanning. Try out different programs to see if you are limited by the amount of space for identifications.

Notes

Notes

EVALUATING THE SOFTWARE

1. Read the reviews.
2. Talk with friends.
3. Try a demo.

For More Info

NATIONAL CONFERENCES (ALL HELD ANNUALLY)

Federation of Genealogical Societies <http://www.fgs.org>
GENTECH <http://www.gentech.org/>
National Genealogical Society <http://www.ngsgenealogy.org>

- **Will it allow you to enter one family or many unrelated families?** Photograph collections consist of images of various family members, as well as friends. Unfortunately in most genealogical programs, you may need to scan these images repeatedly in order to link them to the appropriate family group sheet. Most programs let you enter information on unrelated families, but if you are going to create genealogies for friends or clients, you want to make sure you have the flexibility you need.

- **Does the program have photo-editing capabilities?** Unless your family has a history of taking perfect pictures, you are going to want to crop and fix the images you enter into the program. After spending the money to purchase a genealogical software package, are you really going to want to have to purchase separate photo-editing software for the images? While many products, such as genealogy software, scrapbook software, and digital picture organizing packages, have photo editors, as part of the program you may still end up buying more sophisticated software for restoration purposes. If you own a scanner, editing software usually accompanies the equipment.

- **Will the program allow for Web publishing?** Several programs now provide Web publishing software, but not all. If you intend to place your genealogical information on a family Web page with pictures, be sure to purchase a package that lets you do that.

Before purchasing any software package, it is a good idea to listen to the experts. Each year genealogical magazines and some computer magazines review the latest software. Taking the time to read reviews will save you time, money, and aggravation. While these reviews usually concentrate on the features relating to information, outstanding multimedia functions will be mentioned.

Another way to find out information is to talk to the experts. If you have never attended a national genealogical conference, you are missing an educational opportunity. Most of the leaders in the genealogical field attend these conferences and present lectures. Software vendors use these events as a way to have potential customers try out their new products. Their booths feature computer stations where you can try the software and ask questions. One particular conference, GENTECH, concentrates on just the technical aspects of genealogy. Consider these conferences as a way to protect your software investment. You can find out about these conferences and lectures by consulting online event calendars and reading the genealogical periodicals.

ORGANIZING SLIDES

What family doesn't have sheets and trays of slides of family vacations? I have several boxes of them sitting in my closet waiting for help. The easiest way to deal with slides is to keep them in their current storage containers unless they are in pages not made of polyester or polypropylene. As they

---

MAGAZINES THAT REVIEW SOFTWARE

Ancestry, published bimonthly by MyFamily.com, 360 W. 4800 N., Provo, UT 84604 <http://www.myfamily.com>

Genealogical Computing, published quarterly by MyFamily.com, 360 W. 4800 N., Provo, UT 84604 <http://www.myfamily.com>

Genealogical Helper, published bimonthly by Everton Publishers, P.O. Box 368, Logan, UT 84323-0368 <http://www.everton.com>

NGS Newsmagazine, published six times a year by the National Genealogical Society, 4527 Seventeenth St. North, Arlington, VA 22207-2399 <http://www.ngsgenealogy.org>

Family Tree Magazine, published bimonthly by F&W Publications, 1507 Dana Ave., Cincinnati, OH 45207 <http://www.familytreemagazine.com>

---

deteriorate, some plastic pages deposit chemicals on the slides. However, conservators recommend transferring your slides into proper storage materials to protect them from damage.

Slide collections can be organized by date or by box number that you assign. Either works because both systems require an index to find images of individuals. However, when you organize them, you will have to transfer that number to each slide. You can write it in the upper right corner. The caption goes on the bottom edge of the mount. Remember to use a writing implement approved for images. For example, suppose you have twelve slide boxes or twelve pages of slides in your closet that you've gathered over the last ten years. Number each box or page 1 to 12. Then number the slides within the box or on the page in the upper right corner of the slide casing. Box 1's slides would be number 1.2, 1.3, 1.4, etc. The same would be true for the slides on a page. Box 2's slides would be numbered 2.1, 2.2, 2.3, and so on. You can also add the date the slides were taken. This will make it easy to refile images when you take them out to use them.

Technique

Alternative Filing Methods

Keep in mind that there is no perfect system to organize your images. I've presented one method, but you can probably think of some other ways. Just remember to keep it simple and examine the pros and cons before you start.

MUSEUM REGISTRATION METHODS

One of the ways to organize your images is to create a distinct number for each image, much the way that major museums do. For instance, you "catalog" each image separately by assigning a year and number for the type of material and a sequential number for each image. For family images,

I would use the date the pictures were taken, or, in the case of historical photographs, the birth year of the person in the portrait or the year that you begin organizing the pictures. For instance, Prints would be 1, Daguerreotypes 2, and Color negatives 3.

So, the code 1865.2.3 would signify 1865 as the year of creation. The 2 would refer to the type of object, and the 3 would be the third daguerreotype numbered. This works very well in a museum setting, but there are obvious drawbacks for the home collection. In museums, the first number is the year the collection is received. If you use this for all your images, it will act as a locator but tell you nothing about the image. Another drawback is the time it takes to implement a system where each and every image must be numbered on the back. Finally, there is the time it takes to create a list of all of the different types of photographic methods in your collection. This system appeals to some people because they prefer number-based organizational schemes. This also supplies you with a unique identifier that can be used as a database record number. One friend thought this system was too complicated, while another thought it was just what she needed.

CHRONOLOGICAL METHODS

You could hypothetically also use a chronological system for filing your photographs. In this method, all images would be arranged by year, day, and month. This is fine if you are only filing current images, but if your collection includes older photographs and multiple families, you will be mixing everything together. A very good index to personal names is a necessary part of this system.

HIRING A PROFESSIONAL ORGANIZER

Does the process of tackling your family photograph collection still seem overwhelming? Would you prefer to have someone do it for you? Your collection may be too large or complicated to handle yourself. If you lack the time but have the resources, hiring a collections consultant is an option. It is fairly easy to find help. Contact one of the historical societies or libraries in your area to see if it has a list of consultants. **You can also post a job notice at one of the colleges and universities that offers degree programs in library science, archives, or public history.** Use some of the same questions to evaluate the qualifications of organizers that you did for conservators and restorers.

1. What is their training? There are formal degree programs that cover photographic organization in their coursework. Schools that offer classes in archives management, library science, museum studies, and public history usually include a few classes that expose students to working with images. In addition to interviewing candidates about the schools they attended, find out if they have any practical experience working with photographs. On-the-job training as an intern, volunteer, or paid employee is as important as a degree.

Idea Generator

2. Ask for a list of references and call them. If your candidates have experience, then they also have lists of references. It is always important to call references. It assures you that the candidates you are considering hiring have experience.

3. Have they worked with a variety of photographic materials? If your collection contains a variety of material and a candidate has worked only with slides, this is not necessarily relevant. Be knowledgeable about your own collection so that you can answer and ask questions about the work involved.

BECOMING A PHOTO CURATOR

You may decide you like working with images so much that you would like to embark on a new profession. There are several ways to train for a career as a collections consultant or photo curator. Most individuals who end up in this profession pursue graduate studies in library science, archives management, museum studies, or public history. A list of institutions that offer degrees in those areas appears in Appendix H.

The best experience is gained by working with collections. Some individuals find employment or volunteer work a precursor to applying to graduate school. Others complete a degree program and then find applicable opportunities. Anyone can apply for a graduate program in one of these areas. Prerequisites depend on the program and can include a background in the humanities and a foreign language.

Upon graduation it is advisable to maintain membership in at least one professional organization, such as The Society of American Archivists, the American Library Association, the Special Libraries Association, or the American Society of Picture Professionals. Continuing education is available through workshops and conferences offered to members.

SPECIAL CONSIDERATION
Organizing Before You Donate

If no one in your family is interested in continuing or maintaining your collection of family memorabilia including photographs, then you might want to consider donating it. There are several advantages. Archives, historical societies, and special collection libraries preserve historical and genealogical materials for the future. You can be assured that researchers will appreciate your efforts to preserve your family's place in history.

Idea Generator

The first step is to find an appropriate institution to which you can donate your photographs, papers, and artifacts. Most repositories will accept large gifts as well as single items. The important part is to find the right place for your items. Contact the historical society or library in the town that your family is from. For instance, if your photographs mostly depict families living in a particular state, then you should send an inquiry to the state historical society to see if it will accept your gift. A list of state historical

Notes

Notes

**GUIDELINES FOR
DONATING YOUR
PHOTOGRAPHS**

- Choose an appropriate institution.

- Contact the organization prior to donating.

- Understand its policies.

- Ask for a gift agreement.

- Determine whether your collection be accessible to the public.

- Investigate the tax benefits.

societies appears in Appendix B. Most public libraries and academic libraries have directories that can help you find a repository. The *American Library Directory*, the American Association of Museums' *Official Museum Directory*, and Elizabeth Petty Bentley's *The Genealogist's Address Book* are three such guides. You can also go online and search for historical and genealogical societies, or consult the list in Appendix D. The Society of American Archivists may be able to help you make contact. It also publishes a free guide to donating materials.

In general, you want to select an institution or organization that has a history of caring for the collections given to it. **Many small organizations lack staff and monetary resources, so ask them a series of questions.**

- **Is your repository climate controlled?** Before donating material, you want to make sure that the facility will be able to care for your donation. Why donate your precious heritage to an institution that lacks long-term preservation standards of temperature and humidity?

- **Are materials accessible to researchers?** In general, most collections will be open to the public for research purposes, but in certain cases, you might want to limit the accessibility of material relating to living individuals for a span of time. This is what is known as a restricted collection and is quite common. You also want to be assured that your materials can be retrieved for researchers rather than sit in uncataloged sections of the facility forever. Ask what you can do as a donor to help prepare your collection for public use. The repository will appreciate your efforts at assistance. In general, all materials should be identified prior to donation.

- **What are you willing to accept?** Depending on the type of facility, it may accept all or only a portion of what you want to donate. This depends on its collection policy that stipulates what it maintains in its repository. When you locate a possible place for your family photographs, ask what other types of material the organization collects. You might be surprised to discover that you have other items of interest. Researchers are interested in all types of personal and family materials, but some facilities have restrictions on what they can accept.

- **How should I organize items prior to donating them?** Archivists and librarians prefer to be contacted prior to donation. This provides them with an opportunity to advise you on the organization of your collection. It is a natural reaction to think about culling your collection prior to gifting it, but in fact, you could be damaging the research value of the collection. If you live in the area, invite the archivist or librarian to visit your collection before you begin throwing things away. The one thing that these professionals won't object to is making sure that photographs and other materials are identified. As their owner, you are the most capable person to label the items in your collection. Rather than removing sensitive materials from your collection, ask the staff about ways to restrict access.

Some professionals prefer to organize the material themselves. They may ask for a monetary gift to help offset the costs to their organization. While this grant will not usually affect the acceptance of the gift, it will help the nonprofit institution process your materials.

- **What about a gift agreement?** You should inquire about a written gift agreement prior to actual donation. This document outlines the responsibilities of the organization. It is not uncommon for irrelevant material to be disposed of through sale or distribution to another institution. If you would like to have these items returned to you, it is important to put this request in writing. Gifts are permanent, so make sure you understand all the terms of the donation. Archivists and librarians should explain their policies and address your concerns. Most institutions will not accept collections on deposit or loan because of the time and materials that are spent on these.

- **What are the tax benefits of a gift?** As a donor, you may be able to take a tax deduction for donating your collection to an institution. Only a tax accountant or attorney can help you determine the tax benefits. The staff of the facility cannot give tax advice or appraise the monetary value of the collection. The staff is usually able to give you a list of local appraisers. It is up to you, as the donor, to have it appraised. Most professional appraisers will charge a fee for this service.

CHECKLIST: ORGANIZING

✓ Keep your system simple.
✓ Plan it out beforehand.
✓ Think about donating your photographs to an appropriate institution.
✓ Hire a professional curator to help with large projects.

Notes

NINE

Safe Scrapbooking

Reminder

In certain parts of the country, creating albums or scrapbooks of family photographs and memorabilia is extraordinarily popular. The scrapbook phenomenon is sweeping the country as more people become interested in tracing their family histories. If you don't believe me, ask a bookstore information desk for publications on scrapbooks. The number of titles available on this topic will surprise you. Search a little further and you will find magazines and Web sites that relate to this relatively new hobby.

Souzzann Y.H. Carroll, author of *A Lasting Legacy: Scrapbooks and Photo Albums That Touch the Heart*, attributes the beginning of contemporary scrapbooks to Marielen and Anthony Christensen.[1] These two people displayed their albums in 1980 at the World Conference on Records in Salt Lake City, Utah. Interest in creating these albums gradually grew until 1987 when the first commercially produced items appeared from Creative Memories. Using a simple concept of marketing to consumers who sign up for classes with thousands of consultants in the United States, United Kingdom, Taiwan, Canada, and New Zealand, Creative Memories has become one of the most well-established scrapbook companies in the industry. Today hobbyists spend more than $300 million annually on supplies and equipment for scrapbooking.

Creating albums of family photographs is not new; our grandmothers used their spare moments to lay out images in albums in a particular order. Some of the more elaborate examples resemble contemporary scrapbooks in their use of clippings and related artwork. Unfortunately, the techniques employed by our ancestors and by many of today's scrapbook enthusiasts are beautiful pictorial narratives of family history and a preservation nightmare.

Unknown to most people is that techniques recommended in some of the books on scrapbooking will keep photo conservationists busy for centuries, if the scrapbooks last that long. All of the materials inherent to these items, such as albums, papers, inks, and glues, add up to a mess. For example, the glue used to paste the images into the albums can seep through the pictures and make it impossible to remove the photographs from the pages. This doesn't need to be the case. Let's not repeat the unknowing mistakes of past generations; let's use a little common sense and a few basic rules. By using PAT-approved products and avoiding certain behaviors, these albums can be appreciated by future generations. But how do you know if the techniques in the books and magazines are safe for your family photographs?

There are major misconceptions in most scrapbooking manuals. Acid-free is not always archival. This terminology is overused. Archival generally refers to material that will not cause additional damage to your family heirlooms; however, there is no industry standard for the term. Rather than rely on terminology such as acid-free and archival, make sure all your supplies passed the PAT. It is important to read the labels and ask manufacturers for information about your supplies. One company, Creating Keepsakes, is dedicated to preserving family memories. It has an advisory committee of preservationists to insure that products that receive the CK OK stamp of approval really are safe to use. In response to the preservation standards advocated by leaders in the industry, many manufacturers advertise and sell special products specifically for scrapbook enthusiasts. This means that genealogists can create durable, safe, and attractive scrapbooks if they use the right materials.

ALBUMS

In the late 1970s, I created a series of albums using the wrong materials. At the time, I was unaware of the dangers of acidic paper and adhesives. Today those albums are in terrible shape. The acid and the glue in the magnetic album stained the images, while the plastic overleaf disintegrated and stuck to the pictures. All this damage could have been avoided if museum-quality photograph albums were available.

Anyone desiring to create a family photo album has a wide variety of choices. The best albums can be purchased from suppliers in Appendix D. While these cost more than the albums commonly available in discount stores, they are worth the investment. The basic features of a preservation-quality album are PAT-approved paper and boards. Make sure that the adhesive and the covering that holds the album together has passed the PAT. In general, stay away from vinyl Naugahyde because the resulting hydrogen chloride gas will destroy your images.[2] Preservationists recommend selecting an album that comes with a slipcase to protect your images from light and dust.

Paper

Scrapbook paper and card stock come in a variety of colors and textures. Be sure that the paper is not water-soluble. **Another consideration is whether the paper is lignin-free.** Naturally found in trees and plants, lignin is the substance that causes paper to yellow with age. While the acid added to paper during the production process to break down the wood chips causes staining, it is the lignin that helps to create the aged look that paper acquires when left in the sun.

Warning

Definitions

There is a misunderstanding of the word *archival*. In fact there are no archival standards. Instead, look for specific materials that passed the PAT and are certified safe for use with images. Using these materials appropriately will protect your photographs.

Definitions

According to Gayle Humpherys of *Creating Keepsakes* magazine, there are four paper qualities that influence the preservation qualities of your scrapbook. She suggests looking for paper that is acid-free, lignin-free, and buffered and that doesn't bleed color.[3] Again, the best thing you can do to preserve your albums is use materials that fit the PAT standards. Quality papers suitable for use in scrapbooks are labeled acid- and lignin-free. Creating Keepsakes is one company that works with a group of preservationists to guarantee the preservation qualities of its products.

It is easy to check the acid content of paper, but keep in mind that many materials can be rendered acid-free temporarily. You can purchase a pH testing pen from the suppliers listed in Appendix D. If the line you draw on the paper with the testing pen turns purple, the paper is acid-free, which means it has a neutral pH (6.5–7.5) or the pH is higher than 7.0. The presence of other colors indicates that acid is present. It is necessary to use a pH testing strip and distilled water on darker paper. In general, use neutral pH papers with color photographs, which are sensitive to the pH; other items suffer no damage with a pH of 8.0. Using these pH testing devices is not a foolproof way to select preservation supplies. Rely on the PAT for guidance.

Since the dyes in some paper bleed when exposed to water or high humidity, you need to test highly colored papers for stability. This is done by dropping a small dot of water on the paper or by placing a small piece of the paper in a cup of water. If the color comes off, then the paper is not approved for use in preservation-quality scrapbooks. For this reason, some preservationists suggest using papers and cutouts of a neutral color. Fortunately these papers are available from library suppliers and most scrapbook stores.

Buffered paper helps prevent acid from migrating to other items in your album because it contains a chemical, probably calcium carbonate. Eventually all paper is affected by the acid it absorbs. Buffering merely slows the process.

Adhesives

Even if you use PAT-approved albums, the techniques you employ to create the scrapbook may cause your project to fall apart or may damage the images. There are many books that suggest that scrapbooking actually preserves your images and then they tell you to use glue, paint, and other harmful materials as part of your project.

People often show me older photo albums with the images glued to black paper and express dismay over their inability to remove the pictures from the pages. In addition, the adhesive used to stick the images to the page stained the images or caused them to ripple from contact with the glue. I've seen all types of damage caused by the use of adhesives and advocate that scrapbook hobbyists use PAT-approved photo corners rather than any type of glue, including those advertised as safe and archival.

Most photo corners are either clear polyester or decorative paper corners.

Supplies

PAPER RECOMMENDATIONS FROM *CREATING KEEPSAKES*[4]

- Neutral pH (6.5–7.5) for use with color photos; pH of 7.0–8.0 for other uses

- Buffered with 2 percent minimum calcium carbonate

- Lignin-free (1 percent maximum lignin content)

- Free of fugitive (bleeding) dye

Either is recommended for use in albums as long as the materials are safe according to the PAT. Clear corners can be made of the two types of plastics approved for use with images: polyester or polypropylene. When a manufacturer states its corners are made of plastic, you need to verify that they are one or the other. If in doubt, ask the supplier.

All photo corners use an adhesive that doesn't come in contact with the images or documents, but you want to make sure it is reversible, colorless, odorless, solid, and acid-free. In general, I never put adhesive on a document or photograph. Many scrapbook manuals show beautiful layouts with cutouts and stickers placed on the images and documents. Unless you are using copies of all your images, it is best to refrain from placing cutouts and stickers on your images, no matter how safe the manufacturer claims they are.

Another option is to purchase a special paper punch that allows you to create slits in your pages to hold the photographs by their corners. This eliminates the need for special supplies and concerns about adhesives.

If you need to remove adhesive from the back of photographs, you can use un-du adhesive remover by Doumar Products, (888) buy-undu or <http://www.un-du.com>. It has been rated safe by Rochester Institute of Technology, Duke University, and *Creating Keepsakes*. This nonabrasive substance removes most adhesives by neutralizing them. Place a few drops on the area, and use a clean, soft, lint-free cloth to gently wipe away the adhesive, working from the middle to the edges. This will prevent you from bending the image during the process. Be careful that the solution doesn't end up dissolving the adhesive and migrating to the picture. This could cause staining and long-term damage. The product is quick drying.[5]

Supplies

Inks

Labeling your images is an important part of creating any type of scrapbook. After all, you wouldn't want to spend the time to create the album and have a future generation be unable to identify the individuals. In general, all photographs should be labeled by placing information underneath or alongside your pictures. **A basic caption includes the name of the person (with life dates), information about the event, where the picture was taken, and when.** Scrapbook magazines can supply examples of creative labeling. You may want to have a single image on a page with a story surrounding it.

Citing Sources

Before you begin labeling, there are a few precautions. First, never write on the front of the image. Second, never ever use a ballpoint pen or a felt-tip marker. The ballpoint smudges and makes indentations in the image, while the felt-tip marker's water-soluble ink can be absorbed by the image. You *can* use a soft graphite pencil on the back while the image is face down on a hard, clean surface, but never use anything on the picture area. Even if you are using copies, it is not a good idea to write on an image. The pressure of the pencil will leave indentations in the surface of the image. Contemporary photographs are coated with resin that makes them difficult to write on. In this case, most of the pens appropriate for this purpose use ink that takes about half a minute to dry. Look for a pen with a soft tip and waterproof ink if you want to label the back of the resin-coated images. Just be sure to give the ink enough time to dry, or you will end up with ink where you didn't intend it. You can also label your photographs by writing the identification on the outside of a sheet protector.

There are a few new scrapbook pens available from the "archival" suppliers. These contain the only type of ink approved for album use. Even inexperienced genealogists have seen examples of what happens to ink when exposed to water or high humidity. If you have never seen this type of damage, it will only take a few minutes to find an example by visiting a local library or archive.

Always test the solubility of the ink you want to use by writing on a piece of paper and submersing it in water. If it runs, don't use it. A safe pen for scrapbooks is one that passes the nontoxicity standards of the Art and Creative Materials Institute, which recommends that the ink be waterproof, fade resistant, permanent, odorless (when dry), and quick drying. Don't be concerned about the smell of the ink when wet; pens that dry rapidly often contain alcohol that dissipates when dry. You wouldn't want to spend hours composing an entry only to have it smudge or run. Most of the pens commonly available in stationery stores, such as ballpoints, rollerballs, and markers, do not meet these standards. Before purchasing a pen, try it out to see if it passes the test.

In general, permanent black ink is the best choice for captioning since colored inks can fade. While scrapbook manuals advise using color for decorative features, make sure the inks pass the criteria for scrapbook-safe ink. Conservationists do not recommend metallic inks.

Glues and ink are not necessarily safe for use with photographs. If you want to follow the directions provided in most publications on creating memory albums and scrapbooks, use copies and never originals. Place the originals in storage so that future generations can appreciate them unblemished.

Citing Sources

BASIC LABELS

- Full name, date, location

- Additional information beside the image on your scrapbook page

Citing Sources

RUBBER STAMPING

Each month, *Creating Keepsakes* magazine publishes a column called "Making It Last," which features articles on the preservation aspects of different components of scrapbooking. Decorating pages with all types of graphic elements, including rubber-stamped designs, is part of what makes a scrapbook attractive. But is it safe? Catherine Scott decided to find out by interviewing preservation experts. Their recommendations were that while the inks and materials are safe, no one knows if the stamps will fade and change color.[6]

As a precaution, Scott and the experts suggest using inks that are safe for scrapbooks, but be sure to test the water solubility of the ink after it has dried. The experts even stated that embossing powders that raise the stamped image can be used as long as they don't come in contact with your images. In fact, they advised embossing every stamp to seal the ink and protect your images from the chemicals in the ink. Full instructions and safe products appear in the article.[7]

SHEET PROTECTORS

You have the option of protecting your scrapbook pages by slipping them into sheet protectors. This eliminates any abrasive damage that can occur when the pages rub together. Just as it is important to consider the chemicals in paper, you should be aware of the best type of sheet protector. You wouldn't want to spend time and money buying PAT products only to undo your efforts with poor-quality plastics.

Sheet protectors come in a variety of designs; some are top loading, while others have pockets or fold-over edges. You can decide to forgo scrapbook papers in favor of just using specially sized protectors. A list of suppliers is listed in Appendix D.

Supplies

Regardless of the type of protectors you decide to use, make sure they are either polyester or polypropylene. Neither of these types of plastic deteriorates with time nor deposits chemicals on your scrapbook pages. Conservators do not suggest using pages made from polyethylene because of a chemical added during the manufacturing process. This "slip agent" helps the sheets move smoothly through production, but over time it rises to the surface of the pages where it can cause smudging. For this reason, it is not advisable to use protectors made of this material.[8]

There are other factors to consider before purchase. Since your scrapbook pages are heavier than regular photographs, you should purchase durable protectors that are labeled heavyweight. This will add to the bulk in your album, so you should try several different types of heavyweight and medium-weight sheets to see which suits your purposes. Another issue is whether to use nonglare or clear pages. Again there is a preservation concern. Nonglare pages sometimes contain substances to give pages their appearance. Besides, I find that nonglare pages do not give you a clear view of photographs.

STICKERS

Stickers are fun and add to the visual interest of the scrapbook you are creating. Use them freely in your album, but make sure they are PAT approved. As long as you don't place them directly on documents and images, you can use them safely.

FAMILY MEMORABILIA

Part of the process of creating a scrapbook is including the memorabilia that add meaning to the events and people you are documenting. Unfortunately, the types of items you place in the album can adversely affect all the steps you've taken to protect your photographs. Documents transfer acid

Hidden Treasures

to the images, ink in fabrics and yarns can bleed if it isn't colorfast, and flowers will stain. So what materials can be included and how?

Documents and newspaper clippings add another dimension to the story you are trying to tell. However, since the paper is acidic, you want to be careful they don't come in contact with your images. Preservationists recommend deacidification before placing clippings or documents in scrapbooks. Seek the advice of an expert before attempting to use any of the deacidification sprays on the market or before immersing the documents in a special solution in case parts of the document will be damaged by the solution. Spraying entire documents with one of these solutions can cause bleeding dyes and has the possibility of long-term chemical damage. Another option is to make copies on PAT papers.

LAMINATION VS. ENCAPSULATION

There is a common myth that won't die. Many people wrongly believe that laminating their documents will help preserve them. Initially lamination was thought to protect items. Unfortunately, once something is encased in laminate, damage begins to occur almost at once. The acid sealed inside and the plastic covering start to deteriorate documents and photographs. Indeed, the entire process is harmful and irreversible. In addition, exposing items to heat during the lamination process ages the material.

Fortunately, there is another method that has been proven to protect and preserve precious family documents. It involves encapsulating the material in two protective sheets of polyester. This is the method used in most libraries and archives. Encapsulation is safe and reversible, exactly the opposite of lamination. Before encapsulating any document, make sure it has been deacidified using special solutions. This can be used for items too large for ready-made envelopes and sleeves.

ARTIFACTS

We all have small pieces of material we would like to include in the stories of our lives, from wood-based items and flowers to plastic objects to things like rocks and ceramics. You know what I mean—the little trinkets you pick up while you are on vacation or that your children bring home. Unfortunately, natural objects transfer lignin and acid to your scrapbook pages, plastics give off gases, and rock and ceramics are abrasive. Leather is treated with tannic acid, which will leech onto your images and pages. Money is also unsuitable for inclusion until it is cleaned and placed in a protective covering. However, there is hope. Include memorabilia by using specially made polypropylene envelopes that use the same adhesive as the corners. They are available in a variety of sizes from scrapbook suppliers. Some scrapbook suppliers have products that offer creative solutions such as storage compartments and decorative frames. Be sure to check with the manufacturer to be sure that the plastics these items are made from are either polypropylene or polyester.[9]

There are materials that you can safely include in your album, such as most fabrics and yarns as long as they are acid-free, nonabrasive, and colorfast. When in doubt about whether an object or item is safe, include it in a protective covering to be sure you are not inadvertently causing damage.

CREATING THE SCRAPBOOK

Now that you know what supplies are safe to use, it is time to create the scrapbook. Since one of the goals of creating a scrapbook is to tell a story, one of the first things you need to do is select what items will be included. Scrapbooks become a family artifact. They can be used to tell a particular family story or to create a biography of a single family member. By deciding on a theme, you can focus on completely telling that story. It can be as specific as a single event or be a general family photograph album.

Step By Step

There are three basic steps to creating a scrapbook after you decide on a focus.
1. Set up a clean work area that you can use to lay out your photographs and store your materials. Be sure to wash your hands, and wear clean cotton gloves when handling your images.
2. Purchase materials: Be sure to use only materials approved by the PAT to create your album.
3. Lay out the items: Deciding what to include in your album can be a daunting task when faced with boxes and notebooks full of materials. Choose photographs that relate to your theme and are good quality. If you have difficulty taking usable photographs, see the suggestions on pages 179–182.

Consider Using Copies

Many of the cutting and pasting techniques illustrated in popular magazines will cause irreparable damage. When you use copies and duplicate prints, you eliminate the danger of destroying irreplaceable images. Rather than crop original images and obscure identifying information, use a duplicate and place the original in storage. Chapter two explains several techniques for producing copies, from scanning to duplicate prints.

Film developing offers many opportunities for extra prints. When you take film to be developed, you can request extra prints, selectively choose pictures from a Web site, or have them placed on a CD-ROM. In this way, you can experiment with duplicate prints without harming the original. You can place one in storage and the other in an album.

DIGITAL SCRAPBOOKS

Digital imaging offers an alternative to traditional scrapbooking. Genealogy programs and online photo-sharing sites have features that allow individuals to create digital scrapbooks. It is one way to create a safe scrapbook without making copies and buying supplies. You can also purchase a software package specifically for scrapbook hobbyists. Generally they include tools to help you create scrapbook pages to print out or post on the Web. You select the type of page and format from the list of projects then digitally insert your photographs. It accepts images from photo disk, photo CD-ROM, digital camera, scanner, and even those sent to you via the Internet. In addition, this product includes a photo organizer to keep track of your images and a photo editor to digitally enhance, crop, or fix your pictures. If you decide to print the pages rather than post them on a family site, follow the guidelines for printing digital images in chapter two.

Decorate your pages with stickers of acid-free paper and adhesive, or use cutouts that follow safe scrapbook guidelines. As long as you don't place your images in danger through exposure to substances and chemicals that will harm them, be as creative as you can be. Just don't let your excitement allow you to make preservation mistakes.

CONSULT THE EXPERTS

For More Info

If you need advice, look no further than two popular magazines, *Creating Keepsakes* **and** *Memory Makers.* Both magazines feature how-to articles and scrapbook pages submitted by readers. If you don't know where to buy supplies or attend classes in your area, consult the directories in the back of every issue.

To keep track of current trends and new products, consider becoming a member of the International Scrapbook Trade Association (ISTA). Members receive a bimonthly newsletter.

SUPPLIES FOR A SAFE SCRAPBOOK

Supplies

- PAT-approved album: These can be ordered from several of the suppliers mentioned in Appendix D.
- Polypropylene corners: Made of clear polypropylene with an adhesive back, they hold the photographs in place without putting the image in contact with the adhesive.
- Graphite pencil: Pencils can be used to label the images. Write lightly on the back of photographs while placed face down on a clean, flat surface. Coated papers can be written on with a waterproof pen. Never write on the fronts of images.

RULES FOR SAFE SCRAPBOOKING

Notes

1. If you are going to use the methods and techniques presented in many of the more popular books, then your first rule is to make copies. The originals should be preserved for future generations by being stored in a proper environment. Once you have decided to use duplicate prints or copies, you can be as creative as you like without being concerned about the lasting qualities of your scrapbook.
2. If you decide to lay out original photographs in an album, then use

---

BASIC RULES OF SCRAPBOOKING

Golden rule: Don't cause any permanent damage to your irreplaceable images.

Dos

1. Use scrapbook-safe materials.

2. Use copy photos, placing originals in storage.

3. Enhance the value of your album by labeling the images.

4. Use photographs that are of good quality.

5. Create a lasting artifact that future generations can enjoy.

Don'ts

1. Don't use magnetic albums with adhesive pages.

2. Never crop original photographs.

3. Never write on the fronts of images.

4. Don't include images that are of poor quality or in disrepair.

5. Don't place adhesive directly on an image or attach cutouts.

---

    materials that are acid-free—no inks or paints or colored papers—and have passed the PAT.

3. Don't crop or mat original images. You are irreversibly destroying the image by cutting the photograph or gluing a mat over the image.

4. Do not laminate or hand-color the original images. Laminate contains chemicals that destroy the images over time.

5. Identify the images. Some suppliers offer suggestions on how to identify the images without causing damage.

CHECKLIST: SAFE SCRAPBOOKING

  ✓ Use materials that passed the PAT.
  ✓ Take care to identify your images.
  ✓ Use copies.
  ✓ Read about the long-term effects of products before using them.

Notes

TEN

Three Family Collections

Case Study

I n my book *Uncovering Your Ancestry Through Family Photographs*, the last chapter presented two case studies. One featured a photograph from the Emison/Loock family photograph collection. Using the organizing principles and conservation data in previous chapters, let's look at three collections of varying sizes, including revisiting the Emison/Loock photographs.

THE TAYLOR FAMILY COLLECTION

When my eldest aunt died, a small collection of images passed to her brother (my father), who in turn recently gave them to me. At this point, this collection of less than twenty photographs is the only photographic record of the Taylor family. The rest of the material was disbursed between other siblings, and the large collection of newspaper clippings my grandmother kept were tossed when she died more than thirty years ago.

The genealogy of the family shows that while documents exist that provide family information, there is no mention of any images. One of the reasons I've written the books I have is to help others save their photographic heritage before it is lost like mine. All of my grandmother's siblings are deceased and most of my father's, as well. It will take a good deal of effort to try to reconstruct a photo collection. Cousins live in various places across the country and do not keep in touch. Before I begin to re-create a photo collection, I need to care for the few in my possession.

This small group is in poor shape. This was not a family that spent time taking photographs or collecting them. What survived has water damage and cracks. One extremely out-of-focus picture is a group portrait of my grandmother and her siblings. Since I met only her younger brother, I would love this picture to be in focus. The majority of the images are duplicates of my parents' wedding photograph. The two oldest images in the collection are a pair of pictures taken of a group of men and boys at a picnic in the late nineteenth century (see figure 10-1). My father, as the oldest living member of the family, has no idea who is in the pictures, although one man

Figure 10-1.
This is the oldest photograph in the Taylor family collection. It depicts an unidentified outing. *Collection of the author*

has a family resemblance. The purpose of the photographs or the event it documented is currently unknown. A professional photographer probably took the images using glass plate negatives and then mounted the prints on heavy cardboard.

The size of the collection makes it easy to organize and care for. Each image can be placed in an individual folder with the name of the family member. A single oversize box that can accommodate all the images and their folders is all that is needed. The one severely damaged picture is in need of restoration. Thankfully, most of the water damage and the acid board have not affected the two unidentified prints.

Here are the steps necessary to save this collection:

1. Purchase a box and a few folders from one of the suppliers in Appendix D.
2. Send the damaged portrait to a restorer for an estimate on digital restoration.

Step By Step

3. Have copies made of the unidentified prints, and start circulating them among any cousins still living. This is not a family with many children.
4. Reach out to other family members, and try to build the collection.

Case Study

THE BETLOCK/VIRNIG COLLECTION

Lynn Betlock started researching her family as a young girl but only later became interested in family photographs. One event triggered her desire to build a family photograph collection to accompany her genealogical research. In 1991, she wrote to her grandfather's brother Ed and his wife, Evie, asking for some basic genealogical information. Evie wrote back and sent two studio photographs. This was the first time Lynn had ever seen pictures of her great-grandmother Hannah Peterson Betlock and her great-grandfather Joseph Betlock as young adults not as older people. Most of the family photographs had ended up in the dump because Ed's father, Joseph Betlock, decided to discard them after his wife died. Lynn's grandfather Willard preserved those two images and gave them to his brother Ed who in turn gave them to Lynn. A rather circuitous route, but in the end, the photographs stayed in the family. After this letter and images appeared, Lynn began to look for family photographs as well as documents.

Her paternal grandmother, Alma (Bobbie) Flack Betlock, was the youngest of six daughters. She took care of her elderly father and upon his death inherited family photographs. Instead of the collection being distributed among several generations of a family, one individual became responsible for its future. Few images were lost and the integrity of the photographic heritage of the family stayed intact from the late nineteenth century to the current generation. While several generations of the family are represented, about half of the images are childhood photographs of Lynn's father.

The Flacks originated in Norway. John Flak immigrated to the United States in 1889, a younger brother followed later, while the oldest brother stayed in Norway to work the family farm. Over the years, the family lost contact, but Lynn was able to reestablish contact and locate Norwegian relatives still living on the farm. Since there were many images in the collection with captions written in Norwegian, she enlisted her relatives' help with translation and identification. Without their help, those photos would have remained essentially meaningless. With identification and translations, they became heirlooms.

On the Virnig, or the maternal, side of her family, she sought out her grandmother's photo collection and took select images to a photo lab to be copied. Her grandmother had nine children and twenty-four grandchildren, so it seemed prudent to take advantage of the opportunity to make copies while the collection was intact. Lynn then began to network with her second and third cousins. With ten children in every generation, she expects that any family photos that existed from earlier generations would be widely scattered at this point.

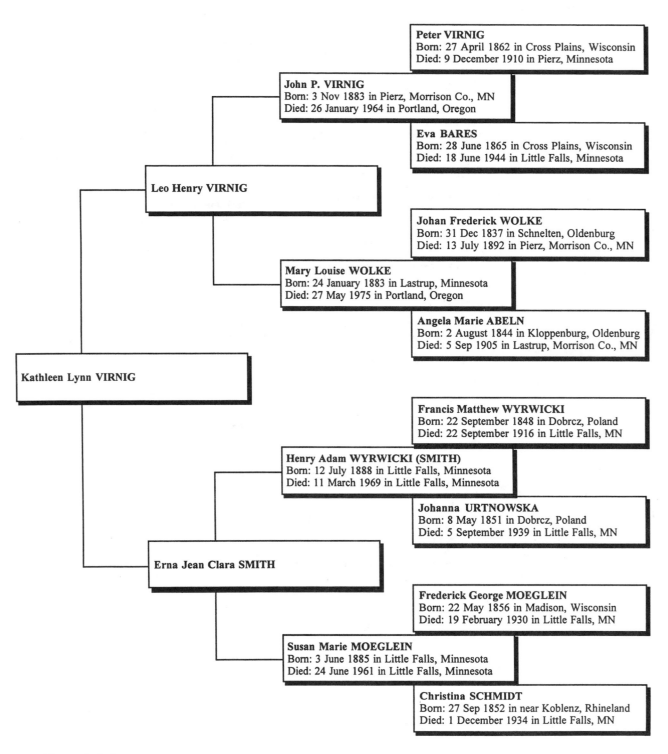

Peter VIRNIG
Born: 27 April 1862 in Cross Plains, Wisconsin
Died: 9 December 1910 in Pierz, Minnesota

John P. VIRNIG
Born: 3 Nov 1883 in Pierz, Morrison Co., MN
Died: 26 January 1964 in Portland, Oregon

Eva BARES
Born: 28 June 1865 in Cross Plains, Wisconsin
Died: 18 June 1944 in Little Falls, Minnesota

Leo Henry VIRNIG

Johan Frederick WOLKE
Born: 31 Dec 1837 in Schnelten, Oldenburg
Died: 13 July 1892 in Pierz, Morrison Co., MN

Mary Louise WOLKE
Born: 24 January 1883 in Lastrup, Minnesota
Died: 27 May 1975 in Portland, Oregon

Angela Marie ABELN
Born: 2 August 1844 in Kloppenburg, Oldenburg
Died: 5 Sep 1905 in Lastrup, Morrison Co., MN

Kathleen Lynn VIRNIG

Francis Matthew WYRWICKI
Born: 22 September 1848 in Dobrcz, Poland
Died: 22 September 1916 in Little Falls, MN

Henry Adam WYRWICKI (SMITH)
Born: 12 July 1888 in Little Falls, Minnesota
Died: 11 March 1969 in Little Falls, Minnesota

Johanna URTNOWSKA
Born: 8 May 1851 in Dobrcz, Poland
Died: 5 September 1939 in Little Falls, MN

Erna Jean Clara SMITH

Frederick George MOEGLEIN
Born: 22 May 1856 in Madison, Wisconsin
Died: 19 February 1930 in Little Falls, MN

Susan Marie MOEGLEIN
Born: 3 June 1885 in Little Falls, Minnesota
Died: 24 June 1961 in Little Falls, Minnesota

Christina SCHMIDT
Born: 27 Sep 1852 in near Koblenz, Rhineland
Died: 1 December 1934 in Little Falls, MN

Created by Lynn Betlock

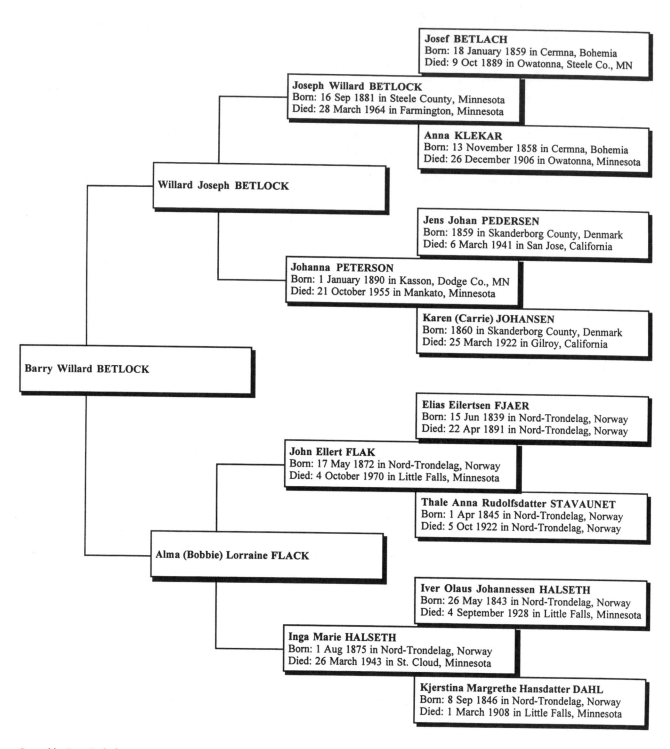

Barry Willard BETLOCK

Willard Joseph BETLOCK

Joseph Willard BETLOCK
Born: 16 Sep 1881 in Steele County, Minnesota
Died: 28 March 1964 in Farmington, Minnesota

Josef BETLACH
Born: 18 January 1859 in Cermna, Bohemia
Died: 9 Oct 1889 in Owatonna, Steele Co., MN

Anna KLEKAR
Born: 13 November 1858 in Cermna, Bohemia
Died: 26 December 1906 in Owatonna, Minnesota

Johanna PETERSON
Born: 1 January 1890 in Kasson, Dodge Co., MN
Died: 21 October 1955 in Mankato, Minnesota

Jens Johan PEDERSEN
Born: 1859 in Skanderborg County, Denmark
Died: 6 March 1941 in San Jose, California

Karen (Carrie) JOHANSEN
Born: 1860 in Skanderborg County, Denmark
Died: 25 March 1922 in Gilroy, California

Alma (Bobbie) Lorraine FLACK

John Ellert FLAK
Born: 17 May 1872 in Nord-Trondelag, Norway
Died: 4 October 1970 in Little Falls, Minnesota

Elias Eilertsen FJAER
Born: 15 Jun 1839 in Nord-Trondelag, Norway
Died: 22 Apr 1891 in Nord-Trondelag, Norway

Thale Anna Rudolfsdatter STAVAUNET
Born: 1 Apr 1845 in Nord-Trondelag, Norway
Died: 5 Oct 1922 in Nord-Trondelag, Norway

Inga Marie HALSETH
Born: 1 Aug 1875 in Nord-Trondelag, Norway
Died: 26 March 1943 in St. Cloud, Minnesota

Iver Olaus Johannessen HALSETH
Born: 26 May 1843 in Nord-Trondelag, Norway
Died: 4 September 1928 in Little Falls, Minnesota

Kjerstina Margrethe Hansdatter DAHL
Born: 8 Sep 1846 in Nord-Trondelag, Norway
Died: 1 March 1908 in Little Falls, Minnesota

Created by Lynn Betlock

162

As she began to look for Virnig information on the Internet, she found a Bares home page that featured a photograph of Peter Virnig (1862–1910) and his wife, Eva (Bares) (1865–1944), Lynn's great-great-grandparents. It is an unusual surname, and she was surprised to find it. The photo, taken around 1888, is the earliest known portrait of these two people (see figure 10-2). The woman who maintained the Bares Web site quickly answered Lynn's request for copies, and they shared information.

After this one success, Lynn began to use family migration patterns to locate additional images. The Virnigs left the Rhineland in the 1840s and 1850s and initially settled in Cross Plains, Wisconsin. A small group of family members eventually left Wisconsin and moved to Morrison County, Minnesota. In this last migration, the entire family did not migrate as a group. Some relatives stayed behind in Wisconsin. This meant that she needed to find her distant relatives to locate more pictures. In one case, she was successful and obtained a photo of four adult sisters. Three of the

Figure 10-2.
Peter Virnig, Eva Bares Virnig, John P. Virnig (center), Christian Virnig (front), Hubert Virnig. This image was found on a family Web page.
Courtesy of Delores Clark

Figures 10-3 and 10-4.
Mathilda and Susan
Moeglein (on the right in
both pictures) as children
and young adults.
Lynn Betlock

Figures 10-3 and 10-4.
Mathilda and Susan Moeglein (on the right in both pictures) as children and young adults.
Lynn Betlock

sisters had stayed in Wisconsin, while Lynn's ancestor, who had moved to Wisconsin as a girl, was able to pose for the photo when she visited later in life. Lynn is continuing to try to locate and contact descendants of other distant relatives.

Lynn's grandmother once quizzed her sons and daughters by pointing to a newly framed photograph in her house and challenging the adult children to identify the two girls in the image. Not a single one could identify their own grandmother Susan Moeglein Smith (Lynn's great-grandmother) in the image (see figures 10-3 and 10-4), even though they had all known her. This is a great example of why identification information needs to appear with a photograph and how easily it is lost even within a lifetime.

The end result of her efforts is that Lynn can now identify most of the people in her collection. Only about 5 percent of the collection of about two hundred images is unidentified. She feels that these photographs, taken in Norway, must be of the Halseth line. The entire Halseth family immigrated to the United States, and she has been unsuccessful in finding relatives in Norway.

Lynn used creative methods to identify the images in her collection. She utilized her genealogical research to follow migration routes and locate distant cousins to help with the process. **She also interviewed family members to learn the stories behind certain photographs.** Part of a photo's history does not exist in the print but in the oral traditions about the images in the family. In this way, she learned about nicknames and personalities. She was able to incorporate this information into her family history. Family events provided opportunities to learn more about the

Oral History

family. At her grandfather Virnig's funeral, she met a previously unknown relative who had genealogical research on other lines of the family. This chance meeting of a distant cousin provided Lynn with photographs of her great-great-grandparents, the Wolkes.

She has invested a great deal of time in building her collection. Maintaining contact with her distant relatives has encouraged them to send her images rather than discarding them. When a great-great-aunt died, her children sent Lynn the images because they knew she was interested. Her collection is slowly growing, and there are few individuals on her family tree for which she lacks photographs.

Lynn is also trying to create a photographic biography of her relatives by photographing places they lived. She accomplishes this by using city directories to find exact addresses. This photo documentation also provides a context for family stories. In one case, she traveled to Hayfield, Minnesota, to photograph a particular building that was a meeting place for her great-grandparents. Her great-grandmother worked as a waitress, serving men working on the railroad, when she met Lynn's great-grandfather, who worked on the Chicago, Milwaukee, and St. Paul Railroad. This romantic tale is now documented both in oral tradition and photographs.

When she agreed to have her collection assessed for reorganization, her first question was, "How can I find the time to organize my collection?" In fact, she has already completed the first steps of the organizational process. She followed a basic rule of organization by starting with a small piece of the project. Her photographs are separated by her grandparents' surnames and stored in boxes that passed the PAT. Genealogical charts provide an index to other surname materials in the boxes. In each storage container, she divided the images by generation and family group. This is her heritage photograph collection.

Figure 10-5.
Lynn Betlock chose to presort her photographs by surname to help her decide how to organize them. *Lynn Betlock*

Lynn has made a distinction between historical images and those that concern her lifetime. A small group of snapshots of her childhood is in a single small envelope; the rest reside with her mother. Any images Lynn takes herself are arranged in albums in chronological order by event.

Step By Step

Using the checklist for steps in organizing family photographs, let's look at the Betlock/Virnig collection.

✓ Look through all the images, and make a list of people, places, and events. Lynn accomplished this by using her genealogical research notes and charts. She could shade the boxes on her charts as a visual reminder of who is represented in the collection or add the images to scrapbook pages provided in the Family Tree Maker genealogical software package she uses.

✓ Decide on an organizational plan. Lynn chose to organize her images in terms of her grandparents. Placing her own photographs in albums as she creates them is a good way to organize contemporary pictures. A list of individuals and a table of contents in the front of each volume will identify what is in each one.

✓ Estimate the supplies you need, and purchase them in bulk. She purchased all the supplies she needs for the project but is having trouble finding the time to complete the project. However, she is almost finished. All her current negatives are stored in polypropylene sleeves, and her photographs are in boxes. The only thing she needs to do is replace the envelopes she is using and place the individual items in approved sleeves or folders.

✓ Set up a work space. She has all her boxes and supplies stored in one place for easy retrieval. When she needs to work on the collection, she uses the kitchen table.

Figure 10-6.
The Union Meat Market in Little Falls, Minnesota. George and Charlie Moeglein are behind the counter. *Lynn Betlock*

✓ Begin sorting. She has completed this phase of the project. Now that she has a basic organizational plan, she can easily incorporate additional images into her collection. Her sorting by surname is simple and flexible.

✓ Create a file of images in need of identification. Not only does she know which photographs need identification, she has taken steps to find help with the project. Only a small portion of her collection is still unidentified.

✓ Create a file of photocopies of pictures requiring conservation or restoration. Her collection is in remarkably good shape. Only a few items can benefit from digital restoration.

✓ Start labeling, boxing, and indexing. Lynn is obviously a very organized person. She began working on her collection in small increments and has almost finished the process. Her boxes are labeled and easily accessible. Her organizational system is self-indexing, and using the genealogical charts is a handy way to refer to both documents and photographs. When she begins placing the images in individual sleeves, she needs to consider writing some identification information either on worksheets or on the sleeves. This is not written on any of the images. This data will be lost unless it is placed with the images.

Figure 10-7.
This is the only photograph of the Halseth family of Norway and Little Falls, Minnesota, in the Betlock Collection. *Lynn Betlock*

In answer to her question about time, I advised her to refolder each individual surname—one in each sitting. By doing so, she will complete the project in a relatively short amount of time. Unbeknownst to her, she has already accomplished a great deal, and with a little effort and patience, she will finish her reorganization.

Her next step is to concentrate on finding other photographs of the Betlock side of her family. Her efforts to locate images of all of her descendants on the Virnig side have been successful (see page 161). There are several ancestors on her paternal side, such as the Betlachs, Klekars, and Fjaers, for which she still needs to try to find images. (Norwegians changed their surnames frequently, sometimes as often as every generation, so these surnames are not necessarily consistent throughout the history of the family.) I have no doubt that with her methodological approach, she will be able to accomplish her goal of having photo documentation for all members of her family tree.

THE EMISON FAMILY COLLECTION

Case Study

Now that we've looked at a small and medium-size collection, let's look at a challenging larger group. The Emison collection is a more typical collection, not in the way it has become the sole responsibility of one person but in its varied contents. Grant Emison inherited the collection after his father died. While his mother is still living, she thought the material would interest Grant. Grant's father was the only descendant in two generations of Emisons. The material Grant received from his father represents more than three generations of family history in documents and photographs. There are at least five boxes of relatively unorganized newspaper clippings, Christmas cards, family photographs, and corporate images from his grandfather's employment at Stauffer Chemical and his involvement at Rice University. Most collections contain ephemera that piece together a family's life such, as postcards, tickets, important documents, and cards. The previous owner of the collection usually retains some of this material, but the reasons are often lost to the current owner. In Grant's case, the collection was kept untouched after the death of his grandparents. It went into storage after Grant's father died and came into Grant's possession a decade later. It arrived in the boxes his grandparents stored it in and in original order.

Notes

When initially assessing a collection, it is necessary to answer a short list of questions in order to understand the contents of the group.

- **What types of photographs are in the collection?** In the Emison boxes are photographs dating from the 1860s to Grant's father's death in 1983. It includes framed images, miscellaneous photographs of his father from birth to death, film negatives, as well as one ambrotype and a tintype.
- **How many different-size pictures are there?** The sizes of the images

vary from a small carte de visite to a few 11″ × 14″ prints. Either every-thing that was oversize was weeded from the collection or nothing larger than a box was ever taken.

- **Are there documents, such as letters, diaries, and birth and marriage certificates, related to the images?** No, not for the Emison side of the family.
- **Are several different families represented?** Yes. Upon preliminary examination, it appears the Emison collection consists of material from his paternal side of the family, including the following sur-names: Emison, Smith, Hutchins, Loock, and Evansich. Unlike with the Betlock collection, photographs do not exist for most branches of the family.

Little is known about how the collection became what it is today. One family story relates how Grant's paternal grandmother so disliked a child-hood photograph that she destroyed all the images of it she could find. As a result, only one copy of that photograph exists (see figure 10-8).

This group of material is more complex than the Betlock/Virnig and the Taylor collections. Therefore, there are more steps involved in organizing it. A preliminary sort of the collection is being done to separate material by

Figure 10-8.
Grant Emison's paternal grandmother disliked this photograph of her-self as a young child and destroyed many copies of it.
Grant Emison

surname. When libraries and archives start to sift through a collection, part of the procedure is weeding out material that would be more appropriate elsewhere. In this case, some of the photographs and ephemera might belong in an institution with related collections. However, the current owners feel that if several generations of the family kept this material together, then it should be kept. However, I would place to one side all of the material unrelated to the Emisons, as well as the miscellaneous corporate material, and concentrate time and efforts on the family photographs. It may become apparent later on that these miscellaneous things should become part of the family archive or be sent to a library. See pages 145–147 for directions on how to donate material.

Notes

Here's the Emison collection in terms of a task list:

- Make a list of people, places, and events. The genealogy of the family provides a starting place for the list. The written material in the boxes has not been incorporated into the family history. Since this collection contains such a wide variety of material, a list of people, places, and events will help orient the owner as he begins to create a plan.

- Decide on an organizational plan. Prior to sorting the collection, it is a good idea to create an outline of who and what is in the boxes. This collection can be organized by surname with subdivisions for individuals as well as travel photos. For instance, Sam Shannon Emison and Frances Mary (Loock) Emison would each have a separate file for photographs of them individually but would also have files for shots of them as a couple and with their son, Sam. As a couple, Sam and Frances traveled extensively, and those images would also have their own files under the Emison surname. Confused? Here's an example.

File folders

Emison (placed either in alphabetical order in the storage container or in terms of generation like this example)

Sam Shannon Emison Jr. (individual images)

    Sam Shannon Emison (individual images)

    Frances Mary (Loock) Emison (individual images) (placed here or with the Loocks as long as a note directs you to the appropriate filing place)

    Sam and Frances Emison (couple)

    Sam, Frances, and Sam (family photos)

    Sam and Frances Emison (travel photos, broken down by trip and date)

      Samuel Grant Emison (individual photos)

The number of images and contents of the collection direct the organizational scheme. Documents for each of these individuals would be interfiled in separate folders.

- Estimate the supplies you need and purchase them. This is the hard part. Grant needs to count each type and size of image in the collection to determine what should be purchased. In Grant's collection, the tintype and ambrotype should either be placed in envelopes or, since there are only two,

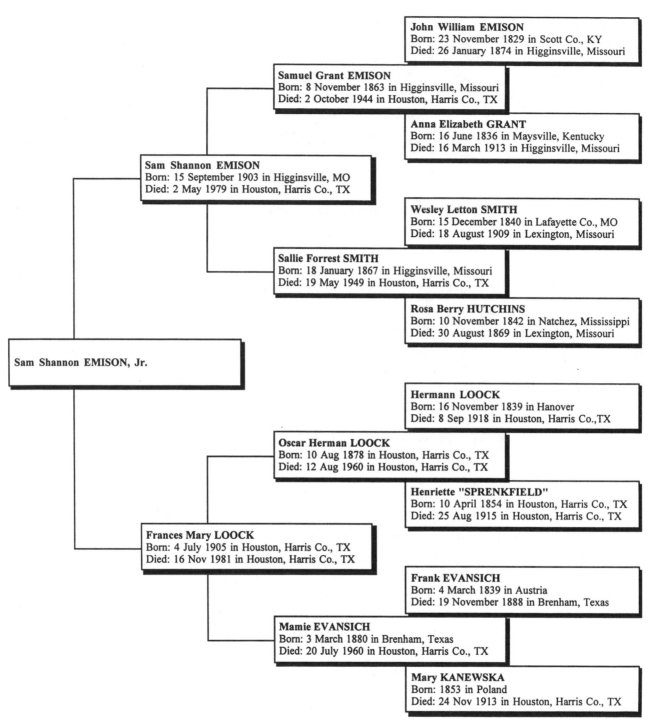

John William EMISON
Born: 23 November 1829 in Scott Co., KY
Died: 26 January 1874 in Higginsville, Missouri

Samuel Grant EMISON
Born: 8 November 1863 in Higginsville, Missouri
Died: 2 October 1944 in Houston, Harris Co., TX

Anna Elizabeth GRANT
Born: 16 June 1836 in Maysville, Kentucky
Died: 16 March 1913 in Higginsville, Missouri

Sam Shannon EMISON
Born: 15 September 1903 in Higginsville, MO
Died: 2 May 1979 in Houston, Harris Co., TX

Wesley Letton SMITH
Born: 15 December 1840 in Lafayette Co., MO
Died: 18 August 1909 in Lexington, Missouri

Sallie Forrest SMITH
Born: 18 January 1867 in Higginsville, Missouri
Died: 19 May 1949 in Houston, Harris Co., TX

Rosa Berry HUTCHINS
Born: 10 November 1842 in Natchez, Mississippi
Died: 30 August 1869 in Lexington, Missouri

Sam Shannon EMISON, Jr.

Hermann LOOCK
Born: 16 November 1839 in Hanover
Died: 8 Sep 1918 in Houston, Harris Co.,TX

Oscar Herman LOOCK
Born: 10 Aug 1878 in Houston, Harris Co., TX
Died: 12 Aug 1960 in Houston, Harris Co., TX

Henriette "SPRENKFIELD"
Born: 10 April 1854 in Houston, Harris Co., TX
Died: 25 Aug 1915 in Houston, Harris Co., TX

Frances Mary LOOCK
Born: 4 July 1905 in Houston, Harris Co., TX
Died: 16 Nov 1981 in Houston, Harris Co., TX

Frank EVANSICH
Born: 4 March 1839 in Austria
Died: 19 November 1888 in Brenham, Texas

Mamie EVANSICH
Born: 3 March 1880 in Brenham, Texas
Died: 20 July 1960 in Houston, Harris Co., TX

Mary KANEWSKA
Born: 1853 in Poland
Died: 24 Nov 1913 in Houston, Harris Co., TX

Created by Lynn Betlock

stored in same-size reinforced boxes from a supplier. These are not a special order. They may cost a little more because he has no need to buy multiples. The film negatives in the Emison collection will require individual sleeves or pages. Standard 35mm negative pages will not work because these are individual negatives not strips. He can use upright boxes with reinforced corners for material smaller than 8″×10″ and use flat storage boxes for larger items. Grant should consult the catalog descriptions to see the storage parameters of the boxes.

- Set up a work space. Finding room to work can be one of the hardest parts of the organizational process. Sorting five oversize boxes of material requires space that in the best of circumstances won't be touched until the process is finished. For this reason, a kitchen or dining room table doesn't work because each is utilized on a daily basis. I suggest Grant purchase a folding table and set it up in an area that doesn't get a lot of traffic. As an alternative, he can try setting aside time to work on one box at a time and store everything between sessions.

- Begin sorting. Before we met to discuss his collection, Grant began sorting his material into groups by surname. This is a good way to begin the process. He should also separate all documents from the photographs, sorting the documents by surname as well. Initially, Grant should keep together the marriage certificate and its associated image in the Emison collection. During the final organization, he needs to make an acid- and lignin-free photocopy of the document and store it with the image. The original document goes in a separate file. He can also place a sheet of PAT paper between the two items in a single folder.

- Create a file of images that need identification. Grant is extremely lucky. There are only a few items that lack identifying information. The most mysterious image in this collection was discussed in *Uncovering Your Ancestry Through Family Photographs*. It is a portrait of two young girls.

- Create a list of images in need of conservation and restoration. Because there was very little interest in these images for a couple of generations, the majority of the material is in pristine condition. A few images suffered abrasive damage through handling. The tintype has lost its glass mat but retained its case. The ambrotype is missing part of its backing and can be restored.

- Label and box. The final stage of reorganizing the Emison collection will take some time. In a large collection, all the steps take longer because you are working with more images and materials. Again, once the organizational scheme is implemented, Grant may decide to track down distant relatives to discover new images to add to the collection. On his Emison line, this would require him to contact descendants of his great-great-grandparents' children since his great-grandparents had three children but only one grandchild, his father. The likelihood of still finding images from that generation may be slim.

THE NEXT STEP

There are similarities and differences in these collections, both in how they were passed on to the current generation and in approach to organizing them. Examine your family collection in terms of its unique qualities before you start to reorganize and lose the original order. These examples only present three approaches. If you need additional information on how to organize the material in your possession, you might want to enroll in an archives class at a local college or university. Another way to learn more about image and organizational methods is to volunteer at a local historical society. That way you can learn firsthand from an experienced individual.

CHECKLIST: POINTS TO REMEMBER

✓ Take your time.
✓ Study the uniqueness of the collection.
✓ Follow the basic steps of organizing a collection.
✓ Reach out and expand your collection.

Notes

ELEVEN

Having Fun With Your Family Photographs

Idea Generator

Y ou've reached the end of your photographic journey. If you have followed the advice in this book and in *Uncovering Your Ancestry Through Family Photographs*, you now have a perfectly organized, restored, and fully identified family photograph collection. No, I'm not crazy. You *will* get there if you gradually invest time and money, but while you are doing that, don't forget to enjoy your family pictures. In our work-driven society, we need to remember to appreciate the small things in life. Our photographs are definitely one of those things. Why not use them for a little stress reduction session by spending some time looking at all your pictures of past vacations? My favorite activity is showing old images to children. They are able to express the joy that we've forgotten. My children love to mimic the expressions and poses from the pictures. **I stock up on disposable cameras when they go on sale so that they can record their own memories of the events in which they participate.** You'll gain a whole new perspective of the world by viewing it through their eyes.

There are so many things you can do with your family images, from remembering to use them in your family history to displaying copies in your home and even creating a game. Photographs can be a large part of a family reunion. I covered reunion activities in *Uncovering Your Ancestry Through Family Photographs*, but I have a few more.

Don't like the quality of the images in your collection? Then follow the steps to improving your images. Looking through a camera's lens is another way of seeing the world—it just takes a few reminders to create images your descendants will enjoy looking at.

USING YOUR PHOTOGRAPHS IN A FAMILY HISTORY

In the first chapter of *Alice's Adventure in Wonderland* by Lewis Carroll, Alice asks, "What is the use of a book without pictures or conversation?" The same is true when applied to a genealogical book. Yet, the majority of genealogies published in the last one hundred years make inadequate use of visual aids. There is usually the obligatory map and a frontispiece portrait of the founding member of the family. But genealogies written around the mid-nineteenth century use illustrations and photographs in ways later compilers seem to have forgotten. While the technology didn't exist to make reproductions of actual photographs, these genealogists hired engravers to make prints based on original photographs. In several instances, these books contain original carte de visite images. It was less expensive to include the originals in a limited edition than commission engravings. A notable example is the *Bolling Family Genealogy* printed in a limited edition of fifty copies in 1868. A review of the book in the *New England Historical Genealogical Register* stated, "The chief value of the book is in the numerous photographs and portraits."[1]

By using family photographs and documents, you can add life and interest to the family history you create. A well-chosen and well-placed image draws readers into the text by piquing their curiosity. The caption should be no more than a couple of sentences and in a genealogy should feature the name of the individuals in the picture, their life dates, and a brief statement about the subject of the photograph. **So how can you utilize the photographs you have in your collection?**

Tip

Using Photographs as Illustrations

1. Make notes on the pages of your manuscript to remind yourself who you have pictures of and what documents are available. If you are using a genealogical computer program, enter these images as attachments to the family group sheet.

2. Select images that are in focus, in good condition (original or restored), and well composed. If a photo doesn't fit those criteria, don't use it even if it is your only picture of an important family member. You want your genealogy to look professional. By including poor-quality images, you are not projecting that impression. Try not to select more than one image of a person.

3. Are the images copyrighted? See chapter two for a review of copyright issues and family photographs.

4. Write clear captions that explain who is in the picture and why you are using it. Be brief. A few sentences are enough.

5. Lack the photographs or documents you need to illustrate the text? Try contacting other relatives to see what they have in their collections. Try including images of places your ancestors lived or activities they pursued. You can also start adding to your collection by following the tips presented in chapter eleven of *Uncovering Your Ancestry Through Family Photographs*.

6. Don't send originals to printers. Have copies made by following the suggestions offered in chapter two.

DISPLAYING FAMILY PHOTOGRAPHS

You don't have to create a family history to show off your images. Some people create a wall of honor in their home. Taking care of your images doesn't mean you can't put them on display as long as you take a few precautions. If you have historical photographs in your possession that are already framed, they need to be taken out of those frames before further damage is caused. A fairly typical nineteenth-century frame has the image flush against the glass, and the backing materials are either cardboard or wood. In these cases, the photograph is exposed to acid from the backing and is in danger of contact with condensation on the glass. What can you do if this is a special family image that you want to continue to display? There are a few easy and relatively inexpensive ways to keep that image on public view.

Use Copies

My historical photographs are too valuable to me to expose them to dangers by framing and displaying them. It is so easy to make copies. Most camera stores can produce same-size duplicates of your images. Since nineteenth- and early-twentieth-century photographs come in a variety of colors, you will want to use a color copying process so that your photographs retain their qualities. However, **if you want a historic feel to the picture, ask the lab to sepia tone it.** This means that the image will appear slightly brown and have the appearance of being old. This is usually available for an additional fee.

In cases where there are already double prints of a particular image, you can display a duplicate without risking the original. This is especially true of the photographs taken today, where you can order second copies when you have the film developed or when you have the negative. Before you copy contemporary photographs taken by a professional photographer, make sure you are not infringing on someone's copyright.

Tip

Reminder

FRAMING CHECKLIST

1. Use materials that have passed the PAT. 2. Select a frame that is baked enamel or aluminum. 3. Mat the image. 4. Find a framer with experience working with museum-quality framing.

Framing Materials

Special materials help you retain the quality of the image you want framed. You can request museum-quality framing methods when you take it to be framed. This means that the glass will offer protection from sunlight and the backing will be lignin- and acid-free. The basic parts of any frame are the glass, frame, and backing. Most professional frame shops carry UV-protection glass or acrylic that filters out the harmful rays of the sun. These ultraviolet rays are the same ones that cause skin cancer. They also cause images to fade or discolor. When selecting a frame, choose one that is baked enamel on metal or aluminum rather than wood. The wood gives off gases and acids that cause staining. The final element of a framed piece is the backing. Ask for acid- and lignin-free materials. If the framer doesn't have the necessary supplies, you can order them from one of the vendors in Appendix D.

There are a few other considerations. First, make sure the photograph is not dry mounted to the backing. Small strips of polypropylene or photo corners that are adhesive will work just as well and are reversible. Acceptable adhesives are wheat starch and rice starch paste. Second, place the

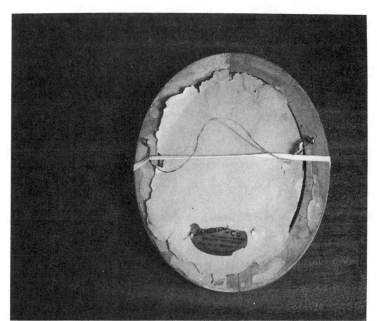

Figure 11-1.
Make sure you use PAT materials for framing so your pictures don't end up looking like this. The acid paper and wood frame may damage your photographs.
Lynn Betlock

photograph in a mat. This is an acid- and lignin-free card stock with an opening for the photograph. The mat prevents the image from resting on the glass and provides for some air circulation. This in turn prevents condensation damage to the image due to fluctuations of temperature and humidity and prevents the image from sticking to the glass.

Where to Display

Unless you don't mind replacing your images every few years, take care to display your images in a place that will extend their life spans. Find an area out of direct sunlight so the light and heat won't damage the prints. Keep in mind fireplaces and other heat sources, such as radiators, generate temperature fluctuations that cause deterioration of the prints. Choose an area that has a low light level. Sunlight and fluorescent light expose the images to UV rays.

Being careful with your photographs does not mean that you need to keep them completely out of sight. As long as you are preservation aware and follow museum-quality framing methods, you can enjoy your family photographs and show them off to visitors.

FAMILY REUNION ACTIVITIES

My husband's family has a reunion every year. This tradition started almost two generations ago, but the photograph albums of the event begin in the 1970s when someone finally appointed herself photographer. The annual event includes a group of zany activities but also includes time for family members to reminisce over the photo albums. The photographer brings all the volumes with her each year. When I attended my first reunion, part of how I learned about the family was to look at the albums. Taking all the

For More Info

CONSULT THE EXPERTS

If you want to frame items yourself, the instructions are provided in *The Life of a Photograph* by Laurence E. Keefe and Dennis Inch. They cover all topics from matting an image to creating a frame.

Tip

SELECTING FRAME SHOPS

1. Ask if they know how to provide museum-quality framing for an item. 2. Do they use PAT-approved materials? 3. Ask for references. For instance, do they work with museums and libraries?

Idea Generator

pictures and compiling the albums is a huge responsibility. Fortunately, the cousin responsible for it all loves the task.

You can use photographs in a variety of ways at family reunions besides compiling albums. **You can play a series of games using your family photographs.**

1. Matching games. If you have baby pictures of several family members, you could set up a matching game for kids and adults. This is a great opportunity to ask individuals to bring pictures with them that are not part of the family collection. The first one to successfully match the baby pictures with the right names wins.

2. Charades. In the late nineteenth century, our ancestors used stereographs of famous statues and scenes to play charades the same way some of us use movie titles and notable scenes. In most families, there is a series of photographs that depicts important family events or images that became family icons. For instance, you can choose to act out a scene from a set of

Figure 11-2.
Is it hard to figure out who the photographer was in your family?
Collection of the author

family images, such as a party or a wedding. Your audience can then try to guess who you are imitating or what scene you are reenacting. Sound confusing? Follow these steps.

- **Select a group of memorable images.** When you spent time with your pictures, you probably discovered that some are more memorable than others. It is not the point of the game to embarrass or ridicule individuals, so try to select images that do neither. Try to find action shots that can be pantomimed.
- **Use copies.** I feel like I've said this a hundred times, but it bears repeating. Use photocopies of images for this activity. The teams will want to handle the images to select an event to act out.
- **Act out the scene.** Once you've selected the images and convinced everyone that this is a fun activity, engage family members in a game of family photograph charades. This works for all ages and really can be a lot of fun.

3. Use images to identify family lines. At the larger reunions, I have trouble understanding extended family relationships. Rather than carrying around a family tree, there are visual ways to present relationships. At the Deely reunion, they decided to use different-colored shirts to identify the various lines of the family from one generation of siblings. You can also use copies of photographs attached to name tags that reinforce the sibling identification. High school reunions use old yearbook photos to jog memories, so why not try it with family photographs?

4. Have a mystery table. A reunion is a great way for relatives to become reacquainted with photographs. Have everyone bring a copy of an unidentified photograph. Post these on a bulletin board and see what happens. The older members of the family can probably help with the identification. You can then write the caption on the back of each copy.

5. Build your collection. Use the reunion as a photo-sharing activity and a way to build your collection. Wouldn't it be great to be able to find photographs of individuals missing from your family collection? This can happen by asking attendees to bring images with them to the reunion. You never know what stories can be added to a family history from a picture or what new knowledge can be gained from photographs held by relatives. Use the suggestions outlined in *Uncovering Your Ancestry Through Family Photographs*.

CREATING A BETTER FAMILY PHOTO COLLECTION

I have a relative, who shall remain anonymous, who takes pictures with her finger in front of the lens. After many years of trying to take good pictures, she decided to give up. It simply isn't something she does well. That doesn't have to be true for you.

Our photograph collections are an amalgamation of professionally posed studio portraits and candids shot by family members and friends. Unless someone in the family is a professional photographer, there are likely to be some

For More Info

FURTHER READING

If you need help planning a reunion, consult Donna Beasley and Donna Carter's *The Family Reunion Planner.*

Reminder

MOMENTS IN THE FAMILY ALBUM

1. The new baby
2. First day of school
3. Graduations
4. Weddings
5. Grandchildren

images in need of improvement. It is easier than ever before to take good pictures of your family. Cameras are available for every budget and skill level.

Every day we are bombarded with images in newspapers and magazines and on television. Through exposure to these pictures, our eyes and brains have learned to distinguish between a well-composed photograph and one of poor quality. While our eyes know the difference, it can be difficult to translate that knowledge into our own photographs. **By following the techniques and tips offered by professional photographers, it is possible to add great photographs to your family archive.**

1. Plan your pictures in advance. Even the most experienced photographer realizes that a certain amount of planning goes into getting a great shot. It is best to be prepared. If you are married, you may remember when your wedding photographer presented you with a list of possible photographic moments to include in your wedding album. Apply this technique to your family. Are there family milestones that you would like to see in your photograph album?

Many families videotape important events, but a still photograph can be a way to intimately record the small details rather than the overall event. Instead of videotaping your daughter's first play from the back row, why not shoot a few images of the preparations and create a story in still photographs? In twenty years, the photographs will still be around, but the videotape will be unusable.

Make a list of what activities or events you would like to see represented in your photograph collection. It isn't necessary to adhere to the list if you see another opportunity. The purpose is to keep you alert to what is important to you. Ask your children what photographs they would like to see in the family album. Not surprisingly, those will differ from your own. By taking their interests into consideration, you will be creating a collection that they will feel a part of.

There is a lot of living missing from the list of five items most apt to be found in contemporary and historical family photograph collections (see sidebar at left). The spontaneity of everyday life does not appear on any checklist. There are spontaneous moments worth documenting. In order to seize a photographic opportunity when it happens, you need to have your camera nearby loaded with film. Just remember that you can't re-create the unexpected.

2. Select an appropriate background. Since most of our pictures are in color, selecting an appropriate background can enhance or detract from the photographic quality. For instance, try to photograph individuals so that the background does not become the focus of the picture. A good example of what not to do is posing someone wearing brightly patterned clothing close to a busy, colorful backdrop. The two will compete visually for your attention. It would be best to contrast the clothing against a plain backing. This will improve the quality of your photograph.

In addition to color, you need to choose the right textural background for the subject and the focus of your image. Subtle textures can convey softness, while sharp edges are harsh and real. A natural background setting is easy to find and can even supply some props.

3. Use props. By now you are wondering how a photograph can be both planned and spontaneous. The answer is in the props. If you are going to photograph children, you will want to bring along a few items to keep them busy. What happens is that in the process of playing with things you brought along for distraction, the kids will begin to improvise. This creates un-planned and wonderful moments. A child in the act of exploring a hat can think of a myriad of ways to wear it or things to carry in it.

The addition of even one item to a photograph makes it more interesting. Props are not necessarily purchased for a photo opportunity. In fact, the best props are those that are found. Use available furniture in a photograph as something for people to sit on or lean against. Show people engaged in everyday activities, such as eating a holiday meal. A large piece of chocolate in a small child's hand is apt to cause a smile. In addition, the contrast between the size of the candy and the child's hand provides additional infor-mation about his age and size. Flowers and trees provide a backdrop for an outdoor portrait but can also double for props. Individuals can hold flowers, wear them in their hair, and even play with them.

The first photographers sought ways to improve their images through the use of simple props. The best photographers would have an assortment of shawls, jewelry, hats, and books to use. Props are a way of discovering new information about the interests of our family. Have relatives pose with favorite sports equipment, near their cars, or with their hobbies. In this way, you are creating a story with a single picture. These photographs become a way to document the interests and lives of your family.

4. Watch for dramatic lighting. Each element of a photograph adds a layer to the total impression of the image. For instance, lighting conveys emotion. It can be used to highlight a smile or the qualities of someone's eyes. Natural lighting can create a dramatic scene, while soft artificial light downplays the emotions. It is all in how you choose to use it.

5. Don't be afraid of the close-up. Probably the worst mistake we make with our images is not getting close enough to our subjects. By maintaining our distance, we allow other parts of our pictures to distract the viewers from our subjects. Photographing people is difficult, and many of us don't like to be photographed.

Tip

The single most important way for you to improve your images is to overcome the distance between yourself and the subject of the picture. This can be done by using a zoom lens or by standing just a little closer to the person. You can test this by taking two pictures of the same person. The first is a close-up where the head and shoulders or just the face fills the frame of the picture. In the second, step back from the subject and include his whole figure and a little bit of the background. Which one is better? Probably, the close-up. By eliminating all background distractions and getting close to the person, you bring him to life. The focus is on him rather than what is happening around him.

6. Take care of your film. One of the causes of poor pictures is film that has expired. This is especially true with Polaroid film. Before you purchase film, check the expiration date. If you are using color film, you can refrigerate it before exposure to protect it from heat and humidity. It might look strange to anyone who opens your refrigerator, but professional photographers use this technique to preserve the quality of their film. After shooting the roll of film, try to have it developed right away. Heat can still damage the film after it has been exposed.

7. Include yourself in family photographs. Is it hard to figure out who the family photographer in your family is? Probably not. It will be apparent just by looking at your pictures. The family photographer is usually missing from most of the images. Add interest to your photograph collection by taking the time to include yourself. Ask other people to take photographs of your family so that you can be included. You can even invest in a small tabletop tripod. This device allows you to set your camera's timer so you can become part of the story.

8. Use more than color. Add a little variety to your family album by shooting a few rolls of black-and-white film. A friend concerned about the stability of color prints had a professional photographer produce all of her wedding pictures in black and white. The photographer chose interesting backgrounds and created a beautiful album regardless of the lack of color.

9. Learn from the experts. Magazines often publish articles that give advice on how to become a better photographer. My relative, despite her best efforts, still includes part of her thumb in all of her pictures. No matter how hard she tries, there is always something wrong with her images. If this sounds familiar, then you will want to read as many manuals and articles as possible. The best part of these lessons is that they show you a photographic mistake and then how to improve it. In most cases, these lessons are easy to duplicate and are worth the expense of film and processing.

10. Practice. Once you have tried to incorporate all these professional tips into your family photographs, you need to practice. Think of every day as a photo opportunity.

Remember that whatever you decide to do with your family photographs, take steps to preserve them for the future. Follow the instructions offered by preservationists and librarians, and give your relatives photographic memorabilia that will last several generations.

CHECKLIST: HAVING FUN WITH YOUR FAMILY PHOTOGRAPHS

✓ Use photographs in your family history.
✓ Find ways to use them at family reunions.
✓ Be creative.
✓ Take better pictures.
✓ Encourage other family members to help you.

For More Info

FURTHER READING

Consult *How to Take Great Photographs With Any Camera* by Jerry Hughes if you are unsure how to improve your picture quality with your type of camera.

Notes

Glossary

Throughout this book are technical terms that may be unfamiliar to individuals who are new to working with family photographs. In addition to the list provided here, two encyclopedias that deal specifically with photographic terminology may be helpful. They are Gloria S. McDarrah, Fred W. McDarrah, and Timothy S. McDarrah's *The Photography Encyclopedia*, and *The Focal Encyclopedia of Photography* (third edition) edited by Leslie Stroebel and Richard Zakia (Boston: Focal Press, 1993). For nineteenth-century terminology, consult *Cassell's Cyclopedia of Photography* edited by Bernard E. Jones (New York: Cassell and Company, 1911, reprinted by Arno Press, 1973).

Abrasion: A type of damage that occurs when prints are rubbed against an object or each other. In certain prints, this will cause image loss and scratches.

Acid-free: Paper with a pH higher than 7.1.

Acidic: Paper having a pH lower than 7.1.

Airbrushing: Technique used for retouching photographs by applying paint with a tool called an air gun. This can be used to eliminate damage from a copy print.

Albumen print: Photographs made by coating paper with a combination of egg white and silver nitrate.

Ambrotype: A piece of glass coated with light-sensitive chemicals, introduced in the mid-1850s.

Archival: Materials or conditions that extend the longevity of the objects stored in them. An example is an acid- and lignin-free storage box with a pH more than 7.1.

Autochrome: Image created by coating grains of potato starch dyed red, green, and blue-violet onto a sheet of glass. They became commercially available in 1907 and were primarily used by professional photographers.

Cabinet card: A type of card photograph that measures 4½″ × 6½″.

Calotype: The first paper negative, invented by William Fox Talbot.

Candid photography: Photographs that lack the formality of studio portraits. It generally refers to pictures taken by amateur photographers after Kodak cameras became available.

Carte de visite: A small card photograph introduced to the United States in 1859. It measures 4¼″ × 2½″.

Collodion: A combination of ether, pyroxyline, and alcohol that was used to make prints and wet-plate negatives. It was also used on wounds during the Civil War.

Conservation: Professional treatments to stabilize a deteriorating object, in this case a photograph.

Contact print: Way of making photographs without enlarging the image. Until the invention of a way to enlarge images became available, all photographs were contact prints.

Copy stand: Special equipment either made at home or commercially manufactured to allow photographers to copy images.

Copyright: Legal right of ownership to an image or text.

Crayon portrait: Photograph enhanced by the use of artists' materials and techniques.

Cropping: Eliminating distracting elements from a photograph. Editors usually crop images prior to publication to improve their quality and to fit a particular space.

Daguerreotype: A one-of-a-kind photograph on a highly polished silver plate, introduced in 1839 by Louis Daguerre.

Developing-out paper: Photographs developed through the use of chemicals rather than those that appear during exposure to light. See *printing-out paper*.

Direct positive: Production of a copy print without the use of a negative.

DPI: Also known as dots per inch. It refers to the number of sensors per inch of scanning width. The greater the DPI, the clearer the image.

Dry-plate negative: Glass plate coated with light-sensitive chemicals and gelatin used when dry.

Emulsion: The light-sensitive part of a negative or paper.

Enhancements: Manipulating the chemicals, film, and exposure times used to copy an image to improve the quality of a faded print.

Ferrotype: See *tintype*.

Foxing: Reddish brown spots that appear on photographs as a result of a chemical reaction due to high humidity.

Generation: Copies of an original print not made with an original negative. It is usually associated with a loss of detail.

Hyalotype: Type of glass slide patented in 1850 by the Langenheim brothers.

Hygrometer: A device that measures and monitors the temperature and humidity in an area.

Image resolution: Refers to the amount of detail in an electronic image.

Improper processing: Photographic processing that fails to wash off residual chemicals.

Lantern slides: Positive images on glass that could be projected. They were popular for more than one hundred years.

Mylar: An inert plastic approved for the storage of negatives and photographs.

Negative: Reversed light and dark areas. In a color negative, the colors are reversed as well.

Nitrate: Nitrocellulose. It is a substance used to create negatives between 1889 and 1939. These negatives are highly unstable and are a fire hazard.

Off-gases: Fumes given off by substances such as plastic containers and carpets. These gases can damage photographs.

PAT: Photographic Activity Test that tests the reactivity of photographs to substances in manufacturer's photographic products.

Polyethylene: A type of plastic once thought safe for use with photographs and negatives. Conservators now caution against using it.

Polypropylene: A type of plastic approved for storing images and negatives.

Printing-out paper: Photograph that develops during exposure to light. See *developing-out paper*.

Relative humidity: The average amount of moisture measured in the air. Most archives maintain a relative humidity of 30 to 50 percent.

Restoration: The process of re-creating the appearance of an image.

RC paper: Photographic paper coated with resin, a type of plastic that became available in the 1960s.

Scanning: The process of converting an image to an electronic format.

Stereograph: Creating the appearance of a 3-D image by photographing the same thing from a similar angle. The images are mounted beside each other and viewed with a stereoscope.

Tintype: A type of photograph, also known as a ferrotype, that consisted of a piece of thin iron coated with light-sensitive chemicals.

Toning: Coating prints with a solution of gold or platinum to change their color and improve stability.

Transference: When two platinum prints are placed together front to back and the image from one transfers onto the back of the first image over time.

Transparency: Another name for a color slide or film positive.

Union case: A case invented by Samuel Peck in 1852 to hold photographs. The cases were manufactured from a combination of gum shellac and fiber but are mistakenly thought to be made of a type of plastic.

Wet plate: Glass negative made with light-sensitive chemicals and collodion that was used while wet. Photographers had to make their own negatives immediately prior to using them.

Sources of Family Photographs

Most state historical societies and other organizations maintain manuscript and photograph collections. Listed below are only those societies that I know to have collections. Find a full list of local historical societies by consulting Elizabeth Petty Bentley's *The Genealogist's Address Book*. Please contact the societies prior to sending them a request for photo research. Different rules and research guidelines may apply for this type of research. Remember that the best sources of family photographs are the collections of other relatives.

Alaska

Alaska Historical Society

1489 C St., Suite 202
P.O. Box 100299
Anchorage, AK 99510-0299
Phone: (907) 276-1596
Internet: http://www.alaska.net/~ahs

Arizona

Arizona Historical Society

949 E. Second St.
Tucson, AZ 85719
Phone: (520) 617-1157

California

California Historical Society

678 Mission St.
San Francisco, CA 94105
Phone: (415) 357-1848
Internet: http://www.calhist.org

Colorado

Colorado Historical Society

Stephen H. Hart Library
1300 Broadway
Denver, CO 80203-2137
Internet: http://www.coloradohistory.org

Denver Public Library

Western History Collection
10 W. Fourteenth Ave. Pkwy.
Denver, CO 80204-2731

Phone: (303) 640-6200

Internet: http://www.denver.lib.co.us

Connecticut

Connecticut Historical Society

1 Elizabeth St. at Asylum Ave.

Hartford, CT 06105

Internet: http://www.chs.org/library

Delaware

Historical Society of Delaware

505 N. Market St.

Wilmington, DE 19801-3091

Phone: (302) 655-7161

Internet: http://www.hsd.org

District of Columbia

Historical Society of Washington, D.C.

1307 New Hampshire Ave. NW

Washington, DC 20036-1507

Phone: (202) 785-2068

Internet: http://www.hswdc.org

National Archives (NARA)

Pennsylvannia Ave. at Eighth St. NW

Washington, DC 20408

Phone: (800) 788-6282

Internet: http://www.nara.gov

Florida

Florida Historical Society

1320 Highland Ave.

Melbourne, FL 32935

Phone: (407) 259-0947

Internet: http://www.florida-historical-soc.org/youfoundus.html

Georgia

Georgia Historical Society

501 Whitaker St.

Savannah, GA 31499

Phone: (912) 651-2128

Internet: http://www.georgiahistory.com

Hawaii

Hawaiian Historical Society

560 Kawaiahao St.

Honolulu, HI 96813
Internet: http://www.hawaiianhistory.org

Idaho
Idaho State Historical Society
450 N. Fourth St.
Boise, ID 83702
Phone: (208) 334-3357
Internet: http://www2.state.id.us/ishs/index.html

Illinois
Chicago Historical Society
1601 Clark St. at North Ave.
Chicago, IL 60614-9990
Phone: (312) 642-4600
Internet: http://www.chicagohistory.org
Illinois State Historical Society
1 Old Capitol Plaza
Springfield, IL 62701-1507
Phone: (217) 524-7216
Internet: http://www.prairienet.org/ishs

Indiana
Indiana Historical Society
Indiana State Library and Historical Bldg.
315 W. Ohio St.
P.O. Box 88255
Indianapolis, IN 46202
Internet: http://www.indianahistory.org

Iowa
State Historical Society of Iowa
Library/Archives Bureau
State of Iowa Historical Bldg.
600 E. Locust, Capitol Complex
Des Moines, IA 50319-0290
Phone: (515) 281-6200
Internet: http://www.iowahistory.org

Kansas
Kansas State Historical Society
6425 SW Sixth Ave.
Topeka, KS 66615-1099
Phone: (785) 272-8681
Internet: http://www.kshs.org

Kentucky
Kentucky Historical Society Library
P.O. Box 1792
Frankfort, KY 40602-1792
Phone: (502) 564-3016
Internet: http://www.kyhistory.org

Louisiana
Louisiana Historical Society
Maritime Bldg.
New Orleans, LA 70130
Phone: (504) 588-9044

Maine
Center for Maine History
485 Congress St.
Portland, ME 04101
Phone: (207) 774-1822
Internet: http://www.mainehistory.com/genealogy.html

Maryland
Maryland Historical Society
201 W. Monument St.
Baltimore, MD 21201
Phone: (410) 685-3750
Internet: http://www.mdhs.org
Steamship Historical Society of America, Baltimore
University of Baltimore Library
1420 Maryland Ave.
Baltimore, MD 21201

Massachusetts
Massachusetts Historical Society
1154 Boylston St.
Boston, MA 02215
Phone: (617) 536-1608
Internet: http://www.masshist.org
New England Historic Genealogical Society
101 Newbury St.
Boston, MA 02116
Phone: (617) 536-5740
Internet: http://www.newenglandancestors.org

Michigan
Historical Society of Michigan
2117 Washtenaw Ave.

Ann Arbor, MI 48104
Phone: (734) 769-1828
Internet: http://www.hsofmich.org

Minnesota
Minnesota Historical Society
345 Kellogg Blvd. West
Saint Paul, MN 55102-1906
Phone: (612) 296-6126
Internet: http://www.mnhs.org

Mississippi
Mississippi Historical Society
P.O. Box 571
Jackson, MS 39205-0571
Phone: (601) 359-6850
Internet: http://www.mdah.state.ms.us/admin/mhistsoc.html

Missouri
State Historical Society of Missouri
1020 Lowry St.
Columbia, MO 65201-7298
Phone: (573) 882-7083
Internet: http://www.system.missouri.edu/shs

Montana
Montana Historical Society
P.O. Box 201201
Helena, MT 59620
Phone: (406) 444-4702
Internet: http://www.his.state.mt.us/

Nebraska
Nebraska State Historical Society
P.O. Box 82554
Lincoln, NE 68501-2554
Phone: (402) 471-4771
Internet: http://www.nebraskahistory.org

Nevada
Nevada Historical Society
1650 N. Virginia St.
Reno, NV 89503
Phone: (702) 688-1190
Internet: http://dmla.clan.lib.nv.us/docs/museums/reno/his-soc.htm

New Hampshire

New Hampshire Historical Society
30 Park St.
Concord, NH 03301-6384
Phone: (603) 271-2236
Internet: http://www.nhhistory.org

New Jersey

New Jersey Historical Society Library
52 Park Pl.
Newark, NJ 07102
Phone: (973) 596-8500

New York

New-York Historical Society
2 W. Seventy-seventh St.
New York, NY 10024
Phone: (212) 873-3400
Internet: http://www.nyhistory.org

North Carolina

Federation of North Carolina Historical Societies
109 E. Jones St.
Raleigh, NC 27601-2807
Phone: (919) 733-7305

North Dakota

State Historical Society of North Dakota
State Archives and Historical Research Library
North Dakota Heritage Center
612 E. Boulevard Ave.
Bismarck, ND 58505-0830
Phone: (701) 328-2668
Internet: http://www.state.nd.us/hist

Ohio

Ohio Historical Society
Archives—Library Division
Interstate Route 71 and Seventeenth Ave.
1982 Velma Ave.
Columbus, OH 43211-2497
Phone: (614) 297-2510
Internet: http://www.ohiohistory.org

Oklahoma

Oklahoma Historical Society
Library Resources Division

Wiley Post Historical Bldg.
2100 North Lincoln Blvd.
Oklahoma City, OK 73105-4997
Phone: (405) 521-2491
Internet: http://www.ok-history.mus.ok.us

Oregon
Oregon Historical Society
Oregon Historical Records Advisory Board
1200 SW Park Ave.
Portland, OR 97205
Phone: (503) 222-1741
Internet: http://www.ohs.org

Pennsylvania
Historical Society of Pennsylvania
1300 Locust St.
Philadelphia, PA 19107-5699
Phone: (215) 732-6200
Internet: http://www.hsp.org
United States Army Military History Institute
Attn: Special Collections
22 Ashburn Dr.
Carlisle, PA 17013-5008
Internet: http://Carlisle-www.army.mil/usamhi/photoDB.html

South Carolina
South Carolina Historical Society
Fireproof Bldg.
100 Meeting St.
Charleston, SC 29401-2299
Phone: (843) 723-3225
Internet: http://www.schistory.org

South Dakota
South Dakota State Historical Society
South Dakota State Archives
Cultural Heritage Center
900 Governors Dr.
Pierre, SD 57501-2217
Phone: (605) 773-3805
Internet: http://www.sdhistory.org/archives.htm

Tennessee
Tennessee Historical Society
Ground Floor

War Memorial Bldg.
300 Capital Blvd.
Nashville, TN 37243-0084
Phone: (615) 741-8934

Texas
Texas State Historical Association
2.306 SRH University Station
Austin, TX 78712
Phone: (512) 471-1525
Internet: http://www.tsha.utexas.edu

Utah
Utah State Historical Society
300 Rio Grande
Salt Lake City, UT 84101-1182
Phone: (801) 533-3500

Vermont
Vermont Historical Society
Pavilion Office Bldg.
109 State St.
Montpelier, VT 05609-0901
Phone: (802) 828-2291
Internet: http://www.state.vt.us/vhs

Virginia
Virginia Historical Society Library
P.O. Box 7311
Richmond, VA 23221
Phone: (804) 342-9677
Internet: http://www.vahistorical.org

Washington
Washington State Historical Society
Special Collections Division
315 N. Stadium Way
Tacoma, WA 98403
Phone: (253) 798-5914
Internet: http://www.wshs.org

West Virginia
West Virginia Historical Society
West Virginia Division of Culture and History
The Cultural Center
Capitol Complex, 1900 Kanawha Blvd. East

Charleston, WV 25305-0300
Phone: (304) 348-2277
Internet: http://www.wvculture.org/history/wvhssoc.html

Wisconsin

State Historical Society of Wisconsin Library

816 State St.
Madison, WI 53706
Phone: (608) 264-6460
Internet: http://www.shsw.wisc.edu

Wyoming

Wyoming State Historical Society

1740 H184 Dell Range Blvd.
Cheyenne, WY 82002
Phone: (307) 635-4881

Timeline of Events

1826/27	Nicephore Niepce, an inventor, uses a camera obscura to capture an image. It takes eight hours to create the picture. A camera obscura projects an image through a hole in a wall of a dark room. Niepce's view wasn't rediscovered until 1952.
1835	William Henry Fox Talbot, a scientist, announces his paper photographic process to the Royal Society of London. He calls them photogenic drawings.
1839	An English patent is issued to Louis Daguerre, an artist who painted theatrical scenes, for a method of capturing images on metal. He was partnered with Niepce from 1826 until Niepce's death in 1833.

- Daguerre writes *An Historical and Descriptive Account of the Various Processes of the Daguerreotype and the Diorama*, a nineteenth-century best-seller.
- Technique for capturing images on glass is invented.
- This may be the first time the word *photography* is used. This is credited to Sir John F.W. Herschel, although a Brazilian inventor, Hercules Florence, may have used the term in 1833.

1840	François Gouraud visits America and demonstrates the daguerreotype process.

- The first daguerreotype portrait studio opens in New York City.
- The first school photograph is taken by Samuel F.B. Morse of the Yale class of 1810.
- Talbot discovers a method for developing an image on paper and patents the process. He calls it the calotype.

1842	Patent for coloring daguerreotypes is issued to B.F. Stevens and L. Morse.

- The cyanotype process is announced.

1844	Talbot publishes *The Pencil of Nature*.
1849	Glass lantern slides can project photographic images.
1850	Mathew Brady publishes *The Gallery of Illustrious Americans*. It contains portraits and biographies of prominent American citizens.

- 1850 census lists 938 males over the age of fifteen with the occupation of daguerreotypist.
- The Langenheim brothers of Philadelphia commercially introduce stereoscopic views.
- The albumen print becomes popular.

- The first photographic journal, the *Daguerreian Journal*, is published.

1851 Frederick Scott Archer introduces the wet-plate, or wet-collodion, negative process. It is faster than all other processes.

1852 Samuel Peck patents the first "union case," consisting of gum shellac and fiber.

1853 Hamilton L. Smith of Ohio introduces the tintype.

1854 James Ambrose Cutting is issued a patent for the ambrotype.

1855 Roger Fenton takes the first battlefield photographs of the Crimean War.

1856 Alexander Gardner introduces a process for making photographic enlargements.

1857 The duke of Parma introduces the carte de visite.

1859 Cartes de visite are brought to America.

1860 The carte de visite is mentioned in an ad in *Frank Leslie's Illustrated Weekly* by S.A. Holmes.
- First aerial photograph is taken in Boston.
- Tintype is used as a campaign medal for the first time.
- Collodion dry plate is introduced.
- First albums are imported into the United States.

1861 First patent is issued for a photograph album.
- Amateur Photographic Exchange Club forms.

1862 Red, yellow, and blue are recognized as basic components of all other colors.

1864 Marcus A. Root publishes *The Camera and the Pencil*, the first history of American photography.

1864–66 Revenue stamps are required for photographs.

1866 Cabinet card photographs are introduced.

1868 Photographic retouching is available.
- H.M. Crider introduces photographic marriage certificates.

1869 Celluloid film, a combination of collodion and camphor, becomes available. This is the beginning of low-cost roll film.

1870 William Henry Jackson photographs Yellowstone. Later the U.S. Congress uses the photographs to decide to make the area a national park.

1878 Factory-produced dry-plate negatives become available.

1880 First photograph appears in a newspaper, the *New York Daily Graphic*.

1881 Professional Photographers of America is established.

1884 Flashlight photography using magnesium light is available.

1888 Kodak roll film camera is introduced. "You press the button, we do the rest."
- Moving pictures are invented.

1895 Lumiere brothers show moving picture films to an audience.

1907 Lumiere brothers invent the autochrome process.

1914	Kodak issues the No.1 Autographic Kodak Jr., which allows a photographer to write date, name, place on film. These were made until 1934.
1929	The first flashbulbs are invented.
1935	Kodak's 16mm movie film becomes available.
1936	Eastman Kodak makes Kodachrome, a low-cost color slide film, commercially available.
1944	Kodak announces Kodacolor, a color negative film.
1947	Edwin Land announces a one-step photo process that develops in less than a minute.
1957	Edwin Land announces full-color Polaroid pictures.
1963	Kodak issues the Instamatic and sells 7.5 million in two years and 70 million in ten years.
1965	Public begins using flashcubes.
1972	Polaroid introduces the SX-70. • Kodak offers 110 camera and film. • Videodiscs are first available.
1978	U.S. Supreme Court rules professional studio photographers own the copyrights to pictures they take for clients.
1980	Marielen and Anthony Christensen display their scrapbooks at the World Conference on Records in Salt Lake City, Utah. • First autofocus cameras become available from Canon.
1982	Kodak markets disc film and camera.
1986	Video camcorders are introduced.
1987	Creative Memories commercially produces scrapbook materials.
1988	Electronic scanners become available.
1991	Kodak makes photo CDs available. • Kodak Professional Digital Camera System weighs more than eleven pounds.
1994	Desktop computers have the capability of printing good-quality digital images.

Important Addresses

Conservators

American Institute for Conservation of Historic & Artistic Works, Inc. (AIC)
Conservation Services Referral System
1717 K. St. NW, Suite 200
Washington, DC 20006
Phone: (202) 452-9545
E-mail: info@aic-faic.org
Internet: http://aic.stanford.edu

Conservation Center for Art & Historic Artifacts (CCAHA)
264 S. Twenty-third St.
Philadelphia, PA 19103
Phone: (215) 545-0613

Northeast Document Conservation Center (NEDCC)
100 Brickstone Sq.
Andover, MA 01810
Phone: (508) 470-1010

Ocker & Trapp
17 A Palisade Ave.
Emerson, NJ 07630-0229

Washington Conservation Guild
P.O. Box 23364
Washington, DC 20026
Internet: http://palimpsest.stanford.edu/wcg

Magazines

Photography Related

Afterimage
31 Prince St.
Rochester, NY 14607
Phone: (716) 442-8676
E-mail: afterimg@servtech.com
Internet: http://www.rit.edu/~vswwww/afterindex.html

Amateur Photographer
IPC Magazines
Specialist Magazine Group
King's Reach Tower
Stamford St.
London SE1 9LS, England
Also available in microform, published since 1884.

American Photo
>Hachette Filipacchi Magazines
>1633 Broadway, 45th Floor
>New York, NY 10019
>Bimonthly since 1978.

Digital Camera Magazine
>Aeon Publishing Group
>88 Sunnyside Blvd., Suite 203
>Plainview, NY 11803
>Bimonthly.

Digital Photographer
>Miller Magazines
>4880 Market St.
>Ventura, CA 93003-7783
>Bimonthly.

Electronic Photography News
>Photofinishing News Inc.
>100915 Bonita Beach Rd.
>Bonita Springs, FL 33923
>Phone: (813) 992-4421
>Internet: http://www.photo-news.com/MainPages/epn.htm

Exposure (Dallas)
>Society for Photographic Education
>P.O. Box 222116
>Dallas, TX 75222-2116
>Semiannually since 1963.

Family Photo
>Petersen Publishing Co.
>110 Fifth Ave., 2d Floor
>New York, NY 10011
>Bimonthly since 1996.

History of Photography
>Taylor & Francis Ltd.
>Rankine Rd.
>Basingstoke, Hants RG24 8PR England
>American subscription:
>Taylor & Francis Inc.
>1900 Frost Rd., Suite 101
>Bristol, PA 19007-1598
>Internet: http://www.tandf.co.uk (U.S. http://www.taylorandfrancis.com)
>Since 1976.

Image
>George Eastman House
>International Museum of Photography and Film
>900 East Ave.

Rochester, NY 14607
Semiannually since 1952.

Petersen's Photographic
Petersen's Publishing Group
6420 Wilshire Blvd.
Los Angeles, CA 90048
Subscription Box 5004
Boulder, CO 80323
Since 1972.

Photo District News
A/S/M Communications Inc.
1515 Broadway
New York, NY 10036
Internet: http://www.pdn-pix.com
Monthly since 1980.

Photo Electronic Imaging
Professional Photographers of America
57 Forsyth St. NW, Suite 16600
Atlanta, GA 30303
Internet: http://www.peimag.com
Monthly since 1958.

Photograph Collector
Photo Review
301 Hill Ave., Suite 2
Langhorne, PA 19047
Monthly since 1980.

Photographica
American Photographic Historical Society
1150 Sixth Ave., 3d Floor
New York, NY 10036-2701
Quarterly since 1969.

Popular Photography
Hachette Filipacchi Magazines, Inc.
1633 Broadway
New York, NY 10019
Subscription: 54912
Boulder, CO 80322
Monthly since 1937.

Shutterbug (annual buying guide)
Patch Communications
5211 S. Washington Ave.
Titusville, FL 32780
Since 1971.

Stereo World
National Stereoscopic Association Inc.
P.O. Box 14801

Columbus, OH 43214
Bimonthly since 1974.

Scrapbook Magazines

Creating Keepsakes
P.O. Box 469007
Escondido, CA 92046-9007
$22.97 for ten issues (one year).

International Scrapbook News
International Scrapbook Trade Association
P.O. Box 295250
Lewisville, TX 75029-5250
Phone: (972) 318-0492
$21.95 for a one-year membership.

Memory Makers
Subscription Services
P.O. Box 7253
Bensenville, IL 60106-7253
Phone: (303) 452-0048
E-mail: letters@memorymakersmagazine.com
$24.95 for six issues (one year).

Societies and Organizations

American Library Association
50 E. Huron
Chicago, IL 60611
Phone: (800) 545-2433
Internet: http://www.ala.org
Organization for professional librarians.

American Photographic Artisans Guild (APAG)
212 Monroe
P.O. Box 699
Port Clinton, OH 43452
Phone: (419) 732-3290
Internet: http://www.apag.net
Founded in 1966 and affiliated with the Professional Photographers of America <http://www.ppa.com>. This organization sponsors educational opportunities for the color artist and retoucher.

American Photographic Historical Society (APHS)
1150 Avenue of the Americas
New York, NY 10036
Phone: (212) 575-0483
Internet: http://www.superexpo.com /aphs
Established in 1969. Members consist of individuals interested in photo history.

American Society of Camera Collectors (ASCC)

4918 Alcove Ave.

North Hollywood, CA 91607

Phone: (818) 769-9160

Established in 1978. Membership is open to collectors of photographic materials and photo historians.

American Society of Media Photographers (ASMP)

14 Washington Rd., Suite 502

Princeton Junction, NJ 08550-1033

Phone: (609) 799-8300

Internet: http://www.asmp.org

Professional organization for freelance photographers founded in 1944. The *ASMP Professional Business Practices in Photography* is a guide for professional photographers and their clients.

American Society of Picture Professionals (ASPP)

409 S. Washington St.

Alexandria, VA 22314

Phone: (703) 299-0219

Internet: http://www.aspp.com

A professional organization for photographers, picture researchers, photo editors, and librarians. The ASPP maintains a membership directory and operates regional chapters.

Association of Professional Genealogists (APG)

P.O. Box 40393

Denver, CO 80204-0393

Internet: http://www.apgen.org

Membership organization of professional genealogists that maintains business practices for members and their clients. The APG publishes a directory of its members both in print and online.

Daguerreian Society

3045 W. Liberty Ave., Suite 7

Pittsburgh, PA 15216-2460

Phone: (412) 343-5525

Internet: http://www.daguerre.org

Membership open to individuals interested in the daguerreotype, an early photograph. It sponsors a yearly conference and publishes the *Daguerreian Annual*, a collection of articles on the history of the daguerreotype.

International Center of Photography (ICP)

1130 Fifth Ave.

New York, NY 10128

Phone: (212) 860-1777

Internet: http://www.icp.org

Founded in 1974. The center maintains a reference library and houses a permanent collection of photographic materials. It also offers a master of arts degree in collaboration with New York University.

International Kodak Historical Society

P.O. Box 21

Flourtown, PA 19031

Phone: (215) 233-2032

Established in 1970. Membership is open to individuals interested in Kodakiana and history of the Eastman Kodak Company.

International Photographic Historical Organization (INPHO)

P.O. Box 16074

San Francisco, CA 94116

Phone: (415) 681-4356

Founded in 1985. Membership consists of individuals and organizations studying photo history. The organization maintains a reference library.

International Scrapbook Trade Association

P.O. Box 295250

Lewisville, TX 75029-5250

Phone: (972) 318-0492

Publishes *International Scrapbook News*, a bimonthly newsletter.

National Stereoscopic Association (NSA)

P.O. Box 14801

Columbus, OH 43214

Phone: (219) 272-5431

Internet: http://www.nsa-3d.org

Promotes the use and history of stereoscopy. It is concerned with both the history of three-dimensional photography and its contemporary applications. Affiliated with the Stereoscopic Society of America, it formed in 1974.

Photo Marketing Association International (PMA)

3000 Picture Pl.

Jackson, MI 49201

Phone: (517) 788-8100

Internet: http://www.pmai.org

Trade marketing association for photographic retailers and photographic processors.

Photographic Art and Science Foundation (PASF)

111 Stratford

Des Plaines, IL 60016-2105

Phone: (708) 824-6855

Established in 1965 by the Professional Photographers of America. It sponsors educational programs on photography and maintains a library that is open to the public.

Photographic Historical Society

P.O. Box 39563

Rochester, NY 14604

Internet: http://www.rit.edu/~andpph/tphs.html

Founded in 1965. This small organization is for anyone interested in the history of photography.

Photographic Historical Society of Canada

P.O. Box 54620

RPO Avenue Fairlawn

Toronto, Ontario M5M 4N5 Canada

Internet: http://web.onramp.ca/phsc

Founded in 1974. This society brings together information and people interested in the history of photography in Canada.

The Society of American Archivists

527 S. Wells St., 5th Floor

Chicago, IL 60607-3922

Phone: (312) 922-0140

Fax: (312) 347-1452

E-mail: info@archivists.org

Internet: http://www.archivists.org

Stereo Photographers Collectors & Enthusiasts Club (SPCEC)

P.O. Box 2368

Culver City, CA 90231

Membership organization established in 1978 for anyone involved with stereo photography.

Suppliers

Conservation Supplies

The companies listed below sell materials for the long-term storage and preservation of photographs, including boxes, folders, protective sleeves, and albums. They also furnish catalogs free of charge.

Archival Products

P.O. Box 1413

Des Moines, IA 50305-1413

Phone: (800) 526-5640

Internet: http://www.archival.com

Bags Unlimited

7 Canal St.

Rochester, NY 14608

Phone: (800) 767-2247

Internet: http://bagsunlimited.com

Clear File, Inc.

P.O. Box 593433

Orlando, FL 32859-3433

Phone: (800) 423-0274

Conservation Materials Ltd.

1165 Marietta Way

P.O. Box 2884

Sparks, NV 89431

Conservation Resources
8000-H Forbes Pl.
Springfield, VA 22151
Phone: (800) 634-6932
Internet: http://www.conservationresources.com

Exposures
1 Memory La.
Oshgosh, WI 54903-3615
Phone: (800) 572-5750

Gaylord Bros.
P.O. Box 4901
Syracuse, NY 13221-4901
Phone: (800) 448-6160
Internet: http://www.gaylord.com

Hollinger
P.O. Box 6185
Arlington, VA 22206
Phone: (800) 634-0491
Internet: http://www.hollinger.com

Light Impressions
439 Monroe Ave.
P.O. Box 940
Rochester, NY 14603-0940
Phone: (800) 828-6216
Internet: http://www.lightimpressionsdirect.com

Metal Edge
6340 Bandini Blvd.
Commerce, CA 90040
Phone: (800) 862-2228
Internet: http://www.metaledgeinc.com

Paige Co.
Parker Plaza
400 Kelby St.
Fort Lee, NJ 07024
Phone: (800) 957-2443

University Products
517 Main St.
P.O. Box 101
Holyoke, MA 01041-010
Phone: (800) 762-1165
Internet: http://www.universityproducts.com

Scrapbook Suppliers

A more complete list of scrapbook suppliers appears in the back of *Memory Makers* and *Creating Keepsakes* magazines. Their addresses appear on page 202.

C-Line Products, Inc.
1100 Business Center Dr.
Mt. Prospect, IL 60056
Phone: (888) 860-9120

Doumar Products, Inc.
12784 Perimeter Dr., Suite B-100
Dallas, TX 75228
Phone: (888) 289-8638
Internet: http://www.un-du.com

Family Treasures
24922 Anza Dr., Unit A
Valencia, CA 91355
Phone: (800) 413-2645

Fiskars
7811 W. Stewart Ave.
Wausau, WI 54401
Internet: http://www.fiskars.com

Generations by Hazel
Eagle OPG, Inc.
St. Louis, MO 63141
Phone: (800) 282-7281
Internet: http://www.generationsbyhazel.com

Keepsake Keepers
Plaid Enterprises
P.O. Box 2835
Norcross, GA 30091
Phone: (800) 842-4197

3D Keepers
Deja Views
Internet: http://www.cthruruler.com

3L Corp.
685 Chaddick Dr.
Wheeling, IL 60090-0247
Phone: (847) 808-1140
Internet: http://www.3l.dk/index.asp

Software
Directory of Genealogy Programs
Ancestral Quest
The Hope Foundation
9547 South 700 East
Sandy, UT 84070
Phone: (800) 825-8864 or (801) 816-1939
Internet: http://www.ancestralquest.com

Family Origins
Parsons Technology

1700 Progress Dr.
P.O. Box 100
Hiawatha, IA 52233-0100
Phone: (800) 779-6000
Fax: (319) 395-7449
Internet: http://www.formalsoft.com

Family Treasures
Family Technologies
P.O. Box 309
Westfield, NY 14787-0309
Phone: (800) 770-0567
Fax: (716) 792-9679
Internet: http://www.famtech.com/FamilyTres.htm

Family Tree Maker
Genealogy.com
P.O. Box 7865
Fremont, CA 94537-7865
Phone: (800) 315-0672
Internet: http://www.familytreemaker.com/ftmvers.html

Generations
Vivendi Interactive Universal
P.O. Box 629000
El Dorado Hills, CA 95762
Phone: (800) 757-7707

Master Genealogist
Wholly Genes Software
5144 Flowertuft Ct.
Columbia, MD 21044
Internet: http://www.whollygenes.com/html/catalog.htm#tmgwin

Reunion (Macintosh)
Leister Productions
P.O. Box 289
Mechanicsburg, PA 17055
Phone: (717) 697-1378
Internet: http://www.leisterpro.com

Scrapbook Software
American Greetings Scrapbooks & More (software)
Call Mattel (800) 395-0277
Internet: http://www.shopmattel.com

Copying and Restoration Services

Copy and Restoration
P.O. Box 7058
San Mateo, CA 94403
Internet: http://www.1800copy.com

Duplitech
P.O. Box 4154
Salem, OR 97302
Phone: (503) 378-0751

Foxchase Photography
4537 Duke St.
Alexandria, VA 22304
Phone: (888) 730-3746
Internet: http://www.foxchasephoto.com

Heritage Photographs
214 First Ave. South
Seattle, WA 98104
Phone: (206) 343-2363
Internet: http://home1.gte.net/peathon

Just Black and White
54 York St.
P.O. Box 4628
Portland, ME 04112
Phone: (800) 827-5881
Internet: http://www.maine.com/photos

Pam Keyes Imaging
109 N. Main
Miami, OK 74354
Phone: (800) 616-1332
Internet: http://www.portraitfixer.com

Photo Synthesis
P.O. Box 9613
Salt Lake City, UT 84109
Phone: (800) 309-8656
Fax: (801) 268-2912
Internet: http://www.xmission.com/~photosyn

Archival Storage Facilities

Iron Mountain
745 Atlantic Ave.
Boston, MA 02111
Phone: (617) 535-4766

Fax: (617) 350-7881

Internet: http://www.ironmountain.com

Safesite Records Management Corporation

96 High St.

P.O. Box 330

North Billerica, MA 01862

Phone: (800) 255-8218

Fax: (978) 670-5406

Cellulose Nitrate Storage

Hazeltine Vaults

7601 Hazeltine Ave.

North Hollywood, CA

Phone: (818) 781-7049

Hollywood Vaults

742 Seward St.

Hollywood, CA 90038

Phone: (213) 461-6464

Internet: http://www.hollywoodvaults.com

WRS Motion Picture and Video Laboratory

1000 Napor Blvd.

Pittsburgh, PA 15205-1501

Phone: (800) 345-6977 or (412) 937-7700

Fax: (412) 922-2418

Conference Lectures—Repeat Performance

Tapes can be ordered from AudioTapes.com, 2911 Crabapple Lane, Hobart, IN 46342 (219) 465-1234 , fax (219) 477-5492, e-mail info@audio tapes.com, Web site <http://www.audiotapes.com>.

Barton, Noel R. "Photograph History and Analysis." Salt Lake City: National Genealogical Society Conference, 1985. Audio tape number SLC-128.

———. "Using Photography in Your Family History Research." Salt Lake City: National Genealogical Society Conference, 1985. Audio tape number SLC-182.

Baylis, Barbara Roberts. "Photography—A Tool for Genealogists." Dallas, Tex.: Federation of Genealogical Societies Conference and the Dallas Genealogical Society, 1997. Audio tape number FGD-T-56.

Davis, Grant. "How to Obtain Pictures and Use Them to Produce Audio-Visual History." Salt Lake City: National Genealogical Society Conference, 1985. Audio tape number SLC-252.

Gartel, E. and J. Cotton. "Basic Techniques for Preservation of Manuscripts and Photographs." Raleigh, N.C.: National Genealogical Society Conference, 1987. Audio tape number RNC-57.

Gehring, Jake. "Multimedia and Scanning." Denver, Colo.: National Genealogical Society Conference, 1998. Audio tape number Den98W25.

Jiloty, Richard S., Bob McKeever, and Terry Deglau. "Copying of Photographs: Electronically and Traditionally." Audio tape number RH-T-44.

———. "Electronic and Traditional Photography and the Genealogy, an Image Scanning Overview." Audio tape number RH-S-105.

Kemp, Leatrice. "Dating Your Photographs." Federation of Genealogical Societies Conference. Audio tape number RNY-131.

Ledden, Larry. "Scanning, Hardware, Software Techniques." San Diego, Calif.: National Genealogical Society Conference, 1995. Audio tape number SD-146.

Lener, DeWayne. "Using Photography for Genealogy." Dallas, Tex.: GENTECH Conference, 1994. Audio tape number GT-07.

———. "Your Camera in Genealogy." Dallas, Tex.: GENTECH Conference, 1995. Audio tape number DTX-F-09.

Miller, Ilene. "Bring Your Family to Life With Photos and Computers." Seattle, Wash.: Federation of Genealogical Societies Conference, 1995. Audio tape number SW-111.

Mishkin, David. "Photographic Identification, Preservation and Restoration." Providence, R.I.: National Genealogical Society Conference, 2000. Audio tape number 00NGS-W35.

———. "Preservation of Modern Imaging Techniques." Providence, R.I.: National Genealogical Society Conference, 2000. 00NGS-S189.

Owen, Chester. "Dating Family Photographs Taken During the Period

1839–1900." Houston, Tex.: National Genealogical Society Conference, 1994. Audio tape number HT-48A. Two tapes.

Reilly, Prof. James M. "Preserving Images Into the Next Millenium." Rochester, N.Y.: Federation of Genealogical Societies Conference. Audio tape number RH-T-20.

Taylor, Maureen A. "Bringing the Past to Light: Understanding and Caring for Your Family Photographs." Richmond, Va.: National Genealogical Society Conference, 1999. Audio tape number NGS-135.

Web Sites of Interest

There is a lot of information online on preserving and identifying photographs. Here are a few of my favorite sites. To locate more, use a standard search engine and search for "photo preservation." You can also find relevant links on Cyndislist.com under "Photographs & Memories."

Ancestors Found
http://www.geocities.com/heartland/prairie/6248/ancestors/found.html
Help for identifying photographs or items that individuals would like to return to the right family.

City Gallery
http://www.city-gallery.com
Offers opportunity to join a mailing list or just read insightful articles on photo history.

Civil War Family Photographs
http://members.tripod.com/~cwphotos
Site for sharing your photographs of Civil War participants.

Clarke Historical Library at the University of Michigan
http://www.lib.cmich.edu/clarke/pres.htm
Online preservation advice that includes information on scrapbooks and electronic media.

CoOL (Conservation Online)
http://palimpsest.stanford.edu
Resources for professional conservators and the general public.

Daguerreian Society
http://www.daguerre.org
Online exhibits of daguerreotypes and useful links.

Document and Photo Preservation by Linda Beyea
http://genweb.net/~gen-cds/faq.html
Answers frequently asked questions pertaining to preservation.

George Eastman House
http://www.eastman.org
Features a timeline of photographic history and access to database of photographers.

Making of America
http://www.umdl.umich.edu/moa
Nineteenth- and early-twentieth-century publications accessible in this digital library.

Minnesota Historical Society
http://www.mnhs.org/preserve/conservation/photpres.html
> Preservation advice from the society's curators and conservationists.

National Archives and Records Administration
http://www.nara.gov/arch/faqs/aboutph.html
> Questions about photographic materials.

Nebraska Gen Web Ancestors Lost and Found
http://www.rootsweb.com/neresour/ancestors/index.html/
> Listings just for Nebraska.

Northeast Document Conservation Center
http://www.nedcc.org
> Online preservation tips from this respected conservation lab in New England.

Wallace Library Guides
http://wally.rit.edu/pubs/guides/photobio.html
> Features bibliographies for nineteenth-century photographic processes.

Scrapbooking Web Sites

dMarie
http://www.dmarie.com
> Has a special section devoted to heritage albums.

Hallmark
www.hallmark.com/
> Offers ideas using acid-free and lignin-free products in the Scrapbooking section of its site. You can purchase these materials online or in one of the Hallmark retail stores.

The Scrapbooking Idea Network
http://www.scrapbooking.com
> Has a monthly article on heritage albums.

ScrapNet
http://www.scrapnet.com
> Virtual classes, contests, and new products.

APPENDIX H

Professional Study Programs

Accredited Degree Programs in Library Science

For a complete list of up-to-date accredited programs, consult the American Library Association, 50 E. Huron, Chicago, IL 60611, (800) 545-2433 <http://www.ala.org>.

Alabama

The University of Alabama
School of Library and Information Studies
P.O. Box 870252
Tuscaloosa, AL 35487-0252
Phone: (205) 348-4610
Fax: (205) 348-3746
Internet: http://www.slis.ua.edu

Arizona

University of Arizona
School of Information Resources and Library Science
1515 E. First St.
Tucson, AZ 85719
Phone: (520) 621-3565
Fax: (520) 621-3279
E-mail: sirls@u.arizona.edu
Internet: http://www.sir.arizona.edu

California

San Jose State University
School of Library and Information Science
One Washington Sq.
San Jose, CA 95192-0029
Phone: (408) 924-2490
Fax: (408) 924-2476
E-mail: office@wahoo.sjsu.edu
Internet: http://witloof.sjsu.edu

University of California, Los Angeles
Department of Information Studies
Graduate School of Education and Information Studies
2320 Moore Hall, Mailbox 951521, Los Angeles, CA 90095-1521
Phone: (310) 825-8799
Fax: (310) 206-3076
Internet: http://is.gseis.ucla.edu

Connecticut

Southern Connecticut State University

School of Communication, Information and Library Science

Department of Library Science and Instructional Technology

Dean: Edward C. Harris

Admissions Contact: Nancy Disbrow

501 Crescent St.

New Haven, CT 06515

Phone: (203) 392-5781

Fax: (203) 392-5780

E-mail: libscienceit@scsu.ctstateu.edu

District of Columbia

The Catholic University of America

School of Library and Information Science

Washington, DC 20064

Phone: (202) 319-5085

Fax: (202) 319-5574

E-mail: cua-slis@cua.edu

Internet: http://www.cua.edu

Florida

Florida State University

School of Information Studies

Tallahassee, FL 32306-2100

Phone: (850) 644-5775

Fax: (850) 644-9763

Internet: http://www.fsu.edu/~lis

University of South Florida

School of Library and Information Science

4202 E. Fowler Ave., CIS 1040

Tampa, FL 33620-7800

Phone: (813) 974-3520

Fax: (813) 974-6840

E-mail: pate@luna.cas.usf.edu

Internet: http://www.cas.usf.edu/lis

Georgia

Clark Atlanta University

School of Library and Information Studies

300 Trevor Arnett Hall

223 James P. Brawley Dr.

Atlanta, GA 30314

Phone: (404) 880-8697

Fax: (404) 880-8977

Internet: http://www.cau.edu/academics/library/index.html

Hawaii

University of Hawaii
Library and Information Science Program
2550 The Mall
Honolulu, HI 96822
Phone: (808) 956-7321
Fax: (808) 956-5835
Internet: http://www.hawaii.edu/slis

Illinois

Dominican University
Graduate School of Library and Information Science
7900 W. Division St., River Forest, IL 60305
Phone: (708) 524-6845
Fax: (708) 524-6657
E-mail: gslis@email.dom.edu
Internet: http://www.dom.edu/academic/gslishome.html
Internet: http://www.stkate.edu (College of St. Catherine)

University of Illinois at Urbana-Champaign
Graduate School of Library and Information Science
Library and Information Science Bldg.
501 E. Daniel St.
Champaign, IL 61820
Phone: (217) 333-3280
Fax: (217) 244-3302
Internet: http://alexia.lis.uiuc.edu

Indiana

Indiana University
School of Library and Information Science
Main Library 012
1320 E. Tenth St.
Bloomington, IN 47405-3907
Phone: (812) 855-2018
Fax: (812) 855-6166
E-mail: iuslis@indiana.edu
Internet: http://www.slis.indiana.edu

Iowa

University of Iowa
School of Library and Information Science
3087 Library, The University of Iowa, Iowa City, IA 52242-1420
Phone: (319) 335-5707
Fax: (319) 335-5374
Internet: http://www.uiowa.edu/~libsci

Kansas
  Emporia State University
    School of Library and Information Management
    P.O. Box 4025
    Emporia, KS 66801
    Phone: (316) 341-5203
    Fax: (316) 341-5233
    Internet: http://slim.emporia.edu

Kentucky
  University of Kentucky
    College of Communications and Information Studies
    School of Library and Information Science
    502 King Library Bldg. S
    Lexington, KY 40506-0039
    Phone: (606) 257-8876
    Fax: (606) 257-4205
    Internet: http://www.uky.edu/CommInfoStudies/SLIS

Louisiana
  Louisiana State University
    School of Library and Information Science
    267 Coates Hall
    Baton Rouge, LA 70803
    Phone: (225) 388-3158
    Fax: (225) 388-4581
    E-mail: slis@lsu.edu

Maryland
  University of Maryland
    College of Library and Information Services
    4105 Hornbake Library Bldg.
    College Park, MD 20742-4345
    Phone: (301) 405-2033
    Fax: (301) 314-9145
    Internet: http://www.clis.umd.edu

Massachusetts
  Simmons College
    Graduate School of Library and Information Science
    300 The Fenway
    Boston, MA 02115-5898
    Phone: (617) 521-2800
    Fax: (617) 521-3192
    E-mail: gslis@simmons.edu
    Internet: http://www.simmons.edu/gslis/

Michigan

University of Michigan

School of Information
304 West Hall Bldg.
550 E. University Ave.
Ann Arbor, MI 48109-1092
Phone: (734) 763-2285
Fax: (734) 764-2475
E-mail: si.admissions@umich.edu
Internet: http://www.si.umich.edu

Wayne State University

Library and Information Science Program
106 Kresge Library
Detroit, MI 48202
Phone: (313) 577-1825
Fax: (313) 577-7563
Internet: http://www.lisp.wayne.edu

Mississippi

University of Southern Mississippi

School of Library and Information Science
P.O. Box 5146
Hattiesburg, MS 39406-5146
Phone: (601) 266-4228
Fax: (601) 266-5774
Internet: http://www-dept.usm.edu/~slis

Missouri

University of Missouri-Columbia

School of Information Science and Learning Technologies
20 Rothwell Gym
Columbia, MO 65211
Phone: (573) 882-4546
Fax: (573) 884-4944
Internet: http://www.coe.missouri.edu/~sislt

New Jersey

Rutgers University

School of Communication, Information and Library Studies
4 Huntington St.
New Brunswick, NJ 08901-1071
Phone: (732) 932-7917
Fax: (732) 932-2644
E-mail: scilsmls@scils.rutgers.edu
Internet: http://www.scils.rutgers.edu/lis/index.html

New York

Long Island University

Palmer School of Library and Information Science

C.W. Post Campus, 720 Northern Blvd., Brookville, NY 11548-1300

Phone: (516) 299-2866

Fax: (516) 299-4168

E-mail: palmer@titan.liunet.edu

Internet: http://www.liu.edu/palmer

Pratt Institute

School of Information and Library Science

Information Science Center

200 Willoughby Ave., Brooklyn, NY 11205

Phone: (718) 636-3702

Fax: (718) 636-3733

E-mail: info@sils.pratt.edu

Internet: http://sils.pratt.edu

Queens College

City University of New York

Graduate School of Library and Information Studies

65-30 Kissena Blvd., Flushing, NY 11367

Phone: (718) 997-3790

Fax: (718) 997-3797

E-mail: gslis@qcunixl.qc.edu

Internet: http://www.qc.edu/GSLIS

St. John's University

Division of Library and Information Science

8000 Utopia Pkwy., Jamaica, NY 11439

Phone: (718) 990-6200

Fax: (718) 990-2071

E-mail: libis@stjohns.edu

Internet: http://www.stjohns.edu/academics/sjc/depts/dlis/index.html

Syracuse University

School of Information Studies

4-206 Center for Science and Technology, Syracuse, NY 13244-4100

Phone: (315) 443-2911

Fax: (315) 443-5806

Internet: http://istweb.syr.edu

University at Albany

State University of New York

School of Information Science and Policy

135 Western Ave., Draper 113, Albany, NY 12222

Phone: (518) 442-5110

Fax: (518) 442-5367

E-mail: infosci@cnsvax.albany.edu

Internet: http://www.albany.edu/sisp

University at Buffalo

State University of New York
Department of Library and Information Studies
534 Baldy Hall
Buffalo, NY 14260-1020
Phone: (716) 645-2412
Fax: (716) 645-3775
E-mail: sils@acsu.buffalo.edu
Internet: http://www.sils.buffalo.edu

North Carolina

North Carolina Central University

School of Library and Information Sciences
1801 Fayetteville St.
P.O. Box 19586
Durham, NC 27707
Phone: (919) 560-6485
Fax: (919) 560-6402
Internet: http://www.slis.nccu.edu

University of North Carolina at Chapel Hill

School of Information and Library Science
CB #3360 100 Manning Hall
Chapel Hill, NC 27599-3360
Phone: (919) 962-8366
Fax: (919) 962-8071
E-mail: info@ils.unc.edu
Internet: http://www.ils.unc.edu

The University of North Carolina at Greensboro

Department of Library and Information Studies
School of Education
P.O. Box 26171
Greensboro, NC 27402-6171
Phone: (336) 334-3477
Fax: (336) 334-5060
Internet: http://www.uncg.edu/lis

Ohio

Kent State University

School of Library and Information Science
Room 314 Library
P.O. Box 5190
Kent, OH 44242-0001
Phone: (330) 672-2782
Fax: (330) 672-7965
Internet: http://web.slis.kent.edu

Oklahoma
University of Oklahoma
School of Library and Information Studies
401 W. Brooks, Room 120, Norman, OK 73019-6032
Phone: (405) 325-3921
Fax: (405) 325-7648
E-mail: slisinfo@lists.ou.edu
Internet: http://www.ou.edu/cas/slis

Pennsylvania
Clarion University of Pennsylvania
Department of Library Science
840 Wood St., Clarion, PA 16214-1232
Phone: (814) 226-2271
Fax: (814) 226-2150
Internet: http://www.clarion.edu/libsci
Drexel University
College of Information Science and Technology
3141 Chestnut St., Philadelphia, PA 19104-2875
Phone: (215) 895-2474
Fax: (215) 895-2494
Internet: http://www.cis.drexel.edu
University of Pittsburgh
School of Information Sciences
505 IS Bldg., Pittsburgh, PA 15260
Phone: (412) 624-5230
Fax: (412) 624-5231
Internet: http://www2.sis.pitt.edu

Puerto Rico
University of Puerto Rico
Graduate School of Library and Information Science
P.O. Box 21906, San Juan, PR 00931-1906
Phone: (787) 763-6199
Fax: (787) 764-2311

Rhode Island
University of Rhode Island
Graduate School of Library and Information Studies
Rodman Hall, Kingston, RI 02881
Phone: (401) 874-2947
Fax: (401) 874-4964
E-mail: gslis@etal.uri.edu
Internet: http://www.uri.edu/artsci/lsc

South Carolina

University of South Carolina

College of Library and Information Science

Davis College, Columbia, SC 29208

Phone: (803) 777-3858

Fax: (803) 777-7938

Internet: http://www.libsci.sc.edu

Tennessee

University of Tennessee

School of Information Sciences

804 Volunteer Blvd., Knoxville, TN 37996-4330

Phone: (423) 974-2148

Fax: (423) 974-4967

Internet: http://www.sis.utk.edu

Texas

Texas Woman's University

School of Library and Information Studies

P.O. Box 425438, Denton, TX 76204-5438

Phone: (940) 898-2602

Fax: (940) 898-2611

Internet: http://www.twu.edu/slis

University of North Texas

School of Library and Information Sciences

P.O. Box 311068, NT Station, Denton, TX 76203-1068

Phone: (940) 565-2445

Fax: (940) 565-3101

E-mail: slis@unt.edu

Internet: http://www.unt.edu/slis

The University of Texas at Austin

Graduate School of Library and Information Science, Austin, TX 78712-1276

Phone: (512) 471-3821

Fax: (512) 471-3971

E-mail: info@gslis.utexas.edu

Internet: http://www.gslis.utexas.edu

Washington

University of Washington

School of Library and Information Science

328 EEB, P.O. Box 352930, Seattle, WA 98195-2930

Phone: (206) 543-1794

Fax: (206) 616-3152

Internet: http://www.ischool.washington.edu

Wisconsin

University of Wisconsin—Madison
School of Library and Information Studies
Helen C. White Hall
600 N. Park St.
Madison, WI 53706
Phone: (608) 263-2900
Fax: (608) 263-4849
E-mail: uw_slis@doit.wisc.edu
Internet: http://polyglot.lss.wisc.edu/slis

University of Wisconsin—Milwaukee
School of Library and Information Science
Enderis Hall 1110
2400 E. Hartford Ave.
Milwaukee, WI 53201
Phone: (414) 229-4707
Fax: (414) 229-4848
E-mail: info@slis.uwm.edu
Internet: http://www.slis.uwm.edu

Degree Programs in Archival Training

This acts as a supplement to the American Library Association's Directory of Graduate Programs in Library Science. Archival method programs are not accredited by The Society of American Archivists. You can get a more complete guide to these programs from The Society of American Archivists, 527 S. Wells St., 5th Floor, Chicago, IL 60607-3922, phone: (312) 922-0140; fax: (312) 347-1452; Internet: http://www.archivists.org.

Alabama

Auburn University
History Department
310 Thach Hall
Auburn University, AL 36849-5207
Phone: (334) 844-4360
Fax: (334) 844-6673
Internet: http://www.grad.auburn.edu

California

University of California—Riverside
Program in Historic Resources Management
Department of History
University of California
Riverside, CA 92521-0204
Phone: (909) 787-5401, ext. 1437
Fax: (909) 787-5299
Internet: http://www.ucr.edu/history/history.html

Florida

Florida State University

Program in Historical Administration and Public History

Department of History

Florida State University

Tallahassee, FL 32306-2200

Phone: (850) 644-9541

Fax: (860) 644-6402

Internet: http://www.fsu.edu/~history/haph.htm

Georgia

Georgia College and State University

History and Geography Department

CBX 047, Georgia College and State University, Milledgeville, GA 31061-0490

Phone: (912) 445-0949

Fax: (912) 445-0873

Internet: http://www.gcsu.edu

Illinois

Loyola University

Public History Program

Loyola University of Chicago

Department of History, 6525 N. Sheridan Rd., Chicago, IL 60626

Phone: (773) 508-2238

Fax: (773) 508-2153

Internet: http://www.luc.edu/depts/history

New York

New York University

Program in Archival Management and Historical Editing

Department of History

New York University, 53 Washington Square South, New York, NY 10012-1098

Phone: (212) 998-8601

Fax: (212) 995-4017

Internet: http://www.nyu.edu/gsas/dept/history/programs/archival

North Carolina

North Carolina State University—Raleigh

M.A. in Public History Program

North Carolina State University, Raleigh, NC 27695-8108

Phone: (919) 515-3715 or (919) 515-2483

Fax: (919) 515-3886

Internet: http://www2.acs.ncsu.edu/grad/

Pennsylvania
Duquesne University
Archival, Museum, and Editing Studies
Department of History
Duquesne University
Pittsburgh, PA 15282
Phone: (412) 396-6470
Internet: http://www.duq.edu/liberalarts/gradhistory/graduateprog
AME.html
Temple University
Department of History (025-24)
Temple University
913 Gladfelter Hall
Philadelphia, PA 19122
Phone: (215) 204-7461
Fax: (215) 204-5891

Washington
Western Washington University
Graduate Program in Archives and Records Management
Department of History
Western Washington University
Bellingham, WA 98225-9056
Fax: (360) 650-7789
Internet: http://www.ac.wwu.edu/~history/archives.html

Digital Photography and Restoration

Contact the Professional Photographers of America for a list of courses and
programs offered under its auspices.

American Photographic Artisans Guild
International Photography School
School Director: Sylvia Happe, PPA Certified, M.Artist., Cr.
7657 West 500 North
McCordsville, IN 46055
Phone: (317) 823-4544
E-mail: happe7657juno.com
California Photographic Workshops
School Director: James Inks, Cr. Photog.
2500 N. Texas St.
Fairfield, CA 94533
Phone: (888) 422-6606
Fax: (707) 422-0973
E-mail: Calif_School@juno.com
Internet: http://www.homestead.com/cpw99

Carolina Art and Photographic School
School Director/Contact: Toby Hardister
P.O. Box 970, Clemmons, NC 27012-0970
Phone: (336) 766-5337
E-mail: tobyhardister@juno.com

East Coast School Photographic Workshops
School Director/Contact: Rex C. Truell
705 Randolph St., Suite E, Thomasville, NC 27360
Phone: (336) 476-4938
Fax: (336) 476-4857
E-mail: clatruell@aol.com
Internet: http://www.ppofnc.com

Florida School of Professional Photography
School Director: Robin Phillips
1505 S. Florida Ave., Lakeland, FL 33083
Phone: (941) 682-6958
Contact: Terri Crownouer
13424 White Cypress Rd.
Austula, FL 34705
Phone: (800) 330-0532
Fax: (352) 243-1136
Internet: http://www.floridaphotographers.org

Georgia School of Professional Photography
Assistant Director/Contact: Tom McCollum
P.O. Box 933, Lilburn, GA 30048
Phone: (770) 972-0619 or (800) 805-5510
Fax: (770) 972-8708
E-mail: GPPAED@Mindspring.com

Golden Gate School
School Director/Contact: Julie Olson
Golden Gate School
P.O. Box F
San Mateo, CA 94402-0018
Phone: (650) 548-0889
Fax: (650) 347-3141
E-mail: ggs@goldengateschool.com
Internet: http://www.goldengateschool.com

Great Lakes Institute of Photography
School Director: Ron Nichols, M. Photog., Cr.
Contact: Ronald Tocco, Cr. Photog.
19276 Eureka Rd.
Southgate, MI 48195
Phone: (734) 283-8433
Fax: (734) 283-0950
E-mail: PPofMich@aol.com
Internet: http://www.glip.org

Illinois Workshops
School Director: Stephen Humphrey
Contact: Bret Wade
229 E. State St., P.O. Box 318, Jacksonville, IL 62650
Phone: (217) 525-2722
Fax: (217) 243-2472
E-mail: bcinc@fgi.net
Internet: http://www.angelfire.com/il/ilworkshops

Kansas Professional Photographers School
School Director: Dave Mencl, PPA Certified, M. Photog., Cr.
Contact: Ron Clevenger
P.O. Box 591
Ottawa, KS 66067
Phone: (785) 242-7710
Fax: (785) 242-1546
E-mail: rstudio@idir.net
Internet: http://www.kpps.com

Long Island Photo Workshop
School Director: Anthony Marchisoto
Contact: Ronald Krowne
216 Lakeville Rd.
Great Neck, NY 11020
Phone: (516) 487-1313

Mid-America Institute of Professional Photography
Contact: Charles Lee
220 E. Second St.
Ottumwa, IA 52501
Phone: (515) 683-7824
Email: lees@pcsia.com
Internet: http://www.maipp.com

Mid-Atlantic Regional School of Professional Photography
School Director: James Bastinck
Phone: (888) 267-MARS
Fax: (888) 267-MARS
E-mail: marschool@nac.net
Internet: http://www.photoschools.com

Mount Carroll Center for Applied Photographic Arts
School Director: Doug Bergren
Contact: Laurel Bergren
301 N. Division
Polo, IL 61064
Phone: (815) 946-2370
Fax: (815) 946-2370
E-mail: mccapa@aol.com
Internet: http://www.mtcarrollcenter.com

New England Institute of Professional Photography
  Seacrest Resort, N. Falmouth, Massachusetts
  School Director: John Ouellette
  659 Sandy La.
  Warwick, RI 02886
  Phone: (401) 738-3778
  Fax: (401) 732-0852
  E-mail: sgenuario@sprynet.com
  Internet: http://www.ppane.com

PPSNY Photo Workshop
  School Director: Linda Hutchings
  P.O. Box 403
  Elmira, NY 14902
  Phone: (607) 733-6563
  E-mail: PPSNYWORKSHOP@email.com
  Internet: http://www.PPSNY.com

Pacific Northwest School of Professional Photography
  School Director/Contact: Russell Rogers
  6203 Ninety-seventh Ave. Court West
  Tacoma, WA 98467
  Phone: (253) 565-1711
  Fax: (253) 564-4013
  E-mail: ReneeCrist@worldnet.att.net
  Internet: http://www.ppw.org

South Carolina Professional Photography School
  School Director: Charles Jordan
  Phone: (864) 646-8361, ext. 2237
  Fax: (864) 646-8256
  E-mail: cjordan@tricty.tricounty.tec.sc.us

Texas School of Professional Photography
  School Director/Contact: Don Dickson, M. Photog., Cr.
  1501 W. Fifth
  Plainview, TX 79072
  Phone: (806) 296-2276
  Fax: (806) 293-5124
  E-mail: DDickson@lonestarbbs.com
  Internet: http://www.tppa.org/school.htm

Triangle Institute of Professional Photography
  School Director/Contact: Samuel Pelaia
  441 State St.
  Baden, PA 15005
  Phone: (724) 869-5455
  Fax: (724) 869-7777
  E-mail: tpa@timesnet.net
  Internet: http://www.trianglephotographers.org

West Coast School Professional Photographic Workshops
School Director: Kathy Trerotola
1172 N. Via Verde Dr.
San Dimas, CA 91773
Phone: (800) 439-5839
Fax: (909) 305-2117
E-mail: wcs@reachme.net
Internet: http://www.PPConline.com

Wisconsin Indianhead Photographers School at Treehaven
School Director: Dennis McGill
Contact: Phil Ziesemer
120 S. Mill St.
Merrill, WI 54452
Phone: (715) 536-4540
E-mail: ziesemer@dwave

Endnotes

Chapter One

1 Brad Edmondson, "Polaroid Snaps the Customer," *American Demographics* 9 (February 1987): 23.

Chapter Two

1 Brenda M. Bernier, "A Study of Poly (Vinyl Chloride) Erasers Used in the Surface Cleaning of Photographs," *Topics in Photographic Preservation* 7 (1997): 10–18.

2 Peter Kolonia, "How to Preserve Your Prints," *Popular Photography* (October 1993): 47.

3 David Mishkin, Just Black and White <http://www.maine.com/photos/nerv.htm>.

4 "Choosing the Right Graphics Format," *Digital Album* <http://www.city-gallery.com/digital/graphics_formats.html>.

5 Larry Ledden, *Complete Guide to Scanning.*

6 M. David Stone, "Capture the Color," *PC Magazine* <http://www.zdnet.com/pcmag/features/scanners/intro.html>.

7 Henry Wilhelm, "The Intimate Relationships of Inks and Papers: You Can't Talk About the Permanence of One Without Considering the Other" <http://www.wilhelm-research.com>.

8 Ibid.

9 Richard Wilson, "Editing Your Ancestor's Images" (Providence, R.I.: National Genealogical Society Conference, 2000), audio tape number F-150.

10 Arthur H. Bleich, "Pioneer Websteads (and Other Great Online Resources) on the PhotoDigital Frontier," *Digital Camera* (April 2000): 17–20.

11 Andrew D. Epstein, "Photography and the Law," *Lawyering for the Arts* 7, Richard C. Allen et al, eds.

12 "Copyright, Photography and the Web" (7 March 1997) <http://www.chimwasmp.org/photoweb/copyrite.htm>.

Chapter Four

1 Klaus B. Hendriks and Rudiger Krall, "Fingerprints on Photographs," *Topics in Photographic Preservation* 5: 8–13.

2 James M. Reilly, *Care and Identification of Nineteenth Century Photographic Prints*, 31.

3 Ibid, 23.

4 Henry Wilhelm and Carol Brower, *The Permanence and Care of Color Photographs*, 599.

5   William C. Darrah, *Cartes de Visite in Nineteenth Century Photography*, 8, 9.

6   Ibid.

7   Ibid.

8   Floyd Rinhart, Marion Rinhart, and Robert W. Wagner, *The American Tintype*, 74.

9   "Preserving Family Albums" <http://www.eastman.org/4_educ/4_prsrv.html>.

10 Ibid.

11 Sarah S. Wagner, "Some Recent Photographic Preservation Activities at the Library of Congress," *Topics in Photographic Preservation* 4 (1993): 140–142.

12 Sarah S. Wagner, "Approaches to Moving Glass Plate Negatives," *Topics in Photographic Preservation* 6 (1995): 130–131.

13 Paul Messier, "Preserving Your Collection of Film Based Photographic Negatives," Conservators of Fine Arts and Material Culture, Rocky Mountain Conservation Center <http://palimpsest.stanford.edu/byauth/messier/negrmcc.html>.

14 Ibid.

Chapter Five

1   Louis Walton Sipley, *A Half Century of Color*, 9.

2   Ibid.

3   Ibid.

4   Douglas Collins, *The Story of Kodak*, 277.

5   Ivan Dmitri, *Kodachrome and How to Use It*, 11.

6   Wilhelm and Brower, 1–60.

7   Leslie Stroebel and Richard Zakia, eds., *The Focal Encyclopedia of Photography* (Boston: Focal Press, 1993): 640.

8   Sarah S. Wagner, "Cold Storage Handling Guidelines for Photographs," 1991 <http://www.nara.gov/arch/techinfo/preserva/maintena/cold.htm>.

9   "Lantern Slides," National Museum of Photography, Film and Television <http://www.nmsi.ac.uk/nmpft/collections/con3.html>.

Chapter Six

1   "A Bit About Photographs: Digital Photography Is Developing Rapidly. How Quickly It Will Overtake Conventional Cameras and Film, Though, Is Debatable," *The Economist* 341 (21 December 1996): 117–119; John C. Dvorak, "Total Exposure," *PC/Computing* 10 (May 1997): 79; "Digital," *Petersen's Photographic* 26 (September 1997): 12.

2   Amy Johnson Crow, "The Life Span of Compact Discs," *Genealogical Computing* (Winter 2000): 23–26.

3   "Special Topics in Digital Photography, Photo Sharing Websites: A

Comparative Review" <http://www.shortcourses.com/book03/sharin
g.htm>.

4 Ibid.

5 "What Does 'Archival' Mean in the Digital World?" *Digital Album*
<http://www.city-gallery.com/digital/what_is_archival.html>.

Chapter Seven

1 Betty Walsh, "Salvage Operations for Water Damaged Archival
Collections: A Second Glance," *WAAC Newsletter* 19, no. 2 (May
1997) <http://palimpsest.stanford.edu/waac/wn/wn19/wn19-2/wn
19-206.html>.

2 Ibid.

Chapter Eight

1 Rick Crume, "Getting With the Program," *Family Tree Magazine* (June
2000): 30–37.

Chapter Nine

1 Souzzann Y.H. Carroll, *A Lasting Legacy: Scrapbooks and Photo
Albums That Touch the Heart*, 9.

2 Jeanne English and Al Thelin, *SOS: Saving Our Scrapbooks*, 44.

3 Gayle Humpherys, "Pulp Fact, Not Fiction," *Creating Keepsakes*
(November 1999): 59–61.

4 Ibid.

5 "Questions and Answers," *Creating Keepsakes* (March 2000): 26.

6 Catherine Scott, "The Ins and Outs of Rubber Stamping," *Creating
Keepsakes* (February 2000): 65–67.

7 Ibid.

8 Gayle Humpherys, "The Skinny on Sheet Protectors," *Creating
Keepsakes* (September/October 1999): 63–66.

9 Deanna Lambson, "Can You Keep It?" *Creating Keepsakes* (March
2000): 55–62.

Chapter Eleven

1 "Review of a Memoir of a Portion of the Bolling Family in England
and Virginia," *NEHGR* 24 (January 1870): 95.

Bibliography

General

American Association of Museums. *The Official Museum Directory*. Biannual. Washington, D.C.: American Association of Museums, 2000.

American Library Directory. Biannual. New York: R.R. Bowker, 1999–2000.

Baldwin, G. *Looking at Photographs: Guide to Technical Terms*. Santa Monica, Calif.: J. Paul Getty Museum in Association with British Museum Press, 1991.

Capa, Cornell, ed. *International Center of Photography Encyclopedia of Photography*. New York: Crown Publishers, Inc., 1994.

Coe, Brian. *Kodak Cameras: The First Hundred Years*. Hove: Hove Foto, 1988.

Coe, Brian, and Mark Haworth-Booth. *A Guide to Early Photographic Processes*. London: The Victoria and Albert Museum in Association with Hurtwood Press, 1983.

Collins, Douglas. *The Story of Kodak*. New York: Harry N. Abrams, Inc., 1990.

Crawford, William. *The Keepers of Light: A History and Working Guide to Early Photographic Processes*. Dobbs Ferry, N.Y.: Morgan and Morgan, 1979.

Dunkelman, Mark. "An Interview With Michael J. Winey, Curator at the U.S. Army Military History Institute." *Military Images* (November/December 1993): 9–16.

Dunkelman, Mark and Michael Winey. "Precious Shadows: The Importance of Photographs to Civil War Soldiers, as Revealed by a Typical Union Regiment." *Military Images* (July/August 1994): 6–13.

Edmondson, Brad. "Polaroid Snaps the Customer." *American Demographics 9* (February 1987): 23.

Eskind, Andrew H., and Greg Drake, eds. *Index to American Photographic Collections*. 3d enlarged ed. New York: G.K. Hall & Co., 1996.

Farber, Richard. *Historic Photographic Processes*. New York: Allworth Press, 1998.

Foresta, Merry A. *American Photographs: The First Century*. Washington, D.C.: Smithsonian Institution Press, 1997.

Frizot, Michel, ed. *A New History of Photography*. English ed. Cologne, Germany: Konemann, 1998. French edition. Paris: Bordas, 1994.

Gernsheim, Helmut, and Alison Gernsheim. *The History of Photography From the Camera Obscura to the Beginning of the Modern Era*. New York: McGraw-Hill, 1969.

Johnson, William S., ed. *International Photography Index*. Annual. 1979, 1980, 1981. Boston: G.K. Hall & Co., 1983–.

———. *Nineteenth Century Photography: An Annotated Bibliography, 1839–1879*. Boston: G.K. Hall & Co., 1990.

"Lantern Slides." National Museum of Photography, Film and Television <http://www.nmsi.ac.uk/nmpft/collections/con3.html>.

Mace, O. Henry. *Collector's Guide to Early Photographs*. 2d ed. Iola, Wis.: Krause Publications, 1999.

McDarrah, Gloria S., Fred W. McDarrah, and Timothy S. McDarrah. *The Photography Encyclopedia*. New York: Schirmer Books, 1999.

Morris, Andrew J. "Photography and Genealogy" <http://www.genealogy.org/~ajmorris/photo/pg.htm>.

Newhall, Beaumont. *The History of Photography*. New York: The Museum of Modern Art, 1982.

Palmquist, Peter E., ed. *Photographers: A Sourcebook for Historical Research*. Brownsville, Calif.: Carl Mautz Publishing, 1991.

Public Record Office. *An Introduction to Nineteenth and Early Twentieth Century Photographic Processes*. Public Record Office Series: Introduction to Archival Materials. London: Public Record Office, 1996.

Roosens, Laurent, and Luc Salu. *History of Photography: A Bibliography of Books*. 2 vols. New York: Mansell, 1989.

Sandweiss, Martha A., ed. *Photography in Nineteenth-Century America*. Fort Worth, Tex.: Amon Carter Museum, 1991.

Sennet, Robert S. *Photography and Photographers to 1900: An Annotated Bibliography*. Garland Reference Library of the Humanities. New York: Garland Publishing, 1985.

Taft, Robert. *Photography and the American Scene: A Social History, 1839–1889*. 1938. Reprint, New York: Dover Publications, 1964.

Walrath, Paul. "Photography and Kodak: A Path to the Past." *FGS Forum* 9 (1997): 4–7.

Welling, William. *Photography in America: The Formative Years, 1839–1900*. New York: Thomas Y. Crowell Company, 1978.

Young, W. Arthur, Thomas A. Benson, George T. Eaton, and Joseph Meehan. *Copying and Duplicating: Photographic and Digital Imaging Techniques*. 2d ed. Rochester, N.Y.: Silver Pixel Press, 1996.

Color

Dmitri, Ivan. *Kodachrome and How to Use It*. New York: Simon and Schuster, 1940.

Dresser, A.R. *Lantern Slides and How to Make Them*. 1892.

Elmendorf, Dwight Lathorp. *Lantern Slides: How to Make and Color Them*. New York: E. & H.T. Anthony & Co., 1895.

Henisch, Heniz, and Bridget A. Henisch. *The Painted Photograph, 1839–1914: Origins, Techniques, Aspirations*. University Park: Pennsylvania State University Press, 1996.

Krause, Peter. "How Long Will Your Color Prints Last?" *Popular Photography* (April 1999): 76–94.

Polaroid Corporation. *Storing, Handling, and Preserving Polaroid Photographs: A Guide*. Cambridge, Mass.: Polaroid Corporation, 1983.

Richter, Heinz. "The History of Color Photography." *F32—The Online Photography Magazine* <http://www.ff32.com/Articles/art020.htm>.

Sapwater, E., Kirsten Mortensen and Helen Johnston. "Images on Ice: Cold Storage Freezes Time for Photographic Film and Prints." *PEI* (April 1999): 36–44.

Sipley, Louis Walton. *A Half Century of Color*. New York: Macmillan Co., 1951.

Wagner, Sarah S. "Cold Storage Handling Guidelines for Photographs." NARA Preservation Programs, 1991 <http://www.nara.gov/arch/techinfo/preserva/maintena/cold.htm>.

Wilhelm, Henry, and Carol Brower. *The Permanence and Care of Color Photographs: Traditional and Digital Color Prints, Color Negatives, Slides, and Motion Pictures*. Grinnell, Iowa: Preservation Publishing Co., 1993.

Wood, John, ed. *The Art of the Autochrome*. Iowa City: University of Iowa Press, 1993.

Computer Software

Clay, Betty. "What Genealogy Software Should I Buy?" *Genealogical Computing* (Fall 1999): 27–31.

Crow, Amy Johnson. "The Life Span of Compact Discs." *Genealogical Computing* (Winter 2000): 23–26.

Crume, Rick. "Getting With the Program." *Family Tree Magazine* (June 2000): 30–37.

Conservation of Photographs

Bernier, Brenda M. "A Study of Poly (Vinyl Chloride) Erasers Used in the Surface Cleaning of Photographs." *Topics in Photographic Preservation* 7 (1997): 10–18.

Beyea, Linda L. "Document and Photo Preservation FAQ" <http://genweb.net/~gen-cds/faq.html>.

Caring for Photographs: Display, Storage, Restoration. Life Library of Photography. New York: Time-Life Books, 1972.

Dear Myrtle's Genealogy Column. "Preserving Old Photos." (27 April 1998) <http://www.ancestry.com/columns/myrtle/april98/my980427.htm>.

Derby, Deborah, with assistance from M. Susan Barger, Nora Kennedy, and Carol Turchan. "Caring for Your Photographs." Washington, D.C.: American Institute of Conservation, 1997.

"Document and Image Preservation and Repair" <http://www.classyimage.com/preserv.htm>.

Ewbank, Lynn. "Photographic Memories." *Family Tree Magazine* (January 2000), 62–67.

Hendriks, Klaus B., and Rudiger Krall. "Fingerprints on Photographs." *Topics in Photographic Preservation* 5: 8–13.

Keefe, Laurence E., and Dennis Inch. *The Life of a Photograph*. Boston: Focal Press, 1990.

Kolonia, Peter. "How to Preserve Your Prints." *Popular Photography* (October 1993): 47.

McComb, Robert E. "Taking Care of Your Photographs." *Petersen's Photographic* 26 (March 1998): 26–28.

"Photo Preservation: How to Care for Your Photographs" <http://www.ajmorris.com/a06/photopres.htm>.

"Preserving Family Albums" <http://www.eastman.org/4_educ/4_prsrv.html>.

"Saving Your Family Treasures" <http://www.myhistory.org/saving/photographs.html>.

Seefeldt, Paula A. "How to Preserve Your Photographs." *Good Housekeeping* 210 (March 1990): 243.

Wagner, Sarah S. "Approaches to Moving Glass Plate Negatives." *Topics in Photographic Preservation* 6 (1995): 130–31.

———. "Some Recent Photographic Preservation Activities at the Library of Congress." *Topics in Photographic Preservation* 4 (1993): 140–42.

Walsh, Betty. "Salvage Operations for Water Damaged Archival Collections: A Second Glance." *WAAC Newsletter* 19, no. 2 (May 1997) <http://palimpsest.stanford.edu/waac/wn/wn19/wn19-2/wn19-206.html>.

Wilhelm, Henry. "The Intimate Relationships of Inks and Papers: You Can't Talk About the Permanence of One Without Considering the Other" <http://www.wilhelm-research.com>. Article no longer available at Web site.

Wilson, Bonnie. "Ask an Expert: Preserving Your Photographs: Windows to the Past." Minnesota Historical Society <http://www.mnhs.org/preserve/conservation/photpres.html>.

Copyright

Allen, Richard C., et al. *Lawyering for the Arts*. Boston: Massachusetts Continuing Legal Education, 1991.

ASMP Professional Business Practices in Photography. 5th ed. New York: Allworth Press, 1997.

"Copyright, Photography and the Web" (7 March 1997) <http://www.chimwasmp.org/photoweb/copyrite.htm>.

Cottrill and Associates. "Copyright Table" <http://www.progenealogists.com/copyright_table.htm>.

Elias, Stephen. *Patent, Copyright, and Trademark*. 3d ed. Berkeley, Calif.: Nolo Press, 1999.

Epstein, Andrew D. "Photography and the Law." In *Lawyering for the Arts*, edited by Richard C. Allen, et al., 7.

Everyone's Guide to Copyrights, Trademarks, and Patents. Philadelphia: Running Press, 1990.

Goad, Mike. "Copyright and Genealogy" <http://www.rootsweb.com/~mikegoad/copyright1.htm>.

Hoffman, Gary B. "Who Owns Genealogy?" <http://www.genealogy.com/genealogy/14_cpyrt.html>.

Strong, William S. *The Copyright Book: A Practical Guide*. 4th ed. Cambridge, Mass.: MIT Press, 1993.

"When Works Pass Into the Public Domain" <http://www.unc.edu/~unclng/public-d.htm>.

Daguerreotypes

Barger, Susan M., and William B. White. *The Daguerreotype: Nineteenth Century Technology and Modern Science*. Washington, D.C.: Smithsonian Institution Press, 1991.

Berg, Paul. *Nineteenth Century Photographic Cases and Wall Frames*. Huntington Beach, Calif.: Huntington Valley Press, 1995.

The Daguerreian Annual. Pittsburgh: The Daguerreian Society.

Field, Richard S., and Robin Jaffee Frank. *American Daguerreotypes From the Matthew R. Isenburg Collection*. New Haven, Conn.: Yale University, 1989.

Foresta, Merry A., and John Wood. *Secrets of the Dark Chamber: The Art of the American Daguerreotype*. Washington, D.C.: Smithsonian Institution Press, 1995.

Krainik, Clifford, and Michele Krainik, with Carl Walvoord. *Union Cases: A Collector's Guide to the Art of America's First Plastic*. Grantsburg, Wis.: Centennial Photo Services, 1988.

Newhall, Beaumont. *The Daguerreotype in America*. New York: Duell, Sloan & Pearce, 1961. Reprint. New York: Dover Publications, Inc., 1976.

"Preservation of the Daguerreotype Collection" <http://lcweb2.loc.gov/ammem/daghtml/dagprsv.html>.

Rinhart, Floyd, and Marion Rinhart. *American Miniature Case Art*. New York: A.S. Barnes & Co., 1969.

———. *American Daguerrean Art*. New York: Clarkson N. Potter, 1967.

———. *The American Daguerreotype*. Athens: University of Georgia Press, 1981.

Rudisill, Richard. *Mirror Image: The Influence of the Daguerreotype on American Society*. Albuquerque: University of New Mexico Press, 1971.

Wood, John. ed. *America and the Daguerreotype*. Iowa City: University of Iowa Press, 1991.

———. *The Scenic Daguerreotype: Romanticism and Early Photography*. Iowa City: University of Iowa Press, 1995.

Digital

Bleich, Arthur H. "Pioneer Websteads (and Other Great Online Resources) on the PhotoDigital Frontier," *Digital Camera* (April 2000): 17–20.

"Bringing Family Photographs into The Digital Album." *Digital Album* <http://www.city-gallery.com/digital/album.html>.

"Choosing the Right Graphics Format." *Digital Album* <http://www.city-gallery.com/digital/album.html>.

Eggers, Ron. "An Introduction to Digital Imaging." *Petersen's Photographic* (April 1998): D3–4.

———. " The Art of Scanning." *Petersen's Photographic* (April 1999): 18–19, 21.

Freeman, Angela. "From Snapshots to Web Sites." *PC World* (December 1997): 347–50.

Gormley, Myra Vanderpool. "Adventures in Cyberspace," <http://www.ancestry.com/columns/myra/Shaking_Family_Tree07-09-98.htm>.

Johnston, Peter. "Image Archiving Aids Digital Service." *Graphics Arts Monthly* 67 (February 1995): 72.

King, Julie Adair. *Digital Photography for Dummies*. 3d ed. New York: IDG Books, 2000.

Kolonia, Peter. "Digital Saves the Day: Pro Photographers Are Turning Rejects Into Winners—Digitally." *Popular Photography* 61 (April 1997): 30–36.

Rodier, Elizabeth. "What to Do With All Those Scanned Pictures." *Digital Album* <http://www.city-gallery.com/digital/albumtips1.html>.

Special Topics in Digital Photography, Photo Sharing Websites: A Comparative Review <http://www.shortcourses.com/specialtopics/sharing.htm>.

"Steps to Storing Family Photographs." *Digital Album* <http://www.city-gallery.com/digital/archive_steps.html>.

"What Does 'Archival' Mean in the Digital World?" *Digital Album* <http://www.city-gallery.com/digital/what_is_archival.html>.

Film

Gordon, Paul L., ed. *The Book of Film Care*. Rochester, N.Y.: Eastman Kodak Co., 1992.

Slide, Anthony. *Nitrate Won't Wait: A History of Film Preservation in the United States*. Jefferson, N.C.: McFarland, 1992.

Genealogical Research

Beasley, Donna, and Donna Carter. *The Family Reunion Planner*. New York: IDG Books, 1999.

Bentley, Elizabeth Petty. *The Genealogist's Address Book*. 4th ed. Baltimore: Genealogical Publishing Co., 1998.

Croom, Emily Anne. *Unpuzzling Your Past: The Bestselling Basic Guide to Genealogy*. 4th ed. Cincinnati: Betterway Books, 2001.

Helm, Matthew L., and April Leigh Helm. *Genealogy Online for Dummies*. 2d ed. New York: IDG Books, 1999.

McClure, Rhonda. *Complete Idiot's Guide to Online Genealogy*. Indianapolis: Alpha Books, 2000.

Radford, Margaret Grove. "Climb Your Family Tree With These 5 Steps." *Memory Makers* (January/February 2000): 61–64.

Sturdevant, Katherine Scott. *Bringing Your Family History to Life Through Social History*. Cincinnati: Betterway Books, 2000.

Negatives

Patti, Tony. "Historically Speaking. Discovery of the Collodion Process in Photography." *PSA Journal* 60 (January 1994): 7.

Organization

Begole, Christine. "Saving Family Memories," *Family PC* (September 1996): 181–84.

Carmack, Sharon DeBartolo. *Organizing Your Family History Search*. Cincinnati: Betterway Books, 1999.

Morris, John. "Negative Filing: How to File 3600 Negs on Your Next Day Off." *Petersen's Photographic* 13 (November 1984): 72–74.

Traylor, Gary D. "Slide Filing: A Computerized System for People Who Don't Own a Computer." *Petersen's Photographic* 13 (November 1984): 76–78.

Photographic Technique

Bearnson, Lisa, and Siobhan McGowan. *Mom's Little Book of Photo Tips*. Orem, Utah: Creating Keepsakes Books, 1999.

Hart, Russell. *Photography for Dummies*. Foster City, Calif.: IDG Books, 1998.

Hughes, Jerry. *How to Take Great Photographs With Any Camera*. Dallas: Phillips Lane, 1999.

Myers, Allison. "Ten Common Photo Mistakes: Learn How to Avoid Them." *Creating Keepsakes* (November 1999): 101–5.

"Kodak's Guide to Better Pictures," <http://www.kodak.com/ciHome/photography/bpictures/pictureTaking/pictureTaking.shml>.

Shull, Wilma Sadler. *Photographing Your Heritage*. Rev. ed. Orem, Utah: Ancestry, 1988.

"Twenty-five Handy Pro Tips: Tricks of the Trade You Can Use Too." *Petersen's Photographic* (October 1999): 28–33.

Zuckerman, Jim. "Five Instant Techniques to Improve Your Photography." *Petersen's Photographic* (March 1999): 33–35.

Preservation

Albright, Gary. "Which Envelope? Selecting Storage Enclosures for Photographs." *Picturescope* 31, no. 4 (1985): 111–13.

Burgess, Helen D., and Carolyn G. Leckie. "Evaluation of Paper Products: With Special Reference to Use With Photographic Materials." *Topics in Photographic Preservation* 4 (1991): 96–105.

Hendriks, Klaus B., and B. Lesser. "Disaster Preparedness and Recovery: Photographic Materials." *American Archivist* 46 (Winter 1983): 52–68.

Messier, Paul. "Preserving Your Collection of Film-Based Photographic Negatives." Conservators of Fine Arts and Material Culture, Rocky Mountain Conservation Center <http://palimpsest.stanford.edu/byauth/messier/negrmee.html>.

Norris, Debbie Hess. "The Proper Storage and Display of a Photographic Collection." *Picturescope* 30 (Spring 1982): 34–37.

Romer, Grant B. "Can We Afford to Exhibit Our Valued Photographs?" *Picturescope* 32 (1987):136–37.

Topics in Photographic Preservation. American Institute for Conservation. Photographic Materials Group. Issued biannually. 1987–1997.

Walsh, Betty. "Salvage Operations for Water Damaged Archival Collections: A Second Glance." *WAAC Newsletter* 19, no. 2 (May 1997) <http://palimpsest.stanford.edu/waac/wn/wn19/wn19-2/wn19-206.html>.

Wilbur, Anne. "How Stable is a Photograph?" *Memory Makers* (Spring 1998): 10.

Prints

Darrah, William C. *Cartes de Visite in Nineteenth Century Photography.* Gettysburg, Pa.: W.C. Darrah, 1981.

Gagel, Diane VanSkiver. "Card and Paper Photographs, 1854–1900." *Ancestry* 15 (September/October 1997):13–17.

Reilly, James M. *Care and Identification of Nineteenth Century Photographic Prints.* Rochester, N.Y.: Eastman Kodak Co., 1986.

Restoration

Benedetti, Wendell. "How to Restore Your Damaged Treasures." *Petersen's Photographic* (April 1998): D8.

Bethel, Brian. "Photo Restoration Techniques Have Come a Long Way," <http://www.reporternews.com/1999/features/photo0809.html>.

Scanning

Bone, Jeff. "The Scanning FAQ" (1993–97) <http://www.infomedia.net/scan>.

Fulton, Wayne. "A Few Scanning Tips" <http://www.scantips.com>.

Ledden, Larry. *Complete Guide to Scanning.* New York: Family Technologies, 1998.

"Scanning for Beginners or Basic Scanning Techniques," <http://home.att.net/~cthames>.

Stone, M. David. "Capture the Color." *PC Magazine* <http://www.zdnet.com/pcmag/features/scanners/intro.htm>.

Scrapbooking

Braun, Bev Kirschner. *Crafting Your Own Heritage Album.* Cincinnati: Betterway Books, 2000.

Carroll, Souzzann Y.H. *A Lasting Legacy: Scrapbooks and Photo Albums That Touch the Heart.* Bountiful, Utah: Living Vision Press, 1998.

Coombs, Patti. "The Lowdown on Labeling Photographs." *Creating Keepsakes* (May June 1999): 58–60

English, Jeanne, and Al Thelin. *SOS: Saving Our Scrapbooks.* Orem, Utah: Creating Keepsakes Books, 1999.

"Heritage Albums: Saving the Past for the Future," *Memory Makers* (Spring 1998): 21–25, 59.

Heritage Scrapbooks. Escondido, Calif.: Porch Swing Publishing, 1999.

Humpherys, Gayle. "Pulp Fact, Not Fiction." *Creating Keepsakes* (November 1999): 59–61.

———. "The Skinny on Sheet Protectors." *Creating Keepsakes* (September/October 1999): 63–66.

Lambson, Deanna. "Can You Keep It?" *Creating Keepsakes* (March 2000): 55–62.

Scott, Catherine. "The Ins and Outs of Rubber Stamping." *Creating Keepsakes* (February 2000): 65–67.

Wilbur, Anne. "Preserving a Legacy." *Memory Makers* (January/February 2000): 108–09.

Stereographs

Bennett, Mary, and Paul C. Juhl. *Iowa Stereographs: Three-Dimensional Visions of the Past.* Iowa City: University of Iowa Press, 1997.

Darrah, William C. *Stereo Views: A History of Stereographs in America and Their Collection.* Gettysburg, Pa.: Times and News Publishing Co., 1964.

———. *The World of Stereographs.* Gettysburg, Pa.: W.C. Darrah, 1977.

Waldsmith, John. *Stereoviews, An Illustrated History and Price Guide.* Raonor, Ohio: Wallace-Homestead Book Co., 1991.

Terminology

Bellardo, Lewis J., and Lynn Lady Bellardo. *A Glossary for Archivists, Manuscript Curators, and Records Managers.* Chicago: Society of American Archivists, 1992.

Daniels, Maygene F. "Introduction to Archival Terminology." NARA <http://www.nara.gov/arch/geninfo/terms.html>. First published in *A Modern Archives Reader: Basic Readings on Archival Theory and Practice.* 1984.

Tintypes

Burns, Stanley B. *Forgotten Marriage: The Painted Tintype and the Decorative Frame 1860–1910: A Lost Chapter in American Portraiture.* New York: The Burns Collection, Ltd., 1995.

Lindgren, C.E. "Caring for Tintypes and Creating New Ones." *PSA Journal* 59 (January 1993): 17–18.

Rinhart, Floyd, Marion Rinhart, and Robert W. Wagner. *The American Tintype.* Columbus, Ohio: Ohio State University Press, 1999.

Index

Abrasion
 of daguerreotypes, 44
 of paper prints, 60
 photographic albums
  and, 70
 of tintypes, 49
Acid-free, meaning of
 term, 1
Acid-free paper, 149-150
Acid paper, 26, 71
Adhesives, 64-65, 71,
 150-151
Adobe Photoshop, 33
Afga
 color paper, 81
 digital services, 95-96
 film, 89
Airbrush restoration,
 121-122, 124
Albumen prints, 55-56, 65,
 123
Albums
 adhesives for, 150-151
 black paper, 71-72
 digital. *See* Family Web
  sites
 inks for, 151
 magnetic, 4, 71-73
 photographic print,
  66-73
 scrapbook, 149-152
 See also Photographic
  albums
Ambrotypes, 13, 45-46
 conservation of, 114
 drying wet, 118
 major characteristics of,
  48
Ansco film, 89
AOL "You've Got
 Pictures," 95
Archival, use of term, 1-2,
 73, 149
Archival boxes, 26
Archival inks, 35
Archival paper, 35
Archival processing, 59
Artifacts, 154. *See also*
 Memorabilia
Attic, storing photos in, 25
Autochrome, 80, 86-87

Backgrounds, 180-181
Basement, storing photos
 in, 25
Bessette family collection,
 12-13
Betlock/Virnig collection,
 160-168
Biological damage, 18-19
Black-and-white
 photographs, 182
Black paper albums, 71-72
Boudoir card photographs,
 58
Boxes, 26, 137-138
Brady, Matthew, 69
Bronzing, 65
Buffered paper, 150

Cabinet card, 58, 70
Caption, 11. *See also*
 Identifying images;
 Labeling
Carbon print, 56
Card file, 139
Card photographs, 56-58
Cartes de visite, 13, 56, 58,
 68-69
Cased images, 48-53
 drying wet, 117-118
 See also Ambrotypes;
  Daguerreotypes;
  Tintypes
CDs, photo, 93-94
Cellulose acetate film, 77
Chemical damage, 20
Chromolithographs, 80
Cleaning
 daguerreotypes, 43-45
 photographs, 23-24
Cold storage, 84-85
Collodion
 on ambrotype, 46
 gelatin printing and, 56
 on glass negatives, 74
 matte, 56
 light sensitivity of, 55
 problems with, 65
Color photographs, 79-84
Color scanning, 33
Compression, file, 32, 97
Conservation, 7
 ambrotypes, 114

cost of, 114
daguerreotypes, 109-111
disaster preparedness
 and, 112, 115
glass negatives, 75-76
negatives, 111-112
paper prints, 114,
 116-117
phases of, 113
professional, 107-109.
 See also Conservator
tintype, 113
water damage and, 115,
 117-118
when to consider, 113
Conservator
 becoming a professional,
  130-132
 choosing, 108
 evaluating, 108-109
 See also Conservation
Contact prints, 55
Copying methods, 30-31
Copyright law, 35-39
Copy stand, 30-31
Costs
 of conservation, 114
 of outside storage, 30
 reducing photo-care, 27
 restoration, 123
Costume encyclopedias, 10
Cracked emulsion, 59-60
Cracking, 65, 82
Crayon portrait, 72
Curling, of paper prints,
 60
Cyanotypes, 22, 55, 56,
 65

Daguerre, Louis, 41
Daguerreotypes, 41-45
 airbrush restoration for,
  121-122
 cleaning, 43-45
 conservation for,
  109-111
 drying wet, 118
 family portrait, 13-14
 identifying, 43
 major characteristics of,
  48
 scratches on, 44-45

sizes of, 42
Damage
 biological, 18-19
 chemical, 20
 to color photographs,
  82-83
 environmental, 20-23.
  See also Humidity;
  Temperature
 to negatives, 76
 to paper prints, 59-62
 pest-caused, 19
 photocopying and, 22
 physical, 18
 types and results of, 23
 water, 115, 117-118
Digital images
 online information
  about, 35-39
 printing, 34-35
 storing, 93
 traditional prints from,
  105
 See also Digital
  photography
Digital photography
 community Web sites, 96
 computer files and, 93
 history of, 92
 online photo community
  and, 94
 photo CDs, 93-94
 planning for
  obsolescence and,
  94
 preservation issues,
  98-99
 suppliers for, 94-98
 See also Digital images
Digital restoration, 122,
 125-126
 at home, 127-130
 results of, 125
 software tools for,
  129-130
 when to conclude, 130
Digital scrapbooks,
 155-156
Direct positive prints, 31
Disaster
 outside storage facility
  and, 29

preparing for, 112, 115
what to save, 119
Discoloration, 82
Displaying photographs, 175-177
Donating photograph collections, 145-147
DPI (dots per inch), 31, 33-35, 101
du Hauron, Louis Ducos, 80

Eastman, George, 58
Ektachrome, 81, 89
Electronic formats, 31-32
Emison family collection, 12, 168-173
Emulsion
  cracked, 59-60
  missing, 114
  on negatives, 73
  removed, 111
Encapsulation, 154
Envelope
  acid paper, 26
  negative, 73
Environmental damage
  humidity and, 20-21
  light and, 22
  pollution, 23
  temperature and, 21
Erasers, 23
Events
  captions for, 11
  organizing by, 135

Fading
  color photographs, 79-80, 82-83
  paper prints, 61
  photographic enhancements for, 126-127
  pre-1900 photographs, 123
"Fair use," 36-37
Family history, photographs in, 14, 67-68, 174-175
Family photograph collection
  adding to your, 11-13
  creating a better, 179-180
  omissions from, 66

types of photographs in, 13-14
Family photographs
  decisions about, 7
  disaster plan for, 119
  displaying, 175-177
  future of, 105
  games using, 178-179
  including yourself in, 182
  reasons for taking, 5-6
  See also Photographs
Family portraits, historic, 13-14
Family reunion activities, 177-179
Family Web sites, 99-101
  designing family home page for, 99-100
  evaluating, 100-101
  list of, 100
  privacy issues and, 101, 103-105
Ferrotypes, 47. See also Ambrotypes
Film
  expiration date on, 182
  Kodacolor, 81
  movie, 88-89
  nitrate, 76, 89
  sheet, 117
  storing unused, 27
  undeveloped, 90
Film-based negatives, 75-78
Film slides, 86-88
Filtering programs, 104
Fingerprints, 8, 18, 62, 83
Flatbed scanners, 32, 34
Fluorescent lights, 86
Folders, acid paper, 26
Foxing, 61
Frames
  for displaying photographs, 176-177
  resin-coated prints in, 66
  wood, 19, 50-51
Fuji digital services, 95-96

Garage, storing photos in, 25
GEDCOM file, filtering programs for, 104
Gelatin developing, 56
Gelatin printing, 56

Genealogical software packages, 141
GENTECH conference, 142
GIF format, 31-32
Glass negatives, 74-76
  drying wet, 117-118
  See also Glass slides
Glass slides, 86-88. See also Glass negatives
Gloves, cotton, 8, 18, 78
Gouraud, François, 41
Group portraits, 133

Halo of corrosion, daguerreotype, 44
Hand-coloring, 63-64
Handheld scanners, 32
Handling
  glass negatives, 74-75
  photographs, 8
  See also Gloves, cotton
Home movies, 88-89
Humidity
  film negatives and, 77
  paper prints and, 59-60
  photo CDs and, 93
  storage and, 20-21
Hyalotype, 86

Identification techniques, 10-11
Identifying images, 3. See also Caption; Labeling
Imperial (life-size) card photographs, 58
Indexing systems, 139
Inks, 35, 151-152
Inpainting, 114
Insect damage, 19
Intellectual property law, 35
International Standards Organization (ISO), 7
Inter-negative, 90
Internet
  publishing Web pages on, 101-103
  search engines, 104
  speed of access, 97, 99
Internet Service Provider (ISP), 99
Inventory, 139

Jewelry, photographic, 16
JPEG format, 31-32, 33

Kodachrome movie film, 89
Kodachrome slides, 86-87
Kodacolor film, 81
Kodak
  color negatives, 86
  Conservation of Photographs, 88
  early cameras, 58
  Kodachrome slides, 80
  PhotoNet online, 94-95
  Picture Maker system, 30, 31
  processing choices from, 94-95
  use of resin-coated (RC) papers, 65
  Web site, 38, 94-96

Labeling
  organizing photographs and, 137-138
  original order and, 9
  RC papers and, 65
  scrapbook, 151-152
  Web page images, 102
  See also Caption; Identifying images
Lamination, 154
Land, Edwin, 81
Langenheim, William and Frederick, 86
Lantern slides, 86-87
Law, copyright, 35-39
Library of Congress, 36, 38
Light damage, 22
Lignin-free paper, 149
Lumiere, Auguste and Louis, 80

Magic Rub erasers, 23
Magnetic albums, 4, 71-73
Mailing photographs, 28
Market value, 14-17
Mars Plastic erasers, 23
Matte collodion, 56
Memorabilia, 153-154
Mildew damage, 20, 61
Model releases, 37, 103
Moisture, color prints and, 82
Mold damage, 20, 61
Movie film, 88-89

Museum registration
organizing, 143-144

Negatives
color, 84
conservation for,
111-112
damage to, 76
deteriorated, 77,
111-112
drying wet, 117
film-based, 76-78. See
also Film-based
negatives
glass, 74-76
materials in, 73
storing, 78
See also Film
Nitrate film, 76, 89
Nitrocellulose negatives, 76

Online photo community,
94
Oral history, 164
Organizing photographs,
3, 133-147
boxes for, 137-138
chronological methods,
144
databases for, 140-142
by events, 135
by family, 134-135
indexing systems for,
139-140
labeling, 137-138
by medium, 136
museum registration
methods, 143-144
planning for, 136
professional organizers
for, 144-145
software for, 140-142
sorting, 137
supplies for, 137
to-do list for, 138
work space for, 137
Organizing slides, 142-143
Oversize photographs
organizing, 135
restoring, 125

Panel card photographs, 58
Paper
acid, 26, 71
acid-free, 149-150
archival, 35

buffered, 150
lignin-free, 149
recommended
scrapbook, 150
Paper prints
conservation of, 114,
116-117
drying wet, 117-118
photographic
enhancements of,
126-127
See also Photographic
prints
Paper supports, 62-63
Papier-mâché case, 51
PAT (Photographic Activity
Test), 7
Peck, Samuel, 51
Pellicle, 111
Photo CDs, 93-94
Photocopying, damage
from, 22
Photo corners, 150-151
Photo curator, 145
Photo-editing tools, 97,
129, 142
Photograph collection,
13-14. See also Family
photograph collection
Photographer, hiring
professional, 89-91
Photographic Activity Test
(PAT), 7
Photographic albums
acid paper in, 71
adhesives in, 71
black paper albums,
71-72
cabinet card, 70
carte de visite, 68-69
family history and, 67-68
learning from, 66-67
magnetic, 71. See also
Magnetic albums
preserving, 70-71
scrapbooks, 70
storing, 71
tintype, 69
Photographic cards. See
Card photographs;
Cartes de visite
Photographic copies,
30-31, 124. See also
Photographic prints
Photographic
enhancement,

122-123, 126-127
Photographic family
history, 14
Photographic jewelry, 16
Photographic prints
adhesives with, 64-65
albums for, 66-73. See
also Photographic
albums
candid, 58-62
card photographs, 56-58
damage to, 59-62
hand-coloring of, 63-64
identifying process of,
55-56
nineteenth century,
54-56
paper supports on, 62-63
resin-coated (RC) papers,
65-66
storing, 66
surface treatments of,
63-65
toning of, 64
water vs. chemical
processing, 91
See also Paper prints
Photographs
additional sources of, 13
color. See Color
photographs;
Copying methods
drawings of, 72
in family histories,
175-177
handling, 8. See also
Gloves, cotton
historical vs.
contemporary, 14
identifying. See
Identification
techniques
mailing and shipping, 28
original order of, 9
preserving new images,
26-27
rolled, 72
See also Family
photographs
Physical damage, 18
PICT format, 31-32
Picture Publisher software,
33
Plastic containers, 25-26, 83
Platinotype, 56
Platinum print, 55, 65

Polaroid, 81-82, 86, 90,
182
Polyester sleeves, 25
Portraits
crayon, 72
formal, 13
group, 133
historic, 13-14
Preservation
digital photography and,
93, 98-99
ink-jet printers and, 35
photograph damage and,
18-23. See also
Damage
Printers, ink-jet, 35
Privacy issues, online
sharing and, 97, 101,
103-105
Promenade card
photographs, 58

Releases, model, 37, 103
Resin-coated (RC) papers,
65-66, 80-81
Restoration, 119-132
airbrush, 121-122, 124
cost of, 123
daguerreotypes, 44
defined, 7
evaluating experts,
120-121
professional, 130-132
Retrieval
of computer files, 93
from outside storage
facility, 30
with photo CDs, 93
Rolled photographs, 72
Roll film, 75
Rubber stamping, 152-153
Rust, on tintypes, 49

Safe-deposit boxes, storage
in, 30, 124
Salted paper prints, 56, 65
Scanning photographs,
31-34, 131
Scrapbooks, 148-157
albums for, 70, 149-152
artifacts in, 154
creating, 155
digital, 155-156
family memorabilia in,
153-154
lamination vs.

encapsulation, 154
rubber stamping in,
    152-153
rules for safe, 156-157
sheet protectors for, 153
software for, 141
stickers in, 153
supplies for safe,
    156-157
Sharing images
online, 96-98
originals, 28
Sheet film, 75, 117
Silver mirroring, 59, 114
Silverfish, 19
Sleeves, protective, 25, 124
Slides
contemporary, 87
drying wet, 117
Ektachrome, 81
film, 86-88
glass, 86-88
handling, 88
Kodachrome, 80
making prints from, 90
organizing, 142-143
storing, 88, 90
Smith family collection,
    140

Software
digital restoration, 129
organizing, 140-142
scanning, 33-34
scrapbooking, 141
Stabilization, 114
Stereographs, 57-58
Storage
of cased images, 52-53
cold, 84-85
of color photographs,
    84-85
considerations, 24-26
containers for, 25-26
damage from improper,
    20-23
of digital images, 93
environment for, 25
of film-based negatives,
    77-78
of glass negatives, 74
humidity and, 20-21
of negatives, 77-78
outside facility for, 28-30
of paper prints, 66
of photographic albums,
    71
safe deposit box for, 30
selecting materials for, 26

of slides, 88, 90

Talbot, William Fox, 55
Tarnishing, daguerreotype,
    44
Taylor family collection,
    158-160
Temperature
color prints and, 82-83
film negatives and, 77
photo CDs and, 93
storage and, 21
Texas GenWeb Project,
    103, 105
TIFF format, 31-33
Tintypes, 13, 47-48
albums for, 69
conservation of, 113
damage to, 48-49
digital restorations of,
    122, 125-126
drying wet, 118
major characteristics of,
    48
Toning, 55, 64
Transference, with paper
    prints, 60-61
TWAIN interface, 33-34

Union case, 50-51
U.S. Copyright Office,
    36, 38
U.S. Supreme Court, 36

Victoria card photographs,
    58
Videotape, 105-106, 180

Water damage, 115,
    117-118
Web sites
digital information, 35
digital photo services,
    94-98
family, 99-101
photo-sharing, 98
scanning techniques, 34
Weeping, daguerreotypes,
    44
Wet plate, 74
Wilson, Richard, 34
Woodburytype, 56

Zoom lens, 181